THE SATURDAY EVENING POST

Time to Entertain Cookbook

OTHER BOOKS BY CHARLOTTE TURGEON

THE SATURDAY
EVENING POST

TIME TO
ENTERTAIN
COOKBOOK

Menus, Recipes and Serving Hints
by Charlotte Turgeon. Wine Suggestions and a
Special Section on Wines by Charles Turgeon.

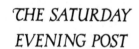

BONANZA BOOKS
NEW YORK

The Saturday Evening Post Time to Entertain Cookbook
Editor: Jean White
Art Director and Designer: Sandra Strother
Copy Staff: Louise Fortson, Dorothy B. Life, Robyn Kimble
Compositors: Gloria McCoy, Penny Allison, Geri Watson, Joy Droeger
Art and Production Staff: Jinny Sauer, Sarah White, Marianne Roan,
Greg Vanzo, Dwight Lamb

This edition is published by Bonanza Books,
distributed by Crown Publishers, Inc.,
by arrangement with The Curtis Publishing Company.
h   g   f   e   d   c   b   a
BONANZA 1981 EDITION

Manufactured in the United States of America

Library of Congress Cataloging in Publication Data

Turgeon, Charlotte Snyder, 1912–
   The Saturday evening post time to entertain
cookbook.

   Reprint. Originally published: Indianapolis,
Ind. : Curtis Pub. Co., c1978.
   Includes index.
   1. Entertaining.   2. Cookery.   I. Turgeon,
Charles F.   II. Saturday evening post.
III. Title.   IV. Title: Time to entertain
cookbook.
TX731.T797   1981   642'.4   81-10083
ISBN 0-517-35391-1   AACR2

Contents

WINES FOR YOUR TABLE

Introduction

One of life's most pleasant experiences is to share a meal with friends, a meal that has been thoughtfully planned and attractively prepared. By the same token, there is nothing more chilling than to be received into a home where the host and/or hostess seem worn to a frazzle from having worked at fever pitch up to the last moment. Somehow the guest feels guilty about having caused trouble.

Let's not pretend that a wonderful meal can be achieved by waving a wand. It can't. Cooking involves work—enjoyable, but still time-consuming. The better the meal, the longer the preparation. The secret of entertaining with ease lies very simply in the timing, and the purpose of this book is to show how to prepare for parties of every description well in advance so that the cook can be relaxed and refreshed when guests arrive.

· In the following pages you will find menus and recipes for every sort of occasion that might take place in your home or mine, from small intimate dinners to parties for large groups. All have been designed so that most of the cooking can be done a day or two in advance at *your* convenience, no matter whether you spend most of the day in office or classroom or at home being a busy parent. Early morning and late evening are great times for precooking.

Include table setting in your plans because that is an art in itself and deserves a little of your undivided attention.

The cardinal rule is that all but the final touches of a meal are accomplished several hours in advance so that the cook can do something strictly nonculinary and look forward to the party as much as the guests. Even unexpected guests can be greeted with genuine enthusiasm if you follow my plan for reserved shelves in cupboard and freezer.

Party food has changed in recent years. Growing concern about nutritional values and caloric content has made us abandon some traditionally festive foods that are overly hearty, and caused us to introduce dishes that avoid the overuse of refined sugars, grains, and flours. This is all to the good, but a party is no place for gastronomical martyrdom and I recommend a middle-of-the-road approach so that menus are intriguing and delectable while subtly healthful.

A meal is a party meal when there are more than two courses. Beginning with an appetizer or taste-awakening soup arouses interest and it often helps with the timing; it gives the guests something to do while the main course readies itself in the kitchen.

In this book each unit begins with one or two menus and a shopping list for all but basic staples. A star next to the name of a dish means that the recipe appears elsewhere in the book and can be found in the index. The recipes are divided into two parts to show what can be done in advance and what can be done without fuss or muss just before serving.

Wine is becoming an integral part of every dinner party. The trouble is that most of us are ignorant of this subject and depend on our dealers to tell us what to serve. Wine, like music, is much more enjoyable if you really know something about it. To this end I have asked Washington, D.C., wine expert Charles F. Turgeon (who is most conveniently and helpfully my son) to share his knowledge and know-how in selecting and serving wines by describing both European and American sources. He will also suggest both a small and a not-so-small list of wines to store either on a closet shelf or in a modest wine cellar.

You will notice that, whenever possible, I use some of the remarkable modern kitchen appliances that are now available. I am not in the business of selling machines and no gadget is indispensible to the preparation of these menus, but I do believe in getting as much help, electric and electronic, in the kitchen as you find in the family garden or at the tool bench. The appliances I recommend save a great deal of

time, and time is what this book is all about. One word of caution:
Don't try to master completely these silent servants as soon as you
purchase them. Extraordinary and mind-boggling recipes and instructions accompany each machine. Take your time and adapt the
machines to your style of cooking. Counter space, I know, presents a
problem, but most of these appliances can be stored in cupboards. A
microwave oven can be put on a wheeled cart and stored in another
room when not needed.

The machines used in the preparation of this book were the following: Cuisinart Food Processor, General Electric Microwave (Jet 110),
Kitchen Aid Mixer, Litton Microwave Oven 540, and the Vita Mix
3600.

The greatest gadget of all is an extra refrigerator to use on special
occasions. If this isn't a possibility, start getting ready for a party by
using up all leftovers, and in this way freeing as much refrigerator space
as possible.

In brief, *Time to Entertain* means timing yourself so that you can
give a party with as much pleasure to yourself as to your guests. And
that is what entertaining is all about.

CHARLOTTE TURGEON

An asterisk (*) indicates a recipe appearing elsewhere in this book, with another menu or in the chapter on Specialties and Supplies. Consult the index for page number.

DINNER PARTIES

Dinners for Two
Dinners for Four
Dinners for Six
Dinners for Eight

Dinners for Two

If dinner for two is a party for two, then it must be of very special significance. Such an occasion calls for a small, beautifully set table, candlelight, and flowers. The food and wine must be better than any restaurant can provide and prepared so that few moments are lost in the kitchen during dinner time.

DINNER FOR TWO I

Small Terrine of Pâté
Gherkin Pickles
French Bread

Trout Véronique
Fresh Pea Puree
Tomato Cup Salad

Apricot Meringue Shortcake
Coffee

WINE SUGGESTIONS:

With the first course—
Domestic: Fumé Blanc, or
Imported: Pouilly Fumé (Loire)
With the second course—
Domestic: Johannisberg Riesling, or
Imported: Wehlener Sonnenuhr
(Mosel)

SHOPPING LIST:

½ pound bacon

½ pound pork

¼ pound veal

¼ pound chicken livers

⅓ pound boiled ham

French bread

Gherkin pickles

2 trout (fresh or frozen)

1 small bunch seedless white
  grapes

Green peas (fresh or frozen)

1 small (3 ounce) package
  cream cheese

Sour cream

2 tomatoes

1 small cucumber

1 small package dried apricots

Bay leaf

Allspice

Ground cloves

Nutmeg

Thyme

Onion

Stick cinnamon

Garlic

Brandy

Cointreau or Grand Marnier
  liqueur

Cream

Lemon

Dry white wine

Lettuce

Parsley

Small Terrine of Pâté

A delicious meat pâté is a leisurely beginning to a special meal. It should be made two to three days in advance so it can mellow. With a food processor or a meat grinder, this takes very little time to prepare. Specialty shops have small rectangular terrines that are intended for these pâtés. Lacking one, use a ½-pound loaf tin.

1 onion, chopped

1 clove garlic, minced

1 tablespoon butter

4 slices bacon

8 ounces clear pork

4 ounces boneless veal

4 ounces chicken livers

1 egg, slightly beaten

4 tablespoons cream

⅛ teaspoon allspice

Small pinch cloves

Small pinch nutmeg

¾ teaspoon salt

¼ teaspoon freshly ground
    black pepper

2 tablespoons brandy

½ bay leaf

⅓ pound boiled ham, sliced
    ⅛ inch thick

GARNISH:

Gherkin pickles

ADVANCE PREPARATION:

Sauté the onion and garlic in butter in a small skillet over low heat just until the onion is tender.

Line a small terrine (or 3-cup loaf tin) with 3 slices of bacon, letting the ends come up the sides.

Chop the meats briefly in the food processor, using the stop-start motion. They should not be pureed. Or, put the meats through a grinder, using the largest blade.

Combine the meats with the onion and garlic and all the other ingredients except the bay leaf and ham.

Cut the ham into ¼-inch strips about 3 inches long. Reserve a third of the strips.

Spread half the mixture in the bottom of the terrine or tin. Cover with a layer of ham strips and then with the remaining mixture, smoothing the top evenly with a small spatula. Arrange the reserved ham strips decoratively on the top.

Divide the remaining strip of bacon in fourths and place on top of the ham. Lay the bay leaf on the ham, too. Cover with the terrine top sealed with kitchen paste made of flour and water, or with two sheets of aluminum foil tied in place with twine.

Place the container in a pan of hot water, deep enough to come halfway up the sides. Bring the water to a boil on top of the stove and then place it in a 350-degree F. oven for 1 hour.

Let the terrine or mold cool until lukewarm before removing the cover (or foil lid).

Remove the bacon pieces and bay leaf. Cover the pâté with another small loaf tin filled with weights or other heavy objects. Cool and then chill in the refrigerator. This will keep for a week.

TO SERVE:

Place the terrine on a small platter. Cut three or four slices for easier serving. Decorate with gherkins. If you have used a loaf tin, turn the pâté onto a plate and then back onto a small serving platter so that the ham design shows. Garnish with the pickles.

Serve with warm French bread and sweet butter.

Trout Véronique

A lovely New Orleans hostelry, the Pontchartrain, serves a specialty that this recipe attempts to duplicate. If fresh trout are not available, use the frozen variety, thawing them almost completely before boning them.

2 small trout
1¼ cups water
4 tablespoons dry white wine
2 teaspoons butter or margarine
½ teaspoon salt
½ bay leaf
Pinch of thyme
1 thin slice lemon

SAUCE:

2 egg yolks
2 tablespoons heavy cream
2 teaspoons lemon juice
¼ teaspoon salt
⅛ teaspoon cayenne
4 tablespoons butter
½ cup seedless white grapes, halved

ADVANCE PREPARATION:

Using a sharp knife, cut the fish down the back, cutting from tail to head. Cut down at the "neck" on one side of the fish as far as the backbone. Holding the knife parallel to the backbone, cut away the flesh from the bones and ribs. Lift the fillet off in one piece. Turn the fish and do the same thing on the other side. Repeat the process with the second fish.

Combine the water, wine, butter or margarine, salt, bay leaf, thyme, and lemon in a shallow skillet. Bring to a boil. Cover and simmer 10 minutes.

Place the fish fillets carefully in the simmering water. Bring to a boil. Cover and simmer gently for 5 minutes. Remove the fish and turn skin side up on a small platter. Cool. Slip off the skin and cover with a lightly buttered piece of aluminum foil. Store in the refrigerator until 1 hour before dinner.

To make the sauce: Whisk the egg yolks, cream, lemon juice, and seasonings over moderate heat just until the mixture is hot and begins to thicken. Remove from the heat and whisk in half the butter. Whisk vigorously for a moment, returning the sauce to the heat briefly. Add the rest of the butter and beat just until it is incorporated. Remove from the stove and pour into a glass measure. Taste for seasoning.

Prepare the grapes and place them in a small bowl or plastic bag. Keep at room temperature.

BEFORE SERVING:

Place the fish in a 175-degree F. oven, still covered with the foil, during the first course (10 to 12 minutes).

Just before serving, stir the grapes into the sauce. Cover the fish with the sauce and brown under the broiler. Since it browns in just a few minutes, it should be watched carefully. Serve immediately.

Fresh Pea Puree

1 pound fresh peas (1 cup
    shelled) or ½ package frozen
    peas
1 medium-sized potato

1 tablespoon butter or
    margarine
½ small package cream cheese
2 tablespoons sour cream
Salt and pepper

ADVANCE PREPARATION:

Shell the peas if fresh. Boil fresh or frozen peas in ¼ cup of water in a covered saucepan for 10 minutes, adding ½ teaspoon of salt. Remove the cover and let the peas cook almost dry without allowing them to scorch. Place the peas in a food processor or blender.

Meanwhile, peel and quarter the potato and steam or boil it until tender. Drain and add the potato to the peas. Add the butter, cream cheese, and sour cream. Spin until smooth. Taste for seasoning and add salt and pepper as needed.

Divide the puree between two individual soufflé dishes or ramekins.

BEFORE SERVING:

Reheat the ramekins in a pan of boiling water 25 minutes in a 325-degree F. oven or covered on top of the stove if you have but one oven. In a microwave place the ramekins at least an inch apart in a glass dish containing boiling water. Cover and microwave 8 minutes.

Tomato Cup Salad

2 medium-sized round tomatoes
1 small cucumber
Vinaigrette *

1 small head garden lettuce
Chopped parsley

ADVANCE PREPARATION:

Dip the tomatoes in boiling water for a minute and slip off the skins. Scoop out the centers from the stem ends and sprinkle the interiors with salt. Turn upside down on a rack to drain.

Peel and split the cucumber and scoop out the seeds. Cut in small balls or cubes and cover with a little vinaigrette. Place in the refrigerator.

Wash the lettuce. Dry it well and keep in the hydrator to crisp.

BEFORE SERVING:

Line small individual salad plates with lettuce. Fill the tomatoes with the cucumbers and place on the lettuce. Spoon a little more vinaigrette over the tomatoes and sprinkle with chopped parsley. These should be served very cold.

Apricot Meringue Shortcake

When the menu includes a sauce made from egg yolks—as for the Trout Véronique—plan on a dessert that will use up the egg whites. You may prepare these meringues a day or two before the party and store them in an airtight container.

2 egg whites
⅛ teaspoon cream of tartar
Pinch of salt
8 tablespoons sugar
½ cup dried apricots
½ cup water

1 inch stick cinnamon
4 tablespoons Cointreau or
    Grand Marnier liqueur
1 tablespoon sugar
4 tablespoons sour cream

ADVANCE PREPARATION:

Preheat the oven to 450 degrees F.

Beat the egg whites with the cream of tartar and salt until stiff. While beating continually, gradually add the sugar and keep beating for 5 minutes.

Line a baking sheet with kitchen parchment or brown paper, and drop 4 spoonfuls of the mixture on it. Place the meringues in the oven, turn off the heat, and forget them until the next morning (6 hours is a minimum). Remove from the paper and store in an airtight container.

Place the apricots, water, and cinnamon in a small saucepan. Boil, covered, for 5 minutes. Remove the cover and add the liqueur and sugar. Cook 5 minutes longer. Discard the cinnamon stick. Spin in a food processor or blender or force the apricots and liquid through a food mill. Cool and chill.

TO SERVE:

Place a meringue on each of two dessert dishes. Spread thickly with the apricot puree. Cover with another meringue and spread with a thinner layer of apricot. Top with sour cream—or, if you prefer, sweetened whipped cream.

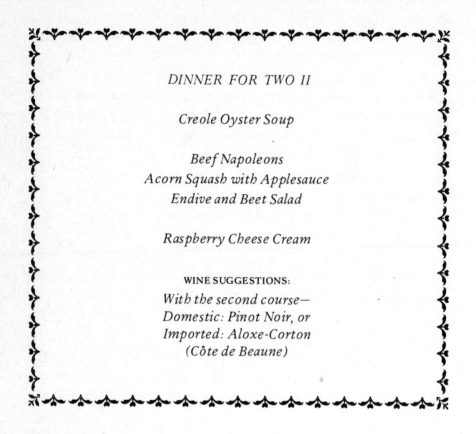

DINNER FOR TWO II

Creole Oyster Soup

Beef Napoleons
Acorn Squash with Applesauce
Endive and Beet Salad

Raspberry Cheese Cream

WINE SUGGESTIONS:

With the second course—
Domestic: Pinot Noir, or
Imported: Aloxe-Corton
(Côte de Beaune)

SHOPPING LIST:

½ pint shucked oysters
2 tenderloin steaks (see recipe)
1 acorn squash
3 Belgian endive
1 small can (8¼ ounces) sliced
   beets
Walnuts
1 10-ounce box
   frozen raspberries
1 package (3 ounces) cream
   cheese

½ pint sour cream
Shallots or scallions
¼ pound mushrooms
1 slice ham
Madeira
Watercress
Canned foie gras or liver pâté
   (optional)
Applesauce

Creole Oyster Soup

More than one recipe claims this name, but this one is so simple and the results so delicious that it gets my vote. The soup should be rich brown in color.

½ pint shucked oysters
3 tablespoons butter or
    margarine
2 tablespoons chopped shallots
    or scallions

3 tablespoons flour
½ teaspoon salt
⅛ teaspoon cayenne

ADVANCE PREPARATION:

Put the oysters in a small saucepan with ½ cup of water. Bring to a boil and simmer just until the edges curl. Drain the liquid into a 2-cup measure. Add enough fish stock, bottled clam broth, chicken broth, or water to fill the measuring cup.

Heat the butter or margarine in the top of a small double boiler over direct heat. Sauté the shallots or scallions for 1 minute. Add the flour and cook until the flour is dark brown, stirring continuously. Whisk in the oyster broth and mix until smooth and slightly thickened. Cover and simmer 5 minutes. Add the oysters, salt, and cayenne. Cool. Cover and refrigerate.

BEFORE SERVING:

Reheat the soup in the top of a double boiler over boiling water, or microwave, covered, in bouillon cups for 2 minutes.

Beef Napoleons

These individual pastry-wrapped steaks are called "Napoleons" because they are a smaller variation and version of Beef Wellington. To my mind this is one time Napoleon beats Wellington. Prepare these a day in advance and keep in the refrigerator.

2 tenderloins (3 inches in
   diameter and 1¼ inches
   thick)
2 tablespoons butter or
   margarine
Pie pastry*
¼ pound mushrooms
Salt and pepper
Pinch of nutmeg

SAUCE:
2 tablespoons butter or
   margarine

1 tablespoon chopped shallots
2 tablespoons diced ham
2 tablespoons flour
2 tablespoons Madeira
⅔ cup bouillon
Salt and pepper
1 egg yolk

GARNISH:
Watercress
Foie gras or liver pâté
   (optional)

ADVANCE PREPARATION:

Heat 1 tablespoon of butter or margarine in a skillet and, when it is very hot, sear the steaks very briefly on each side. Remove from the skillet to a plate and discard the browned butter. Season with salt and pepper. Cool the steaks completely. Cover and refrigerate.

Make a 2-crust pie pastry. Let it rest 20 minutes.

Trim the stem ends of the mushrooms. Wash the mushrooms briefly. Pat dry with toweling and chop coarsely in the food processor or by hand. Heat a tablespoon of butter or margarine in the skillet and sauté the mushrooms until almost dry. Strain through a small strainer, forcing the liquid into a small bowl with the back of a spoon. The mushrooms should be very dry. Season them with salt, pepper, and a little nutmeg. Let them cool.

Put the second two tablespoons of butter or margarine in the same skillet and heat it, scraping the bottom to incorporate any of the juices. Sauté the shallots and ham for 2 minutes, stirring frequently. Sprinkle with the flour and stir until the flour disappears. Stir in the mushroom liquid, the Madeira, and the bouillon. Stir until thickened. Season to taste with salt and pepper. Pour into a small bowl. Cool. Cover and refrigerate.

Roll out the pastry ⅛ inch thick. Cut four 4-inch circles, using a saucepan cover if necessary. Moisten the edges with water.

In the centers of two of the circles, spread a layer of mushrooms, leaving a ¾-inch rim. Place the cold steaks on top of the mushrooms and cover with the remaining pastry circles. Pinch the edges together firmly. Place on a small baking sheet.

Cut decorative motifs (lattice strips, stars, leaves, or crescents) from the unused pastry. Moisten them slightly on the bottom and affix to the tops and sides of the "Napoleons." Prick the surface with the tines of a fork.

BEFORE SERVING:

Paint the top and sides of each Napoleon with the egg yolk mixed with 1 tablespoon of water. Bake 12 minutes in an oven preheated to 425 degrees F.

Reheat the sauce either in a double boiler or for 2 minutes in the microwave. Serve the sauce in a separate bowl.

Place the Napoleons on individual heated plates. Garnish with watercress and, if desired, a slice of foie gras or a teaspoon of chilled liver pâté.

Acorn Squash with Applesauce

1 acorn squash	Salt and pepper
1-2 teaspoons butter or	⅓ cup applesauce
margarine	1 teaspoon horseradish

ADVANCE PREPARATION:

If using a conventional range, split the squash in half and scoop out the seeds and fibers. Place cut side down on a rack in a deep saucepan. Add 2 inches of water and steam for 25 minutes. Turn the squash over in an ovenproof dish. Put 1 to 2 teaspoons of butter or margarine in each and sprinkle with salt and pepper.

With a microwave oven, wash the squash and prick it in several places. Microwave 8 to 12 minutes, according to the size of the squash, on a glass or ceramic plate. Let stand until cool enough to handle, then cut in half and remove seeds and fibers. Season with butter, salt, and pepper as above.

BEFORE SERVING:

In a conventional oven, bake at 350 degrees F. 25 minutes or until very tender. In a microwave, reheat 3 minutes. Mix together the applesauce and horseradish and spoon it into the squash halves.

Endive and Beet Salad

1 small can (8¼ ounces) sliced	⅛ teaspoon black pepper
beets	2 tablespoons chopped scallions
1 tablespoon red wine vinegar	(green part)
1 teaspoon Dijon mustard	3 Belgian endive
3 tablespoons olive oil	2 tablespoons chopped walnuts
½ teaspoon salt	

ADVANCE PREPARATION:

Cut the beet slices into small matchsticks. Combine the vinegar and mustard in a small bowl. Whisk in the oil, salt and pepper, and scallions. Stir in the beets. Cover and refrigerate.

Trim the ends of the endive and separate the leaves. Wash and pat dry. Place the leaves in a small salad bowl. Cover and refrigerate.

BEFORE SERVING:

Combine the beets with the endive and the walnuts. Toss lightly and serve in the salad bowl.

Raspberry Cheese Cream

1 small box frozen raspberries
1 package (3 ounces) cream
  cheese

4 tablespoons sour cream
1 tablespoon sugar

ADVANCE PREPARATION:

Thaw the raspberries for 1 hour. Spin in a food processor or blender and force through a sieve to remove the seeds.

Blend the cream cheese, sour cream, and sugar.

Spoon alternate layers of the raspberries and cheese mixture into parfait glasses. Chill in the refrigerator.

TO SERVE:

Serve very cold. Iced-tea spoons are the best utensils for this dessert.

Dinners for Four

A dinner party for four with close friends is one of the best ways in the world to spend an evening. Set the table as elaborately or as simply as you wish; the menus will fit either decor. What makes it a party is that there are three courses—four, if you prefer to serve the salad alone. You and the silent servants—the mechanical aids in your kitchen—can prepare everything in advance except for a few last-minute touches, and your guests will be flattered and impressed by the results.

DINNER FOR FOUR I

Ham Rolls with Rye Rounds

Sole Normande
Duchess Zucchini Boats
Tomato and Endive Salad
Homemade Hard Rolls*

Strawberry Almond Soufflé

WINE SUGGESTIONS:

With the first course—
Domestic: Gewurztraminer, or
Imported: Gewurztraminer (Alsace)
With the second course—
Domestic: Fumé Blanc, or
Imported: Sancerre (Loire)

SHOPPING LIST:

4 thin slices boiled ham
⅓ pound liverwurst
1 can consommé (with gelatin)
Walnuts
1½ pounds flounder fillets
½ pound shrimp
½ pound mushrooms
4 zucchini about 6 inches long
2 medium-sized potatoes
2 Belgian endive
4 tomatoes
1 small head romaine lettuce
1 small head Boston lettuce
1 box frozen strawberries
½ pint whipping cream

Slivered almonds
Thin-sliced party rye bread
Dijon mustard
Chives or green onions
Parsley
Shallots
Bay leaf
Thyme
Lemon for juice and grated rind
Cheddar or Gruyère cheese
Black olives
Unflavored gelatine
Cointreau
Madeira
Dry white wine

Ham Rolls

4 slices boiled ham, cut very
  thin
⅓ pound liverwurst
6 tablespoons jellied consommé
1 teaspoon Dijon mustard

2 tablespoons chopped walnuts
2 tablespoons Madeira
2 tablespoons chopped chives
  or green onions
Parsley

ADVANCE PREPARATION:

Trim the ham slices so that they measure approximately 4½ by 3½ inches. Cut the trimmings into thin pieces. Using an electric beater, whip the liverwurst with the consommé (which should be melted but not hot), the mustard, walnuts, Madeira, and chives. Mix until well blended.

Spread each piece of ham with a thick layer of the filling, making sure the edges are well covered. Add the extra strips of ham and roll up. Place seam side down on a plate. Stick parsley flowerets in the filling on each end. Chill in the refrigerator.

BEFORE SERVING:

Remove the ham rolls from the refrigerator 30 minutes before mealtime. Place each roll on a lettuce-lined small salad plate. Add two or three slices of thin-sliced party rye bread.

Sole Normande

The special goodness of this dish, which demands high prices in fine restaurants, lies in the sauce. Its subtle flavor is superb.

3 cups water	1½ pounds flounder fillets
1 cup dry white wine	½ pound mushrooms
1 tablespoon chopped shallots	4 tablespoons butter
½ bay leaf	2 tablespoons flour
⅛ teaspoon powdered thyme	4 tablespoons cream
4 sprigs parsley	2 egg yolks
½ teaspoon salt	1 tablespoon lemon juice
⅛ teaspoon white pepper	Parsley
8 shrimp	

ADVANCE PREPARATION:

Combine the water, wine, bay leaf, thyme, parsley, salt, and pepper in a 2-quart skillet or shallow saucepan. Cover and simmer 5 minutes.

Wash the shrimp, add them to the broth, and simmer for 5 minutes. Remove from the pan with a slotted spoon and set aside.

Carefully add the fillets and, once the broth has returned to a simmer, cover and simmer 5 to 8 minutes, depending on the thickness of the fillets. Remove the fillets with a slotted spatula to a heatproof platter (nonmetal if you have a microwave oven). They should be in a single layer.

Meanwhile, trim the mushrooms and wash them briefly before slicing them in a food processor or with a sharp knife. Caps and stems should be sliced together lengthwise.

Heat 2 tablespoons of butter or margarine in a small skillet and sauté the mushrooms until they have released their juices. Add the mushroom juices to the fish broth and boil the combination down to approximately 1½ cups.

Heat the remaining butter or margarine in a small saucepan. Whisk in the flour and cook over low heat for 3 minutes, whisking constantly. Add the broth and whisk until smooth. Beat the eggs and cream together in a small mixing bowl and beat in the hot sauce gradually. Return the sauce to the saucepan and whisk over moderate heat until slightly thickened. Remove from the heat and add the mushrooms and lemon juice. Season to taste with salt and white pepper. Cool, cover, and refrigerate. If the color of the sauce seems drab, add a drop or two of red vegetable coloring.

Remove the shells and intestinal strips from the shrimp. Wrap in waxed paper. Refrigerate.

BEFORE SERVING:

Take the fish, sauce, and shrimp from the refrigerator at least 1 hour before reheating. Remove any liquid from the fish platter. Spread the sauce over the fillets.

In a microwave oven, reheat 4 minutes, turning the dish after the first 2 minutes. Let stand 5 minutes before serving.

In a conventional oven, reheat 30 to 40 minutes at 300 degrees F.

Garnish with the shrimp and sprigs of parsley.

Duchess Stuffed Zucchini

4 small zucchini
2 medium-sized potatoes
2 tablespoons butter or
  margarine

2 egg yolks
Salt and pepper
3 tablespoons grated cheddar
  or Gruyère cheese

ADVANCE PREPARATION:

Select zucchini approximately 6 inches in length. Wash them well and cut off the tips of both ends. Slice them lengthwise. Scoop out the centers with a pointed spoon and discard. Boil the zucchini halves in salted water for 10 minutes. Drain well.

Peel the potatoes. Cut them in half and boil in salted water for 18 to 20 minutes or until tender. Drain and return to the heat, tossing them until they are dry and mealy on the outside.

Mash the potatoes with an electric beater, adding the butter and one egg yolk. Season to taste with salt and white pepper.

Using a pastry bag fitted with a fluted tip, or a small teaspoon, fill the zucchini centers. Place in an oven-serving dish (nonmetal if you have a microwave oven). Cover and refrigerate.

BEFORE SERVING:

Remove the zucchini from the refrigerator 1 hour before final cooking. Beat an egg yolk slightly with 1 teaspoon of water. Paint the potato filling with the mixture. Sprinkle with grated cheese.

In a microwave oven heat 4 minutes, turning the plate after the first 2 minutes.

In a regular oven bake 20 to 30 minutes at 300 degrees F. For further browning, slip the dish under the broiler for a minute or two.

Tomato and Endive Salad

All parts of a salad can be prepared in advance, but combining them is a last-minute chore. Whether a salad is served as a separate course *à la française* or as part of the main course is up to the host or hostess. In any case, a good salad deserves a separate plate or bowl. Try to use different lettuces in an appetizer and a salad that are to be served at the same meal.

2 heads Belgian endive	*8 pitted black olives*
4 medium to small tomatoes	*2 tablespoons chives*
1 small head romaine lettuce	*Vinaigrette**

ADVANCE PREPARATION:

Wash, trim, and cut the endive into ¾-inch slices. Wrap in plastic film and place in the refrigerator.

Dip the tomatoes in boiling water for 5 seconds and slip off the skins. Place on a small plate. Cover and chill.

Wash the lettuce carefully and dry thoroughly. If space permits, line a shallow salad bowl with broken pieces of the lettuce. Cover the bowl and refrigerate. Otherwise, store lettuce in crisper.

Chop the chives and prepare the basic vinaigrette. Put the vinaigrette in a small serving pitcher. Do not refrigerate.

BEFORE SERVING:

Distribute the endive slices over the lettuce. Quarter the tomatoes and arrange them decoratively over the endive.

Sprinkle with the olives (cut in half) and the chopped chives. Bring the salad to the table for all to admire before tossing it with the dressing.

Strawberry Almond Soufflé

This dish takes a little time to prepare but, since it can be done the day before and because the results are so stupendous, it's worth it. You will need a 3- or 4-cup straight-sided soufflé dish for this recipe. Tie a piece of paper around the dish so that the paper extends 3 inches above the rim of the dish.

4 egg yolks
¾ cup sugar
2 tablespoons lemon juice
1 tablespoon grated lemon rind
1 envelope gelatin softened in
   ¼ cup water
1 box (10 ounces) frozen
   strawberries

2 tablespoons Cointreau
4 egg whites, beaten stiff
1 cup whipping cream
2 tablespoons confectioners'
   sugar
2 tablespoons slivered almonds

ADVANCE PREPARATION:

At least 6 hours before serving time combine the egg yolks, sugar, lemon juice and rind in a glass bowl that will fit over a large saucepan in the manner of a double boiler. The water should not reach the bottom of the bowl, nor should the water be allowed to boil. Beat the mixture with an electric hand beater over the hot water for 10 minutes or until the mixture falls in ribbons. Remove from the heat and beat in the softened gelatin. Continue to beat for 3 minutes.

Drain the thawed strawberries and chill the juice. Spin the berries in a blender or food processor for a second and stir them into the egg mixture. Stir in the Cointreau.

Rinse out the saucepan with cold water and fill it half full of ice cubes. Suspend the bowl over the ice and stir occasionally while the mixture thickens.

Meanwhile, beat the egg whites until stiff, and in a separate bowl whip ¾ cup of the cream. Fold first the cream and then the egg whites carefully and lightly into the strawberry mixture in the glass bowl. Pour into the prepared soufflé dish. Chill in the refrigerator.

BEFORE SERVING:

Remove the soufflé from the refrigerator 2 hours before serving. Just before dinner remove the paper. Whip ¼ cup of cream and sweeten it with the confectioners' sugar. Coat the exposed sides with some of the cream and sprinkle one inch of the top edge with the almonds.

Within the ring of almonds pipe or carefully make an inner circle of cream. The depth of the cream should be about ½ inch. Into the small center circle pour about 2 tablespoons of the reserved chilled strawberry juice.

DINNER FOR FOUR II

Crab Meat Broth

Veal Scallops Vendôme
Honeyed Carrots
Artichoke Salad

Coffee Sherry Jelly

WINE SUGGESTIONS:
With the second course—
Domestic: Cabernet Sauvignon, or
Imported: Château Pavie
(St. Emilion)

SHOPPING LIST:

8 ounces flaked crab meat
1 bottle (8 ounces) clam juice
3 ¼ cups chicken broth
1-1 ¼ pounds veal scallops
½ pound mushrooms
½ pint sour cream
1 pound carrots
1 can artichoke hearts
Garden lettuce
Pecans
½ pint whipping cream

Unflavored gelatin
1 lemon
Oregano
Red onion
Parsley
Soy sauce
Brandy
Madeira
Sherry
Honey

Crab Meat Broth

This delicious broth does just what any good appetizer does. It whets the appetite but is not too filling. Making it twenty-four hours in advance improves the flavor.

8 ounces crab flakes (fresh
  or frozen)
2 tablespoons butter or
  margarine
1 bottle (8 ounces) clam juice

3 cups chicken broth
1 ½ teaspoons soy sauce
1 tablespoon lemon juice
4 tablespoons parslied whipped
  cream (optional)

ADVANCE PREPARATION:

Sauté the crab flakes in the butter for 3 minutes in a heavy 2-quart saucepan. Stir over moderate heat until the crab is completely coated. Add the clam juice, the chicken broth (which should be completely fat-free), the soy sauce, and the lemon juice. Simmer very gently for 10 minutes. Remove from the heat and cool. Store in the refrigerator.

BEFORE SERVING:

Reheat the soup and serve in individual soup cups. If desired, top with 4 tablespoons of whipped cream seasoned with a teaspoon of chopped parsley and ⅛ teaspoon of salt.

Veal Scallops Vendôme

This delicious dish was served to us in Vendôme, France, years ago. It is a taste sensation I have never forgotten and one that fortunately I was able to analyze and duplicate. Not every butcher knows how to cut and pound a proper scallop, but search until you find one. Allow ¼ pound of veal for each person unless you are serving very hearty eaters.

1-1¼ pounds veal scallops
Unbleached white or whole
   wheat pastry flour
Salt and freshly ground
   black pepper
½ pound mushrooms
2 tablespoons finely chopped
   onion

4 tablespoons butter or
   margarine
2 tablespoons salad oil
2 tablespoons brandy
2 tablespoons Madeira
½ pint sour cream

ADVANCE PREPARATION:

Dredge each scallop lightly in flour and sprinkle with salt and pepper. Place on a baking sheet and let stand.

Trim the mushroom stems and wash the mushrooms briefly. Dry on toweling. Save out 4 beautiful caps and groove them with a sharp knife or a French tool made expressly for fluting.

Using the steel blade of a food processor, chop the mushrooms very briefly. Do not puree them. Lacking a food processor, chop medium fine by hand.

Using the same method of chopping, prepare the onion.

Heat 2 tablespoons of butter in a large skillet. Brown the reserved mushroom caps on both sides. Remove with a slotted spoon. Now sauté the chopped mushrooms and onions in the same skillet until the mushrooms become dry. Stir occasionally. Transfer to a bowl.

Heat the remaining butter and the oil together in a skillet. When the fat is bubbling hot, brown the scallops well on both sides, doing them in series if necessary. Pour the brandy over the scallops in the pan and touch with a lighted match. Spoon the brandy over the meat until the flames subside. Remove the meat to a heatproof serving platter (non-metal if you have a microwave oven).

Stir in the Madeira and the chopped mushrooms over moderate heat, incorporating the pan juices. When the mixture comes to a boil, remove from the heat and stir in the sour cream. Taste for seasoning. Spread the sauce over the meat. Cool and store in the refrigerator.

BEFORE SERVING:

Take the veal out of the refrigerator 1 hour before reheating. With a microwave oven, reheat 4 minutes, turning the platter once, and let stand 5 minutes before serving. In a conventional oven reheat the veal for 30 to 40 minutes at 275 degrees F. Garnish with the reserved mushroom caps and parsley sprigs.

Honeyed Carrots

Even nonlovers of carrots will like this recipe. It can be made in a microwave oven or on top of the stove; the only difference is in the amount of broth. Scrub the carrots well but do not peel them.

3 cups sliced carrots	1 tablespoon honey
2 tablespoons butter or	1 tablespoon chopped parsley
margarine	1 teaspoon lemon juice
Chicken broth	Salt and pepper

ADVANCE PREPARATION:

Cut off the tips of the carrots at both ends. Slice in a food processor, using the "thick-slicing" blade, or cut about ⅛ inch thick with a sharp knife.

To prepare in a microwave oven, place the carrots in a glass or ceramic dish with the butter or margarine, 2 tablespoons of chicken broth, and the honey. Cover and microwave 8 minutes, turning the dish once. Remove from the oven and stir in the parsley, lemon juice, and salt and pepper to taste. Cool and refrigerate.

To cook on top of the stove, combine the butter or margarine, ¼ cup chicken broth, and the honey in a small saucepan. Bring to a boil. Add the carrots and cover partially. Cook 15 minutes. Remove from the heat and stir in the parsley, lemon juice, salt and pepper. Cool and refrigerate.

BEFORE SERVING:

Reheat in the microwave 3 to 4 minutes, turning the dish once; in a 300-degree F. oven 25 to 30 minutes, or over hot water in a double boiler on top of the stove.

Artichoke Salad

1 can (8½ ounces) artichoke
   hearts
¾ cup vinaigrette *
½ teaspoon oregano

2 thin slices red onion
Garden lettuce
Salt and pepper

ADVANCE PREPARATION:

Drain the artichoke hearts and mix them gently in a bowl with the vinaigrette dressing and oregano. Let stand 2 hours at room temperature before refrigerating.

Break the red onion slices into rings. Put in a small bowl of water and refrigerate.

Wash and dry the lettuce. Break it into pieces. Crisp in the refrigerator.

BEFORE SERVING:

Combine all the ingredients and taste for seasoning, adding salt and pepper as needed. Bring to the table very cold.

Coffee Sherry Jelly

This very simple dessert becomes party fare when prettily presented. For those avoiding sugar, it can be made with artificial sweetener and served with plain cream.

*1½ tablespoons powdered
    gelatin*
½ cup cold water
*2 cups hot strong coffee or
    4 teaspoons instant coffee
    plus 2 cups boiling water*
½ cup sherry

*½ cup sugar or 1 tablespoon
    artificial sweetener*
½ cup whipping cream
*4 tablespoons confectioners'
    sugar (optional)*
4 tablespoons chopped pecans

ADVANCE PREPARATION:

Soften the gelatin in the cold water. Stir it into the hot coffee. Add the sherry and simmer, stirring until the gelatin has dissolved. Remove from the heat and stir in the sugar or sweetener. Cool slightly and pour into individual dessert glasses.

BEFORE SERVING:

Whip the cream, and stir in the sugar if desired. Top each dessert with the cream and sprinkle with chopped nuts.

Dinners for Six

Six around a table makes for wonderful conversation, especially if the food and wine are very good. The following menus are essentially simple fare, easy to prepare in advance and with very little last-minute fuss and bother; yet they can be termed exceptional.

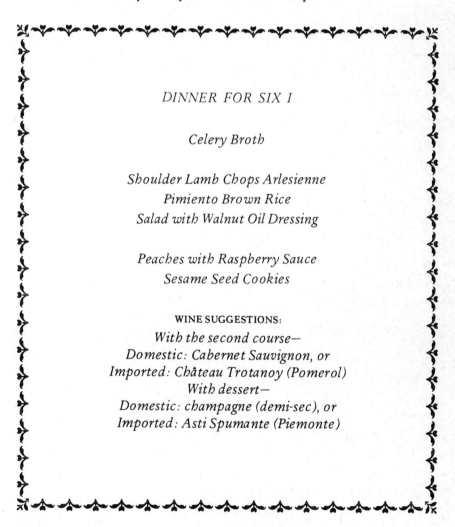

DINNER FOR SIX I

Celery Broth

Shoulder Lamb Chops Arlesienne
Pimiento Brown Rice
Salad with Walnut Oil Dressing

Peaches with Raspberry Sauce
Sesame Seed Cookies

WINE SUGGESTIONS:
With the second course—
Domestic: Cabernet Sauvignon, or
Imported: Château Trotanoy (Pomerol)
With dessert—
Domestic: champagne (demi-sec), or
Imported: Asti Spumante (Piemonte)

SHOPPING LIST:

1 bunch celery

3 cups chicken broth

6 shoulder lamb chops

2 small eggplants

4 large tomatoes

Brown rice

3 cups beef bouillon

Walnut oil (buy at health food
   or specialty shop)

Walnuts

Garden lettuce

Romaine lettuce

Red cabbage

Green pepper

Pimiento

Garlic

Onion

Sour cream or yogurt

Peaches (fresh or frozen)

Frozen raspberries

1 orange

1 lemon

½ cup unhulled sesame seeds

Chives

Parsley

Honey

Dry red wine

Kirsch

Celery Broth

6 stalks celery with leaves

2 tablespoons finely minced
   onion

3 cups chicken broth

3 tablespoons sour cream or
   yogurt

Chopped chives

Salt and pepper

ADVANCE PREPARATION:

Wash the celery and cut it into 2-inch pieces.

Mince the onion in a food processor or with a sharp knife.

If you are using a microwave oven, place the celery, onion, and broth in a glass or ceramic dish. Cover and cook 10 minutes.

If cooking on top of the stove, combine the same ingredients in a saucepan. Bring to a boil. Reduce the heat and simmer covered for 20 minutes. Strain the broth. Taste for seasoning.

BEFORE SERVING:

Reheat the broth in the microwave oven 2 to 3 minutes or on top of the stove until it comes to a simmer.

Pour into individual bouillon cups. Garnish with either sour cream or yogurt and sprinkle with chopped chives, salt, and pepper.

Shoulder Lamb Chops Arlesienne

This dish would not be considered party fare in France because it is essentially a southern peasant dish, but if you agree with me that a dish that is unusual and interesting is good for any occasion you will serve this with pride to your guests.

6 thick (1½ inches) shoulder
   lamb chops
2 small (½ pound) eggplants
Unbleached white or whole wheat
   pastry flour
4 large tomatoes

1½ garlic cloves, minced
6 tablespoons chopped parsley
Olive, corn, or safflower oil
¾ cup dry red wine
Salt and freshly ground pepper

ADVANCE PREPARATION:

Prepare all the ingredients before you start cooking. If you prefer, use two skillets at once, but one will suffice.

Wipe the lamb chops free of any bone dust, using paper toweling.

Wash the eggplants, cutting off the blossom and stem ends, but do not peel. Cut in ½-inch slices and dredge lightly in flour on both sides. Place on a baking sheet.

Wash the tomatoes. Slice off the blossom and stem ends. Cut in ½-inch slices and place on a plate.

Peel and mince the garlic or force through a garlic press into a small bowl. If you like garlic, use 2 cloves.

Chop the parsley in a food processor or blender or with a very sharp knife.

Oil the inside of a large ovenproof nonmetal casserole.

Heat 1½ tablespoons of oil in a large skillet. Brown three of the chops at a time on each side, turning them after 1 or 2 minutes. Place temporarily on a plate or a platter. Repeat with the remaining chops.

Heat 2 more tablespoons of oil and, when it is very hot, brown the eggplant slices on both sides. As the eggplant slices are browned, transfer them to the casserole. Sprinkle with salt and pepper.

Using the same skillet and adding 2 more tablespoons of oil, cook the tomato slices 5 minutes, along with the garlic and half the chopped parsley. Do not let the garlic burn. Turn each tomato slice once with a broad spatula. Place the cooked tomatoes on the eggplant and sprinkle with salt and pepper.

Cover the tomatoes with the chops.

Add the wine to the skillet and bring to a boil, stirring vigorously with a fork so that all the juices on the bottom of the pan will be incorporated. Pour over the chops and sprinkle with salt and pepper.

In a microwave oven, prebake covered for 10 minutes, giving the dish a quarter turn after 5 minutes. In a conventional oven, prebake 30 minutes at 350 degrees F. Allow to cool, then refrigerate.

BEFORE SERVING:

Allow casserole to come to room temperature before reheating. In a microwave oven, cook 10 minutes uncovered, turning the dish once. Let stand 2 minutes before serving. In a conventional oven, bake 30 minutes uncovered at 350 degrees F.

TO SERVE:

Line the chops up in the center of a heated serving platter. Distribute the eggplant and tomatoes around the edge of the dish using a slotted spoon. Pour the sauce over the chops and sprinkle with the remaining chopped parsley.

Pimiento Brown Rice

1 cup raw brown rice	4 tablespoons chopped green
3 cups beef bouillon	pepper
2 tablespoons butter or	4 tablespoons chopped pimiento
margarine	Salt and pepper
2 tablespoons minced onion	

ADVANCE PREPARATION:

Rinse and drain the rice.

Bring the bouillon to a boil and add the rice, stirring once. Reduce the heat, cover, and cook slowly for 45 minutes or until all the liquid is absorbed.

Meanwhile, heat the butter or margarine in a small skillet and cook the onion and green pepper over very low heat until tender. Do not brown. Remove from the heat and stir in the pimiento.

When the rice is cooked, stir in the onion/pepper mixture and blend well. Season to taste with salt and pepper. Place in a small buttered casserole; cover.

BEFORE SERVING:

Bring the rice to room temperature. In a microwave oven cook 2 minutes covered. Stir well and cook 1 minute longer. In a regular oven bake 20 minutes covered at 350 degrees F.

Salad with Walnut Oil Dressing

Walnut oil is very much in vogue right now, for reasons of nutrition as well as flavor. It seems to compliment the southern, sunny Mediterranean characteristics of the main dish of this meal.

1 head garden lettuce
1 head romaine lettuce
1 cup shredded red cabbage
½ cup coarsely ground walnuts

DRESSING:

2 tablespoons red wine vinegar
6 tablespoons walnut oil
1 teaspoon Dijon mustard
½ teaspoon salt
⅛ teaspoon black pepper

ADVANCE PREPARATION:

Wash the lettuce and dry it thoroughly. This is most easily done in a spin dryer. Break the lettuce into small pieces.

Shred the cabbage and plan to use the rest of the head in a Red Cabbage and Apples recipe in the not-too-distant future.

Chop the walnuts.

If refrigerator space permits, put all the ingredients together in the salad bowl you intend to use. Cover and chill.

Combine all the dressing ingredients in a small cruet or pitcher suitable to the table. Do not chill.

TO SERVE:

Bring the salad bowl to the table at the appropriate time and add the dressing at the table, tossing lightly but thoroughly just before serving.

Peaches with Raspberry Sauce

This dessert can be made with frozen or fresh fruit. Anyone who wishes to tuck vanilla ice cream, ricotta, or plain yogurt under the peaches will create a kind of Pêche Melba of varying caloric counts. If you are starting with fresh peaches, cut them in halves. Frozen peaches always come sliced.

6 fresh peaches or 2 10-ounce
   boxes sliced frozen peaches
1 lemon
1 10-ounce box frozen
   raspberries

2 tablespoons honey
2 tablespoons kirsch

ADVANCE PREPARATION:

Dip fresh peaches in boiling water for 5 seconds and slip off the skins. Rub the outsides with the cut side of a lemon to keep them from discoloring.

If using frozen peaches, thaw until just soft. Sprinkle with lemon juice.

To make the sauce, spin partially thawed raspberries in a blender or food processor until smooth. Drain through a stainless steel strainer to remove the seeds. Mix the puree with the honey and kirsch.

TO SERVE:

Spoon the peaches into individual dessert glasses, adding the raspberry sauce at the last minute.

Sesame Seed Cookies

(3 dozen)

These cookies are quick to make, extremely nutritious, and delicious to eat. I recommend them for party fare and for children fare.

½ cup unhulled sesame seeds
½ cup (1 stick) butter or
   margarine
½ cup light brown sugar or
   ¼ cup liquid brown sugar
1 teaspoon vanilla

1 tablespoon grated orange peel
⅓ cup unbleached white flour
⅓ cup whole wheat pastry flour
¼ teaspoon baking powder
1 egg
2 tablespoons orange juice

Preheat the oven to 375 degrees F.

Heat the sesame seeds in an ungreased skillet over moderate heat, tossing occasionally until they are lightly toasted. This takes 2 or 3 minutes.

Beat the butter or margarine and the sugar with an electric beater until they are blended. Add the remaining ingredients and continue beating slowly until all are well mixed.

Drop by teaspoonfuls onto an ungreased baking sheet and bake 8 minutes. Remove the cookies to a wire rack to cool.

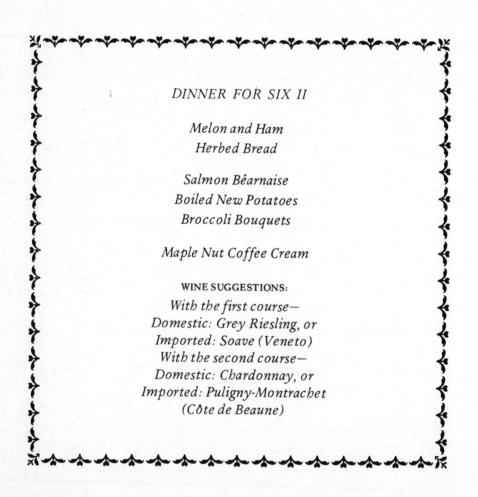

DINNER FOR SIX II

Melon and Ham
Herbed Bread

Salmon Béarnaise
Boiled New Potatoes
Broccoli Bouquets

Maple Nut Coffee Cream

WINE SUGGESTIONS:
With the first course—
Domestic: Grey Riesling, or
Imported: Soave (Veneto)
With the second course—
Domestic: Chardonnay, or
Imported: Puligny-Montrachet
(Côte de Beaune)

SHOPPING LIST:

1 small honeydew melon
*6 slices prosciutto or country
  ham*
1 loaf French bread
White wine vinegar
6 salmon steaks
Small new potatoes
2 pounds broccoli
1 small jar pimientos
Garlic

Dill
Tarragon
Sage
Basil
Parsley
Shallots or scallions
Walnuts
½ pint heavy cream
Maple syrup
1½ pints coffee ice cream

Melon and Ham

Honeydew melon and prosciutto, an Italian specialty, is often served in restaurants but it is very easy to prepare for home dining. If you can find prosciutto in an Italian food store or delicatessen, remember that one large paper-thin slice per person is sufficient. If prosciutto is not available, ask your butcher to cut 6 paper-thin slices of country-cured ham. Make sure that the melon is ripe before cutting.

ADVANCE PREPARATION:

    Cut the melon in half and remove the seeds. Cut each half in thirds and remove the rind with a sharp knife. Wrap each section in a slice of prosciutto or ham and place on a small platter. Cover well with wax paper or plastic film and chill in the refrigerator.

BEFORE SERVING:

    Place the melon sections on individual salad plates and have them on the table before your guests sit down.

Herbed Bread

4 tablespoons butter or
   margarine
1 clove garlic

1 tablespoon chopped parsley
   or 1 tablespoon mixed chopped
   herbs (tarragon, sage, basil,
   parsley)
1 long loaf French bread

ADVANCE PREPARATION:

Heat the butter or margarine in a small skillet. Add the garlic, forced through a press or minced very fine. Cook over very low heat for 3 minutes, stirring occasionally so that the garlic will not brown. Remove from the heat and add the herbs. Cover and let stand 20 to 30 minutes.

Cut the bread in ¾-inch slices without cutting through completely. Using a pastry brush, paint each slice with the herb butter. Wrap the loaf in aluminum foil and keep in a cool place.

BEFORE SERVING:

Ten minutes before serving, slip the bread into a preheated (300 degrees F.) oven. When it is warm, place it in a napkin-lined basket on the table, so people can help themselves.

Salmon Béarnaise

Salmon steaks can be cooked either in a microwave or in a regular oven. We will give directions for both. (If you are cooking frozen salmon by the microwave method, plan to turn on the broiler of your regular stove for a few minutes of browning, unless your microwave has a special browning unit.) This dish is a delight to the eye as well as to the taste buds.

6 salmon steaks (5-6 ounces)   Salt and freshly ground black
  1 ½ inches thick   pepper
½ cup salad oil   Paprika (optional)
Juice of 1 lemon   Béarnaise sauce (see the next
Fresh or dried dill   recipe)

ADVANCE PREPARATION:

If you have a microwave, line a glass baking dish with paper towels.
Lay the steaks on the paper and brush with oil. Sprinkle with lemon
juice, dill, salt and pepper. Cover the dish with a piece of wax paper and
refrigerate.

If you will be using a conventional oven, line a baking sheet with
aluminum foil and paint with a little oil. Place the steaks on the foil and
brush with oil. Sprinkle with lemon juice, dill, salt and pepper. Cover
with a sheet of oiled aluminum foil and refrigerate.

BEFORE SERVING:

Microwave on "high" for 5 minutes. Give the dish a half turn and
continue to cook for 7 minutes. Let stand 3 minutes to complete the
cooking.

Or, bake the salmon 30 minutes in a preheated 350-degree F. oven.
Remove the top sheet of foil and bake 15 minutes longer.

With a sharp knife and small spatula remove the skin from each steak
before transferring it to a heated ovenproof platter. Sprinkle the steaks
with more lemon juice, dill, salt and pepper, and, if desired, a little
paprika. Slip under the broiler for a minute or two to brown lightly.

TO SERVE:

Top each steak with a little Béarnaise. Surround with alternating
bouquets of broccoli and clusters of potatoes. Serve the rest of the
sauce in a sauce dish. The sauce serves for the vegetables as well as for
the salmon.

Béarnaise Sauce

Béarnaise, one of France's greatest culinary inventions, is not difficult to make. An elaboration of Hollandaise, it can be made in the classic manner or quickly in a blender or food processor, in advance or at the last minute. Make the sauce in a stainless steel or enamel-lined saucepan. Béarnaise should always be served lukewarm, not hot.

4 tablespoons white wine
  vinegar
1 teaspoon chopped shallots or
  scallions
2 teaspoons chopped parsley
1½ teaspoons chopped tarragon

¼ teaspoon salt
⅛ teaspoon black pepper
5 egg yolks
1½ sticks butter or margarine
2 tablespoons heavy cream
  (for reheating)

ADVANCE PREPARATION:

Classic Method: Boil the vinegar with the shallots and half the parsley and tarragon in a small saucepan or the top part of a double boiler until most of the vinegar has evaporated. This is a matter of minutes. Remove from the heat. Add the salt and pepper and cool to lukewarm.

Whisk the egg yolks in a bowl until blended and add slowly to the lukewarm herbs, whisking constantly. Place over low heat or over simmering water and whisk until the mixture starts to thicken. Add the butter 2 tablespoons at a time and keep whisking until the sauce is smooth and thick. Add the remaining chopped herbs. Taste for seasoning. Serve immediately or pour into a glass jar and refrigerate.

Quick Method: Boil the vinegar and shallots for 1 minute or until 1 tablespoon of the vinegar remains.

Chop the parsley and tarragon together in a blender or food processor. Remove about 2 teaspoons of the mixture.

Melt the butter until liquefied but not bubbling.

Add the vinegar to the parsley and tarragon in the machine. Spin 3 seconds. Add the salt, pepper, and egg yolks and spin 3 seconds. Add the butter gradually and spin until smooth and thick. Stir in the reserved herbs. Serve immediately or pour into a glass jar for refrigeration.

BEFORE SERVING:

If sauce has been refrigerated, reheat it to lukewarm, adding the cream to prevent separation. Warm in a small pan over low heat or place uncovered in the microwave oven for 20 seconds. Whisk before serving.

Boiled New Potatoes

New potatoes boiled in their jackets is a dish traditionally served in New England in early summer when salmon are running. Fortunately salmon and new potatoes are available almost year round, but freshly dug potatoes and equally fresh salmon are far superior to those shipped from far away. Allow 2 to 3 potatoes per person depending on size, both of potatoes and of appetite.

ADVANCE PREPARATION:

Scrub the potatoes thoroughly and place in a saucepan.

BEFORE SERVING:

Before your guests arrive, cover the potatoes with cold water. Add 1 teaspoon of salt and bring to a boil. Set the timer for 25 minutes. Reduce heat and simmer. Test the potatoes; and if a fork slips in easily, drain the potatoes and suspend them in a strainer over a little hot water to dry. Keep warm until time to serve.

Broccoli Bouquets

1 large bunch of broccoli   *1 small jar pimientos*

ADVANCE PREPARATION:

Cut away the hard stalks from the broccoli. Cut the tight green buds and tender stems into small bunches. If necessary, tie several single stalks together with kitchen twine. There should be 12 sturdy little bouquets. Cut 12 thin strips of pimiento to serve as ribbons.

BEFORE SERVING:

Bring to a simmer 4 cups of water and add 1 teaspoon of salt. Just before serving the first course, drop the bouquets into the simmering water. Increase the heat and cook 10 to 12 minutes. Undercook rather than overcook. Drain well.

Arrange the bouquets as suggested in the salmon recipe, removing any kitchen twine. "Tie" the bouquets with the red pimiento strips.

Maple Nut Coffee Cream

1 large egg yolk   *1½ pints coffee ice cream*
¾ cup maple syrup   *6 walnut halves*
¾ cup whipping cream   *4 tablespoons hot maple syrup*
½ cup chopped walnuts   *(optional)*

ADVANCE PREPARATION:

Whisk the egg yolk and maple syrup in the top part of a double boiler over simmering water until the mixture thickens. Turn the mixture into a freezing tray and place in the freezer until thoroughly cold but not frozen.

Whip the cream. Fold the cream and the nuts into the maple syrup mixture and return to the freezer. Freeze for 3 hours, stirring once or twice.

TO SERVE:

Put a tablespoon of the maple mixture in the bottom of each of 6 parfait glasses. Fill each glass three-quarters full with ice cream. Top with its share of the remaining maple syrup mixture and garnish with a walnut half. For an extra touch, you can dribble a little hot maple syrup over each serving.

Dinners for Eight

The perfect number for an elegant dinner party is eight, to my way of thinking. Such a party should be a whole evening's occupation and not something that precedes the theater or any other event. The stellar role of the evening is played by the food and wine, which together make a perfect setting for friendly and animated conversation with new friends or old. Even when the host or hostess doubles as cook and waiter, the dinner can be impressive, and it will be more relaxed than if there were a footman behind each chair.

DINNER FOR EIGHT I

Asparagus Vinaigrette

Gigot of Spring Lamb
Mushroom-Stuffed Tomatoes
Buckwheat Kasha with Sour Cream
or Duchess Potato Nests
Green Peas

Cheese Platter

Lime Meringue Pie or
Grapefruit Cherry Heering

WINE SUGGESTIONS:

With the second course—
Domestic: Cabernet Sauvignon, or
Imported: Château Gloria (Médoc)
With the cheese—
Domestic: Gamay Beaujolais, or
Imported: Fleurie (Beaujolais)

SHOPPING LIST:

3 pounds asparagus

5-pound leg spring lamb

2 cups veal or beef stock

8 medium-sized tomatoes

½ pound mushrooms

2 ounces cheddar cheese

Green peas (fresh or frozen)

Choice: buckwheat groats or
potatoes. To prepare the
buckwheat groats you will
need chicken broth and
sour cream.

Cheese for tray (see suggestions)

Bread (French or sourdough
whole wheat)

Choice of dessert: pie or
fruit. To prepare the pie
you will need 6 small
limes; for the fruit dessert,
4 grapefruits and Cherry
Heering liqueur.

Asparagus Vinaigrette

This recipe is equally good with white or green asparagus. Like most vegetables, asparagus is best when freshly picked, but canned white or frozen green asparagus adapt very well to this manner of serving. Crusty bread is almost a must with this dish.

3 pounds green or white
asparagus

¼ cup red wine vinegar

2 shallots, chopped fine

½ teaspoon salt

⅛ teaspoon black pepper

¼ cup olive oil

¼ cup vegetable oil

2 tablespoons chopped
parsley

2 tablespoons chopped
carrots

ADVANCE PREPARATION:

Trim off the tough ends of the asparagus and wash the asparagus quickly but thoroughly, taking care that no sand lurks behind the stem leaves. Using a potato parer, scrape the bottom 3 inches of the stems. Tie the asparagus into 8 bunches, using kitchen twine. Place upright, stem ends down, in a steaming kettle containing 2 inches of boiling water. Cover and steam for 12 to 14 minutes depending on the thickness of the spears. Remove and drain. Cool and place in the refrigerator.

Combine the vinegar, salt, pepper, and oils in a glass jar. Cover, and shake for a moment or two. Do not refrigerate.

Chop the parsley and carrots very fine in a food processor or by hand. Place in a jar and refrigerate.

BEFORE SERVING:

Place the asparagus bunches on individual salad plates. Remove the twine. Shake the dressing well and pour over the asparagus, allowing 1½ tablespoons per serving. Sprinkle with the chopped parsley and carrots. The plates should be on the table before the guests sit down.

Gigot of Spring Lamb

Ask the butcher to leave the protruding bone on the leg. This is lamb à la française, and the French carve the meat with the grain, parallel to the bone, grasping the leg by the bone. Meat carved this way is particularly tender and flavorful.

1 5-pound leg of lamb
1 large clove garlic
2 tablespoons butter
1 teaspoon rosemary leaves
1 teaspoon salt
Freshly ground black pepper

SAUCE:
2 cups veal or beef stock
Juice of ½ lemon
1 tablespoon butter

ADVANCE PREPARATION:

Remove all visible fat from the lamb with a sharp knife. Make small deep slits at several spots in the meat.

Peel the garlic and cut into small slivers. Insert the garlic in the slits so that they disappear from sight.

Rub the meat with the butter and sprinkle with rosemary, salt, and pepper. If this is done several hours in advance, refrigerate the meat but allow it to come to room temperature at least an hour before roasting.

BEFORE SERVING:

Plan your schedule so that you will remove the meat from the oven and have time to make the sauce before serving the first course.

Preheat the oven to 350 degrees F. and allow 12 to 15 minutes oven time per pound for rare to medium-rare lamb, 25 minutes per pound for well-done. Baste occasionally. Transfer the cooked lamb to a heated platter and keep on top of the stove or in a warming oven.

To make the sauce: Pour off the fat from the pan. Stir in the stock with a fork, taking care to scrape the pan juices. Add the lemon juice and butter and stir until the butter melts. Strain into a small saucepan.

TO SERVE:

Reheat the sauce and pour it into a sauce bowl. Surround the lamb with the stuffed tomatoes.

Mushroom-Stuffed Tomatoes

8 tomatoes
½ pound mushrooms
2 tablespoons butter or
  margarine
2 tablespoons chopped shallots
  or scallions (green onions)

½ cup whole wheat bread
  crumbs
4 tablespoons grated sharp
  cheddar cheese
Salt and pepper

ADVANCE PREPARATION:

Choose tomatoes of the same size. Cut off ¼ inch from the stem end. Cut the tops into small pieces. Scoop out the centers and place upside down on a rack to drain.

Trim the stem ends of the mushrooms and wash briefly, patting them dry in a towel. Chop coarsely in a food processor or by hand.

Heat the butter or margarine in a small skillet. Sauté the shallots for 1 minute over moderate heat. Add the mushrooms and stir well. Continue to cook until the mushrooms are almost dry. Remove from the heat and stir in the chopped tomatoes, the bread crumbs, and the cheese. Season to taste with salt and pepper.

Fill the tomatoes with the mixture. Place on a buttered baking sheet or (if using a microwave) in a glass dish, leaving space between.

BEFORE SERVING:

In a regular oven bake 10 minutes at 375 degrees F. Serve around the meat platter or on a separate platter with the Duchess Potato Nests.

In a microwave oven bake 5 minutes. Serve as above.

Buckwheat Kasha

Buckwheat Kasha has a special nutlike flavor that goes well with lamb. It can be cooked in advance in either a regular oven or a microwave and reheated with the final seasonings, either in a double boiler or in a microwave oven, shortly before serving.

2 tablespoons butter or margarine	*4 cups chicken broth*
3 tablespoons chopped onion	*1 large egg*
1½ cups buckwheat groats (kasha)	*1 cup sour cream*
	2 tablespoons chopped parsley
	Salt and pepper

ADVANCE PREPARATION:

Heat the butter or margarine in a 2-quart ovenproof, nonmetal serving casserole.

Sauté the chopped onion over moderate heat for 1 minute. Add the buckwheat groats and stir well. Reduce the heat to low and cook very gently for 10 minutes, stirring frequently. Do not let the groats scorch.

Heat the chicken broth.

Beat the egg in a small bowl with a whisk and gradually add 1 cup of the hot broth, whisking continuously. Pour the mixture into the rest of the hot broth, still whisking.

Stir the broth into the groats.

BEFORE SERVING:

If using a conventional oven, cover the kasha and cook for 25 minutes at 375 degrees F. Remove from the oven and stir in the sour cream and parsley. Season to taste with salt and pepper. Keep warm if serving is delayed. In a microwave oven, cook uncovered for 6 minutes, stirring twice. Remove from the oven and let stand 5 minutes. Add the sour cream and parsley and let stand 3 minutes longer.

TO SERVE:

Turn the kasha onto a heated platter and quickly smooth into a round. Fashion a well in the center to hold the peas.

Duchess Potato Nests

These decorative and delicious creations can be made well in advance. They can be served as a garnish for the meat platter or on a separate platter along with the stuffed tomatoes.

6 medium to large potatoes   2 egg yolks
3 tablespoons butter or   1 teaspoon salt
  margarine   ⅛ teaspoon white pepper
1 egg

ADVANCE PREPARATION:

Peel the potatoes and cut them in half. Place in a saucepan and cover with cold water. Add 1 teaspoon of salt and bring to a rapid boil. Cook until tender. Drain the potatoes and return them to the saucepan, tossing them over moderate heat until mealy on all sides.

Place the potatoes in an electric mixing bowl and beat, adding the butter or margarine, egg, egg yolks, salt, and pepper. Cool for 5 to 10 minutes.

There are two methods of making the rings, depending on your equipment:

1. Make 8 potato balls, each 2 inches in diameter, by rolling them between the floured palms of your hands. Place them on a small buttered baking sheet. Flour the bottom of a small juice glass and press a well into the center of each ball.

2. Butter a small baking sheet and dust half of it lightly with flour. Using a water glass, mark out 8 circles 1 inch apart. Fill a pastry bag, fitted with a medium cannellated tip, with the potato mixture. Fill in the circles with half-inch layers. Smooth them with a small spatula. Pipe a ½-inch ring around the edge of each circle.

Keep the nests in a cool place.

BEFORE SERVING:

Bake the potato nests 8 to 10 minutes in a 375-degree F. oven. The tomatoes will take the same length of time.

TO SERVE:

Transfer the potato nests and the tomatoes to the edge of the lamb platter, or place them decoratively on a separate platter. Fill the nests with buttered peas.

Green Peas

The peas serve principally as an accent of color and demand very little attention. They can be cooked during the first course.

2 pounds fresh peas or   *2 tablespoons butter or*
  1 box (10 ounces)   *margarine*
  frozen peas   *Salt and pepper*

ADVANCE PREPARATION:

Fresh peas may be shelled in advance and stored in a covered container in the refrigerator until cooking time.

BEFORE SERVING:

Steam the peas over boiling water for 13 to 15 minutes in a covered pan or boil in a very small amount of water 10 to 12 minutes. Drain and stir in the butter or margarine, salt, and pepper.

Cook frozen peas according to package directions.

TO SERVE:

If you are serving Buckwheat Kasha, make a round depression in the center of the mound and fill with the peas.

If you have chosen the Duchesse potatoes, fill the nests with the peas.

The Cheese Platter

A cheese course is often the most popular part of a dinner party. Never serve it before a hot soufflé because it is a course guests linger over while table conversation flourishes. Cheese, like wine, is for both connoisseurs and amateurs and it seems to evoke nostalgic memories that must be reviewed.

A cheese platter can contain as many varieties as your purse affords, but usually it consists of 4 or 5 varieties ranging from a simple domestic cheese to some of the more robust varieties. Sweet butter, good bread, and a sturdy red wine have to be part of the picture. I suggest both a crusty French bread for the milder cheeses and a sourdough whole wheat bread for the stronger varieties. Remember that cheese must always be served at room temperature for full flavor.

Below are listed some of the good cheeses. There are hundreds more.

Brie	*Gruyère*
Cream Havarti	*Triple crème*
Danbo with caraway	*Cheddar*
Stilton	*Liederkranz*
Double crème	*Boursin*
Pont L'Evêque	*Gouda*
Gorgonzola	

Lime Meringue Pie

The thought of making pastry discourages some people from attempting pies. This problem has been solved by the food processor, which magically produces excellent pastry in a matter of seconds. Instructions for making pie pastry this way, and the old-fashioned way, with a variety of flours will be found on page 238. For this pie, plan to use a 10-inch Pyrex or Corning pie plate. I make the shell and filling the day before a party, but I do not fill the shell or put on the meringue until the morning of the festive dinner.

Baked Pie Shell

FILLING:
½ cup cornstarch
1⅔ cups sugar
2 cups water
5 egg yolks
½ cup lime juice

2 teaspoons grated lemon rind
¼ teaspoon salt
Green vegetable coloring

MERINGUE:
6 egg whites
¼ teaspoon salt
¾ cup sugar

ADVANCE PREPARATION:

Put the cornstarch, sugar, and water in the top part of a double boiler. Whisk over direct heat until the mixture comes to the boiling point. Place over simmering water and continue to cook 3 minutes.

Meanwhile, separate the eggs and beat the egg yolks with an electric beater until light. Add the lime juice, lemon rind, and salt. Add very gradually to the cornstarch mixture, whisking hard. Continue cooking, stirring constantly until the mixture is thick.

Remove from the heat and pour into a bowl. Color very lightly with 2 or 3 drops of coloring. Keep in a cool place.

On the morning of the day the pie is to be served, let the egg whites (six) come to room temperature before beating. Add the salt and whip with an electric beater, starting slowly and then increasing the speed of the beater. When the eggs are stiff, start adding the sugar very gradually. Continue beating for 10 minutes.

If you have a plastic turntable, place the pie plate on it. It makes for easier decorating.

Fill the pie shell with the lime filling, smoothing it into place with a spatula. Cover the filling with a ½-inch layer of meringue, making sure that it completely seals in the filling.

If you wish to finish the pie very simply, just spoon small mounds of meringue all over the surface. But if you feel creative, put the meringue in a large pastry bag, fitted with a cannellated tip. Run a ring around the rim. Make a large star in the center and radiate spokes of meringue from the star to the rim, punctuating each end with a small star.

Sprinkle the entire surface very lightly with fine sugar (white or green) and bake in a 275-degree F. oven for 30 minutes. Cool and chill before serving.

TO SERVE:

Place the pie on a round dessert platter and cut at the table.

Grapefruit Cherry Heering

4 grapefruits   *Cherry Heering liqueur*

Allow ½ grapefruit per serving. Halve, seed, and section the grapefruit. Clip out the center core. Pour 1½ tablespoons of Cherry Heering into each half. Place on a tray. Cover with wax paper and chill in the refrigerator.

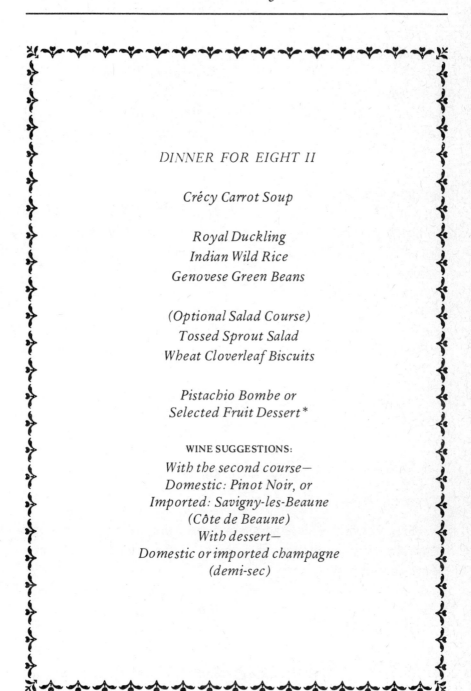

DINNER FOR EIGHT II

Crécy Carrot Soup

Royal Duckling
Indian Wild Rice
Genovese Green Beans

(Optional Salad Course)
Tossed Sprout Salad
Wheat Cloverleaf Biscuits

Pistachio Bombe or
Selected Fruit Dessert*

WINE SUGGESTIONS:
With the second course—
Domestic: Pinot Noir, or
Imported: Savigny-les-Beaune
(Côte de Beaune)
With dessert—
Domestic or imported champagne
(demi-sec)

SHOPPING LIST:

Carrots

4 cups chicken broth

2 ducks

2 oranges

1 lemon

4 bananas

Currant jelly (optional)

Watercress

1 pound wild rice

Italian green beans (fresh or
    frozen)

¼ pound grated Parmesan

Basil

Pinenuts or walnuts

1 large head Boston lettuce

2 cups alfalfa sprouts

Black olives

Cherry tomatoes

1 quart pistachio ice cream

2 ounces pistachios

½ pint cream

Glacé cherries

Parsley

2 medium-sized potatoes

3 onions

Garlic

Madeira

Rum

Cointreau

Amaretto liqueur (optional)

Crécy Carrot Soup

The French word, Crécy, always indicates the presence of carrots, vegetables so healthful that some people feel they shouldn't appear at a party. This soup will convert them.

4 fresh firm carrots (5
    or 6 inches long)

2 medium-sized potatoes

1 onion

¾ teaspoon sea salt

½ teaspoon celery salt

⅛ teaspoon white pepper

4 cups chicken broth

1 tablespoon chopped parsley

1 cup cream (optional)

ADVANCE PREPARATION:

Scrub the carrots well and cut off the tips of each end. Cut off half of one of the carrots and slice the rest in ½-inch slices. Place them in a 2-quart saucepan.

Peel and slice the potatoes and onion and combine with the carrots. Add the seasonings and 1½ cups of the broth. Bring to a boil and simmer 20 to 25 minutes or until the vegetables are very soft.

Meanwhile, slice the remaining carrot half and the parsley into a food processor or blender and spin for 3 seconds. Put the combination in a small bowl. Cover and refrigerate. Or chop the parsley and grate the carrot by hand. Mix together and refrigerate.

Pour the cooked vegetables and broth into a blender or food processor and puree briefly. Add the remaining broth.

BEFORE SERVING:

Reheat the soup in a double boiler, adding the cream if desired. Taste for seasoning.

TO SERVE:

Ladle the soup into warmed individual soup cups. Garnish with the chopped carrot and parsley.

Royal Duckling

This recipe is an adaptation of a regal French recipe. It has the advantage of being both cooked and quartered in advance, a boon to most carvers. It is also defatted after the first cooking, which makes it less caloric than most duck dishes. Of course, the ducks can be cooked entirely in either a regular or microwave oven, but I find the best method is to defrost the ducks (one by one) in the microwave and to roast them in a regular oven. Then either oven can be used for final cooking. Directions will be given for this method and also for using just the regular oven.

2 ducks (4½ pounds each)	2 tablespoons rum
2 onions stuck with 2 cloves each	Watercress
2 oranges	4 tablespoons Madeira wine or 4 ounces currant jelly
1 lemon	Salt and pepper
1 teaspoon cornstarch	3 tablespoons Cointreau
4 small bananas	
1 tablespoon butter or margarine, melted	

ADVANCE PREPARATION:

Since most ducks are sold frozen, one must allow 12 hours at room temperature for defrosting unless your kitchen is graced with a microwave oven.

To defrost in the microwave, allow 5 minutes per pound for each bird. Place the duckling in its store wrapper (the metal closures do not have to be removed) on the floor of the oven. Defrost for half the calculated time (10 to 13 minutes). Remove the duckling from the wrapper and place it in a glass or ceramic dish. Cover the wings, tail, and leg ends with pieces of aluminum foil and defrost for another 10 to 13 minutes. Remove the thawed duck and run cold water through the cavity to dislodge the giblets. Repeat the process with the other duckling.

Preheat the oven to 400 degrees F. Place the livers in a small bowl; cover and refrigerate for your future pleasure.

Put the necks, gizzards, and hearts in a small saucepan with 1½ cups of water, ¼ bay leaf, a pinch of thyme, and ¼ teaspoon of salt. Cover and simmer for 1 hour.

Wash the ducks inside and out with cold water. Pat dry both exterior and interior with paper toweling. Rub in salt and pepper and prick the skin in several places with a fork. Put an onion stuck with cloves in the cavity of each duck.

Place the ducks in an open roasting pan and roast for 12 to 14 minutes per pound depending on preference of doneness. As the ducks cook, remove the fat from the pan every 15 minutes with a bulb baster.

Meanwhile, prepare the garnish: Squeeze the juice of one orange and ½ lemon into a small bowl. Remove the flesh and fibers from the orange and cut the peel into thin shreds with a sharp knife. Throw the shreds into a small pan of boiling water and cook 5 minutes. Drain immediately and discard liquid.

Dissolve the cornstarch in the juices.

Peel the bananas and cut them lengthwise. Place on an ovenproof platter and sprinkle with lemon juice to keep the fruit from discoloring. Brush with the butter or margarine and sprinkle with the rum. Cover with wax paper and keep in a cool place.

Wash and trim the watercress. Place in a small plastic bag and refrigerate.

Cut the remaining orange into thin wedges. Wrap in another small bag and refrigerate.

Transfer the roasted ducks to a platter to cool. Pour off all the fatty drippings from the pan into a bowl. Cool and refrigerate. Drain the giblet broth into the roasting pan and bring to a boil, scraping with a fork the juices adhering to the pan. Strain the mixture into a small saucepan. Add the Madeira or jelly. Simmer 3 minutes. Add the fruit peel and the cornstarch mixture. Bring to a simmer and remove from the heat. Season to taste. Cool and chill.

Cut each cooled duck into quarters. Discard the onions and cut away the large breastbones and backbones (large kitchen scissors are very handy for this operation). Place the duck in a shallow casserole suitable for reheating, nonmetal if using microwave. Cover and refrigerate.

BEFORE SERVING:

With conventional oven arrange the oven racks to accommodate the bananas, the duck, and the rice. Preheat the oven to 350 degrees F.

Allow 40 minutes for the final cooking of the duck, 30 minutes for the rice, 10 minutes for the bananas.

Remove the fat from both refrigerated bowls. Add the duck juices and Cointreau to the sauce. Spread the sauce over the duck. Cook covered for 20 minutes; uncover for the final 20 minutes.

With a microwave oven, the main course can be given its final preparation before serving if you organize a kind of assembly line before your guests arrive. Defat the sauce and drippings. Combine them and stir in the Cointreau. Pour over the duck and cover with a glass cover or wax paper. Place in the microwave oven.

Assemble the dishes containing the bananas, the rice, and the green beans mixed with sauce, and place them near the oven. Have a warm platter, the orange sections, and the watercress at hand.

Just before serving the first course, set the oven on "high" for 8 minutes. After cooking, the duck should be allowed to set for 3 minutes, which allows you time to enjoy the first course with ease.

While someone else is clearing the table, remove the duck and put in the bananas (covered) for 1 minute. Remove from the oven.

Put in the rice and microwave for 2½ minutes. Open the door and stir the rice with a fork. At the same time put in the beans. Microwave 4 minutes. Give the beans a stir after 2 minutes.

TO SERVE:

Place the duck quarters and sauce on a large heated platter. Garnish decoratively with the bananas and orange wedges. Surround with watercress and bring to the table.

Indian Wild Rice

Wild rice is an expensive commodity, but it's worthy of the Royal Duckling. Brown rice, which appears elsewhere in this book, is a good substitute. Connoisseurs of wild rice claim that it must never be boiled and that it should be prepared a day in advance and reheated. The preparation takes no cooking and can be done while preparing the rest of the meal.

ADVANCE PREPARATION:

For eight cups of "cooked" rice, wash 2 cups of raw wild rice under running water, rubbing the rice between the palms of your hands in a colander until the water runs clear. Drain well and place in a deep saucepan. Cover with rapidly boiling water and let stand covered until cool. Drain. Repeat the process three times, making sure that the water is boiling rapidly when you pour it over the drained rice. After the final draining, stir in 4 tablespoons of melted butter or margarine and season with salt and pepper. Cover and keep in a cool place.

BEFORE SERVING:

In a microwave oven, place the rice in a shallow covered Pyrex or Corningware dish. Cover and cook 5 minutes. Remove the cover, stir well, and cook covered for another 1½ minutes.

With conventional range, place the rice in a covered dish. Set in a pan of water in the 350-degree F. oven for 30 minutes. Or, if space is limited, reheat in a covered double boiler on top of the range.

Genovese Green Beans

This dish is made with Italian flat green beans, to my mind the best green beans you can grow in your garden. (They can also be found in the freezer section of the market.) To stand up in flavor to the duck and wild rice, I serve them with a form of Italian pesto. For the faint of heart, I suggest saucing the beans with butter or margarine or sour cream, and salt and pepper. However, the following is a real taste sensation.

2 pounds fresh Italian green
  beans or 3 boxes frozen

SAUCE:
4 tablespoons freshly washed
  basil leaves or 2 tablespoons dried basil
2 cloves garlic, peeled

½ cup freshly grated Parmesan
  cheese
2 tablespoons pinenuts or
  walnuts
1 tablespoon butter or margarine
½ cup olive oil or salad oil
½ teaspoon salt
⅛ teaspoon black pepper

ADVANCE PREPARATION:

Put all the ingredients for the sauce in a blender or food processor. Spin until blended, a matter of seconds. Place in a bowl. Cover and refrigerate.

Wash fresh beans, snip off ends, and break into pieces. Cook in a small amount of boiling salted water (just enough to cover) until barely tender. Remove and drain (saving the water for a future soup).

If using frozen beans, follow directions on the package, allowing 2 minutes less than the prescribed time. Drain, cool, cover, and refrigerate.

BEFORE SERVING:

Heat the sauce in a pan. Stir in the beans, which have been allowed to come to room temperature. Heat just until hot.

If using a microwave oven, place the beans in a nonmetal vegetable dish. Stir in the sauce and heat 2 minutes, stirring once.

Tossed Sprout Salad

You can easily grow your own sprouts, or you will find them in most markets. They are crisp and delicious as well as full of healthy nutrients. You can use soy, chick pea, or mung sprouts in place of the alfalfa.

2 cups alfalfa sprouts
1 large head Boston lettuce
12 cherry tomatoes
8 pitted black olives

DRESSING:
4 tablespoons red wine vinegar

1 clove garlic, pressed
4 tablespoons olive oil
½ cup corn, peanut, or
   safflower oil
1 teaspoon sea salt
⅛ teaspoon black pepper

ADVANCE PREPARATION:

Wash and drain the sprouts. Place in the refrigerator.

Wash the lettuce. Break it into pieces and spin dry or pat dry carefully with clean dish towels.

Wash the tomatoes and cut them in half. Place in a container, cover, and refrigerate.

Halve the olives and place in a small covered jar in the refrigerator.

Combine all the ingredients for the dressing in a small jar or pitcher. Shake well and let stand in a cool place.

TO SERVE:

Line a salad bowl with the lettuce leaves. Cover with the sprouts and sprinkle with the tomatoes and olives. Bring to the table and mix with the dressing at table.

Food Processor
Wheat Cloverleaf Biscuits
(1 dozen)

These biscuits can be mixed and baked in advance and then reheated in a double boiler, or they can be mixed and formed and then refrigerated for baking just before serving. If the biscuits are to go direct from refrigerator to oven, allow an extra 2 minutes baking time.

1 cup unbleached white flour
¾ cup whole wheat flour
4 tablespoons wheat germ
2 teaspoons baking powder

¼ teaspoon baking soda
6 tablespoons frozen butter
1 teaspoon salt
¾ cup buttermilk

ADVANCE PREPARATION:

Preheat the oven to 425 degrees F.

Place the flours, wheat germ, baking powder, baking soda, frozen butter (cut in ¼-inch slices), and salt in a food processor. Spin 10 seconds. Add the buttermilk through the spout and spin 30 seconds or until the dough forms a ball on the blades.

Turn the dough out on a working surface and roll into 36 small balls, each approximately ¾ inch in diameter.

Butter or oil 12 muffin cups, or use unbuttered Teflon-lined tins. Place 3 balls in each cup. Bake 12 minutes.

Pistachio Bombe

A bombe is an easy party dessert that can be made weeks in advance. I keep two on hand in the freezer at all times, one large and one small (half this recipe). It is wonderful both for the unexpected guest and for those times when making a dessert seems too much work.

1 quart pistachio ice cream
1 cup whipping cream
¾ cup confectioners' sugar
½ cup chopped pistachio nuts

½ cup glacé cherries
2 tablespoons amaretto liqueur
   or 1½ teaspoons vanilla

ADVANCE PREPARATION:

Open the quart of ice cream to let it soften a little.

Whip the cream stiff and fold in the sugar, nuts, cherries, and preferred flavoring.

Rinse a 1½-quart mold in cold water. Put three-fourths of the ice cream in the mold and, using the back of a large spoon, push the ice cream against the sides and bottom of the mold, leaving a large hole in the center. Fill the center with the whipped cream mixture and smooth the remaining cup of ice cream over the top.

Cover with aluminum foil and put on the cover. Lacking a cover, use 2 thicknesses of foil and tie in place with kitchen twine.

Place in the freezer for a minimum of 6 hours.

TO SERVE:

Fill a large bowl or dishpan with hot water. Remove the cover from the bombe and lower the mold into the water for 30 to 50 seconds. Turn onto a dessert platter.

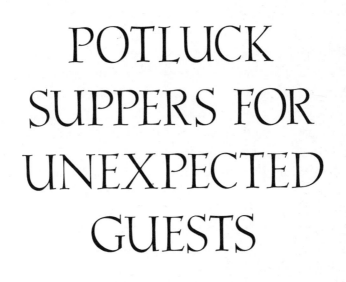

POTLUCK
SUPPERS FOR
UNEXPECTED
GUESTS

Potluck Supper for Four

Potluck Supper for Six

Potluck Supper for Eight

Friends have dropped in for a late afternoon drink. The talk is good, the atmosphere congenial, and it seems a shame to bring it to an end. Or you meet someone coming home on the train who would be better off for an evening with company and you would like to bring him—or her—home with you. This is the time that reserve shelves in both cupboard and freezer come to the rescue. Make a point of stocking your shelves and keeping them stocked along the lines I suggest. It is like money in the bank. "Potluck" suppers are not meant to be elaborate dinners, but it is amazing what you can produce at a moment's notice when the right ingredients are available. (See my suggestions for Reserve Food and Freezer Shelves, pages 261-262.) If children are involved, feed them the meal you had planned for the family while you whisk up the supper party for adults to share with the guests. Sometimes this kind of evening is more fun than the most carefully planned dinner.

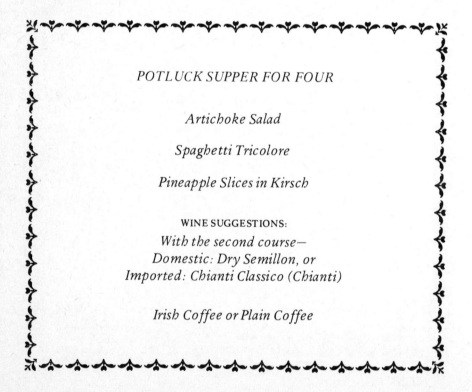

POTLUCK SUPPER FOR FOUR

Artichoke Salad

Spaghetti Tricolore

Pineapple Slices in Kirsch

WINE SUGGESTIONS:
With the second course—
Domestic: Dry Semillon, or
Imported: Chianti Classico (Chianti)

Irish Coffee or Plain Coffee

Artichoke Salad

This should be eaten with French bread or unleavened (Sahara) whole wheat bread (unbuttered).

1 can (20 ounces) artichoke
  hearts
2 tablespoons red wine vinegar
3 tablespoons olive oil
3 tablespoons salad oil
½ teaspoon salt

⅛ teaspoon black pepper
1 tablespoon chopped chives
  (fresh or dried)
Garden lettuce
8 anchovy strips (optional)

ADVANCE PREPARATION:

Drain the artichokes and place them in a small salad bowl. Mix the vinegar, oils, salt, pepper, and chives. Pour over the artichoke hearts. Let stand in the refrigerator while you are preparing the rest of the supper.

TO SERVE:

If you have lettuce leaves in your refrigerator, encircle the top inside of the bowl with them. Drape the anchovy fillets over the artichokes.

In serving, each person will place lettuce on a salad plate and help himself to the artichokes.

Spaghetti Tricolore

When spaghetti is to be the principal feature of an impromptu party, it has to be something extraordinary. It can still be simple. Just serve two or three sauces. My whimsy is to follow the colors of *Il Tricolore*, the Italian flag, and serve tomato sauce, pesto, and clam sauce. Sometimes I spread the sauces in parallel strips on the cooked pasta and other times I serve them in three bowls and offer the spaghetti separately at the table. The secret of success is heated soup plates for the spaghetti and a heated soup tureen or other deep bowl if the spaghetti is to be served at table. If you will read the pages on Reserves, you will be prepared for this entire meal. You will have the tomato sauce and pesto in your freezer and they will only need to be warmed. Allow ¼ pound of spaghetti (semolina or whole wheat) and 2 to 3 tablespoons of each sauce per person.

Tomato Sauce*	2 cloves garlic
Pesto*	1 can minced clams
Spaghetti	½ cup fine bread crumbs
Parmesan cheese	2 tablespoons chopped parsley
	Salt and black pepper

CLAM SAUCE:
¼ pound butter

To make the clam sauce, heat the butter in a small saucepan and add the garlic, pressed or finely minced. Cook over a low flame for 2 minutes. Do not let the garlic brown. Add the clams with 2 tablespoons of the juice, the crumbs, parsley, salt, and pepper. Stir over low heat until well mixed and hot. Set aside and keep warm.

Warm the tomato sauce and pesto.

While you are eating the first course, boil the spaghetti in a large kettle of well-salted water to which 1 tablespoon of salad oil has been added. Once the water comes to its second boil, allow 6 minutes for semolina spaghetti to cook, 10 minutes for the whole wheat variety. The spaghetti must be tender but firm. Drain the spaghetti in a colander and return it to the kettle. Toss with two forks for a minute and add a tablespoon of butter. Serve immediately in either of the suggested ways.

❧ ❧

Pineapple Slices in Kirsch

This dessert does not warrant a recipe. It's just a question of having the supplies on hand.

1 can sliced pineapple   *Kirsch*
  (packed in unsweetened juice)

Chill the pineapple (in the freezer if time is short). Drain the juice and combine ½ cup with 4 tablespoons of kirsch. Place the pineapple slices in individual dessert dishes and spoon over them the kirsch mixture. Garnish, if possible with a red glacé cherry and a sprig of fresh mint.

Irish Coffee

Here is a comforting way to finish supper, especially if it is cold outside. Plain coffee can be served to those who prefer it. For this confection, use Irish whiskey glasses, parfait glasses, or deep stemmed wine glasses.

4 teaspoons sugar   *½ cup cream, whipped*
1½ cups hot strong coffee   *Nutmeg*
1 cup Irish (or bourbon)
  whisky

Put a long silver spoon in each glass.

Dissolve the sugar (some may like it a little sweeter) in ½ cup of hot coffee. Pour 2 tablespoons in each glass.

Add 4 tablespoons of whisky and fill within an inch of the top with the remaining coffee.

Top with whipped cream and sprinkle with a little nutmeg. Serve immediately.

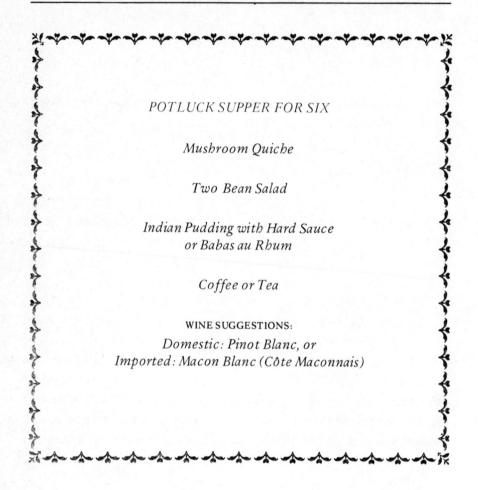

POTLUCK SUPPER FOR SIX

Mushroom Quiche

Two Bean Salad

Indian Pudding with Hard Sauce
or Babas au Rhum

Coffee or Tea

WINE SUGGESTIONS:
Domestic: Pinot Blanc, or
Imported: Macon Blanc (Côte Maconnais)

Mushroom Quiche

If you don't have a prebaked quiche shell (as we recommend in the pages on Reserves) and you do have a food processor, you can make the shell in very short order. Lacking these two options, make a classic pie crust.

FOOD PROCESSOR SHELL:

⅔ cup unbleached white or
  whole wheat pastry flour
½ teaspoon salt
½ stick (4 tablespoons) very
  cold butter
2 tablespoons ice water

FILLING:

2 3½-ounce cans mushroom
  caps

1½ tablespoons butter or
  margarine
4 tablespoons chopped shallots
  or green onions
4 eggs
1 cup cream
1 cup whole milk
½ teaspoon salt
¼ teaspoon white pepper
1 cup grated Gruyère or mild
  cheddar cheese

To make the shell: Preheat the oven to 450 degrees F.

Spin the flour, salt, and butter for 8 seconds in a food processor. Pour the ice water through the tube and continue spinning for about 40 seconds or until the dough forms a ball on the blades. Roll the pastry on a lightly floured surface to a large circle. Place a 9-inch pie plate on the pastry and trim around it with a margin of 1½ inches. Roll the pastry up on the roller and unroll it over the inside of the pie plate, patting it in place with your fingertips. Prick the pastry well, bake 5 minutes, and remove. Reduce the heat to 375 degrees F.

To make the filling: Drain the mushrooms and let them dry.

Heat the butter in a small skillet and sauté the onions over moderate heat for 3 minutes, stirring occasionally so that they will not brown. Set aside.

Beat the eggs with the cream, milk, salt, and pepper, just until blended.

Thirty minutes before serving, spread the shallots or onions over the bottom of the crust. Cover with the grated cheese. Dot with the mushroom caps. Pour in the egg mixture. Bake 30 minutes and serve.

Two Bean Salad

1 can (16 ounces) small green beans	2 tablespoons red wine vinegar
1 can (8¾ ounces) shelled beans	6 tablespoons salad oil
2 small onions	1 teaspoon salt
	¼ teaspoon black pepper
	Lettuce (if you have it)

Drain the beans and place them in a salad bowl.

Peel and slice the onions very thin. Break the slices into rings. Add to the beans.

Mix the vinegar, oil, salt, and pepper in a small jar and pour over the beans. Toss lightly and cover with the lettuce leaves if you have them. Do not toss again until just before serving.

Indian Pudding with Hard Sauce

1 can (16 ounces) Indian pudding	1 tablespoon brandy or 1 teaspoon vanilla
4 tablespoons butter	¼ teaspoon cinnamon
1¼ cup confectioners' sugar	Nutmeg

Open the can and spoon portions of the pudding into 6 ramekins or custard cups.

Cream the butter and sugar together in an electric beater, blender, or food processor. Add the brandy (or vanilla) and cinnamon and mix until smooth. Place in a small serving dish and dust with nutmeg. Refrigerate.

To bake in a conventional oven, place the ramekins in a pan of hot water. Bake at 350 or 375 degrees F. for 25 to 30 minutes. In a microwave oven, cover the ramekins with wax paper and microwave for 2 minutes.

Babas au Rhum

1 can babas au rhum   *Ice cream or whipped cream*
Rum   *Garnish (optional)*

Heat contents of can in the top of a double boiler over simmering water until just lukewarm. Spoon 3 or 4 of the little cakes into each individual dessert glass and cover with the syrup. Sprinkle each with ½ teaspoon rum. Top with a dollop of ice cream or whipped cream and garnish with a candied violet or glacé cherry.

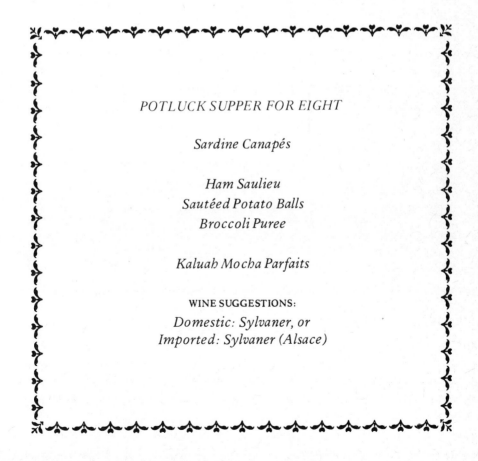

POTLUCK SUPPER FOR EIGHT

Sardine Canapés

Ham Saulieu
Sautéed Potato Balls
Broccoli Puree

Kaluah Mocha Parfaits

WINE SUGGESTIONS:
Domestic: Sylvaner, or
Imported: Sylvaner (Alsace)

Sardine Canapés

8 slices firm whole wheat
   bread
Butter or margarine

2 cans sardines in oil
Lemon
Parsley

Toast and butter the bread.

Arrange the toast on a baking dish. Cover each slice with sardines arranged in neat rows.

Just before serving, slip under a preheated broiler.

Garnish with the lemon and with chopped parsley (fresh if possible). Serve hot on individual salad plates.

Ham Saulieu

2-pound canned ham
Flour
3 tablespoons butter or
   margarine
1 clove garlic, quartered
1 teaspoon tomato paste

¼ cup Madeira or sherry wine
1 can (13 ounces) lobster or
   shrimp bisque
½ pint light cream or
   evaporated milk
Salt and pepper

Remove the ham from the can and remove all the aspic, setting it aside.

Cut the ham in ¾-inch slices and dredge each piece very lightly in flour.

Heat the butter or margarine in a skillet and sauté the garlic over very low heat for 2 minutes. Remove the garlic with a slotted spoon and increase the heat. Brown each slice of ham on both sides and place them all on an ovenproof platter (nonmetal if using a microwave oven), overlapping the slices.

When all the slices are browned, whisk the tomato paste and wine into the skillet. Mix well and add 3 tablespoons of the aspic, the bisque, and the cream. Continue stirring until the mixture comes to a simmer. Remove the pan from the heat and taste for seasoning, taking care not to oversalt.

Pour the sauce over the ham and bake 10 to 15 minutes at 300 degrees F. in a regular oven, or in the microwave, covered, for 6 to 8 minutes, turning the platter once.

Sautéed Potato Balls

2 16-ounce cans potato balls
2 tablespoons butter or
  margarine

2 tablespoons salad oil
Salt

Drain the potato balls and pat them dry with toweling.

Heat the butter or margarine and the oil in an electric skillet (400 degrees F.) or in a frying pan until very hot.

Add the potatoes and brown quickly on all sides, tossing the pan frequently. Reduce the heat to very low and cover, allowing a little space for steam to escape. The potatoes can stand this way for quite a long time if you occasionally toss them. Taste and add salt if needed.

Broccoli Puree

This recipe can be made in a blender but has to be done in sections. The food processor is quicker and easier.

3 packages frozen chopped
   broccoli
3 tablespoons butter or
   margarine
3 tablespoons unbleached white
   or whole wheat pastry flour

1½ cups milk
Salt and pepper
⅛ teaspoon nutmeg

Bring ¾ cup of water to a boil in a saucepan. Add a teaspoon of salt and the frozen broccoli. Using a fork, break the broccoli up; and as soon as the vegetable comes to a boil, cover tightly and cook 5 minutes over moderate heat.

Drain the broccoli over a bowl to save the liquid. Return the liquid to the stove and boil down to ½ cup.

Put the broccoli in a food processor fitted with the steel blade or in a blender.

Add the butter and preferred flour. Puree until the butter is melted.

Add the milk and spin until blended. Add the reduced liquid. The mixture should be creamy and smooth. Season with salt, pepper, and nutmeg.

Place the puree in a heatproof serving bowl and place in a pan of simmering water. Cook a minimum of 10 minutes—but it can be cooked for as long as 30 to 40 minutes without coming to harm.

Kaluah Mocha Parfait

Kaluah is a coffee-flavored liqueur which blends deliciously with ice cream. Serve this dessert in parfait glasses or in deep stemmed wine glasses.

½ cup slivered almonds
½ cup heavy cream
2 tablespoons confectioners'
   sugar (optional)

½ teaspoon vanilla
¾ cup Kaluah
1 pint chocolate ice cream
1 pint coffee ice cream

ADVANCE PREPARATION:

Toast the almonds on a baking sheet under the broiler. Shake the pan frequently and watch closely to make sure the almonds do not burn. Transfer the nuts to a small bowl. Whip the cream, adding the sugar (if desired) and the vanilla. Store in the refrigerator. Arrange the glasses on a tray. Just before dinner, measure 1½ tablespoons of Kaluah into each glass and place the ice cream where it will soften slightly during the main course.

BEFORE SERVING:

Put ¼ cup each of the two kinds of ice cream in each glass. Top with whipped cream. (If you want to be really fancy, put the cream through a pastry tube with a cannellated tip.) Sprinkle with the toasted almonds and serve with long iced-tea spoons, calling your guests' attention to the "gravy" at the bottom of the glass.

MENUS
FOR SPECIAL
OCCASIONS

A Meal of Hors d'Oeuvres

Summer Lunch or Supper for Four

Winter Supper for Eight

Luncheon for Female Friends

Lunch for a Male Foursome

Fish Fare

Hunters' Banquet

A Meal of Hors d'Oeuvres

Not many years ago one of the greatest attractions of traveling in France was lunching at a sidewalk café and feasting on the large assortment of hors d'oeuvres. This was only the first course but someone was bound to say, "I could make a whole meal of just hors d'oeuvres." Such largesse is no longer to be found in most French restaurants but it makes wonderful party fare as a summer noonday lunch on porch or terrace or as a kind of cocktail dinner party. Such a menu should include a minimum of five cold dishes and one hot dish. Guests can fill and refill their plates at will. Plates, forks, and napkins are the only essential equipment other than serving pieces.

I offer no shopping list because it depends on what you choose to serve. I have given several of my favorite recipes. You will think of more. But essential to all such meals is good bread (rye, whole wheat, pumpernickel, and French) and you should have mayonnaise, the makings of a good vinaigrette, parsley, and watercress. Remember that hors d'oeuvres must be as attractive to the eye as to the palate. Refrigerator space must be cleared since everything is prepared in advance.

The buffet table on which the various dishes will be displayed can be arranged on levels with the use of building blocks and children's bed tables covered with napkins. Two more tables, one to serve as a bar and the other for coffee, make this meal almost completely self-service so that the host and hostess can be relaxed.

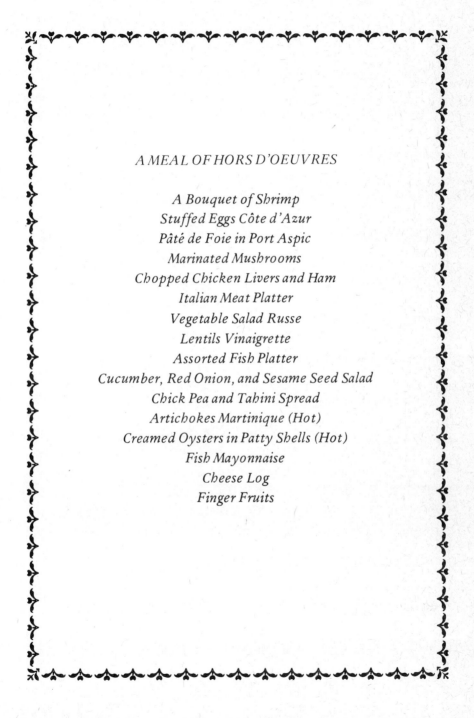

A MEAL OF HORS D'OEUVRES

A Bouquet of Shrimp
Stuffed Eggs Côte d'Azur
Pâté de Foie in Port Aspic
Marinated Mushrooms
Chopped Chicken Livers and Ham
Italian Meat Platter
Vegetable Salad Russe
Lentils Vinaigrette
Assorted Fish Platter
Cucumber, Red Onion, and Sesame Seed Salad
Chick Pea and Tahini Spread
Artichokes Martinique (Hot)
Creamed Oysters in Patty Shells (Hot)
Fish Mayonnaise
Cheese Log
Finger Fruits

A Bouquet of Shrimp

This serves as a centerpiece for the hors d'oeuvre table. Placed on a silver tray and bordered with watercress, it can compete with any florist's display you can buy—and costs about the same. Buy as many shrimp as you can afford; they are never wasted.

2-4 pounds raw shrimp
1 stalk celery
1 onion, sliced
1 bay leaf
1 slice lemon

SAUCE:
1½ cups mayonnaise
1 tablespoon chopped capers

2 teaspoons anchovy paste
2 tablespoons minced scallions
   (green part)
1 clove garlic, pressed
   (optional)
2-3 drops hot sauce (optional)
4 tablespoons catsup
Salt and pepper

ADVANCE PREPARATION:

Wash the shrimp. Remove the shells and intestinal strips. Put the celery, onion, bay leaf, and lemon in 1½ quarts of water. Bring to a boil and simmer covered for 5 minutes. Add the shrimp. Bring to a boil over high heat. Reduce the heat immediately and *simmer* for 6 minutes. Drain. Discard the seasonings. Cool the shrimp, cover, and refrigerate.

Combine the ingredients for the sauce. Place in a covered jar and refrigerate.

TO SERVE:

Put a stemmed goblet filled with the sauce in the center of a pretty glass bowl. Fill the bowl with ice cubes and hang the shrimp all around the rim of the bowl, replacing the shrimp once or twice as necessary.

Stuffed Eggs Côte d'Azur

4-6 large eggs
2-3 basil leaves
1 tablespoon chopped chives
1½ teaspoons chopped capers
4-6 tomatoes

¼ pound soft butter
4 tablespoons olive oil
Salt and pepper
Garden lettuce
2 stuffed olives

Cook the eggs in simmering water for 15 minutes. Drain and crack the shells gently. Place in cold water to cool. Peel the eggs and cut them in half lengthwise. Remove the yolks and place them in a small mixing bowl, a food processor, or a blender.

Parboil the basil leaves for 30 seconds. Drain and chop fine. Combine with the chopped chives and capers.

Choose tomatoes approximately 3½ inches in diameter. They serve as cases for the eggs. Wash them well and cut in half horizontally. Squeeze the halves gently to remove the seeds and scrape out some of the center flesh. Sprinkle with salt and turn upside down on a rack.

Add the butter to the egg yolks and mix thoroughly with a hand beater, food processor, or blender. When they are well blended, add the oil very slowly as though you were making mayonnaise. When that is well incorporated, add ½ teaspoon of salt and ⅛ teaspoon of white pepper. Remove about one-third of the mixture and set aside. Stir the herbs and capers into the rest and use it to fill the egg whites.

Fit an egg half into each tomato half. Spoon the plain egg yolk mixture into a small pastry bag or tube fitted with a small plain tip. Force the mixture in small dots around the tomato rim to look like little mimosa flowers so typical of the French Côte d'Azur. Line a small platter with torn lettuce leaves and place the tomatoes on the lettuce. Garnish each egg with a slice of pimiento-stuffed olive. Refrigerate until time for serving.

Pâté de Foie in Port Aspic

1 pound liverwurst
12 tablespoons soft unsalted
　butter
⅛ teaspoon mace
Salt and pepper
1 can (13 ounces) jellied
　madrilène or beef consommé

1 tablespoon gelatin
4 tablespoons port wine
1 package (3 ounces) chopped
　pistachio nuts
Watercress

ADVANCE PREPARATION:

Chill a 1-quart decorative mold in the refrigerator.

Cut the liverwurst in pieces into an electric mixer bowl or food processor. Add the butter and beat or spin until smooth and fluffy. Season with the mace, salt, and plenty of freshly ground black pepper.

Heat the madrilène or consommé. Soften the gelatin in the port and add to the soup, stirring until the gelatin is dissolved. Pour the soup into a metal bowl and place the bowl in a larger bowl containing ice cubes. Stir until the soup becomes syrupy.

Remove from the ice. Pour 6 tablespoons of the soup into the mold. Tilt the mold so that the aspic reaches all sides of the mold. Place in the refrigerator for 10 minutes (5 minutes in the freezer). Add 6 more tablespoons and repeat the process.

Beat the remaining soup into the liverwurst mixture and stir in the nuts by hand. Gently fill the mold and smooth the top. Cover and chill for several hours.

TO SERVE:

Dip the mold in hot water for 3 or 4 seconds and turn onto a platter. Garnish with watercress.

Marinated Mushrooms

1 pound medium-sized mushrooms
4 tablespoons dry white wine
4 tablespoons tarragon vinegar
¼ cup olive oil
½ cup salad oil (peanut, corn,
  or safflower)
4 tablespoons minced scallions
  (green and white parts)

1 clove garlic, pressed
1 tablespoon grated lemon rind
¾ teaspoon salt
⅛ teaspoon black pepper
Chopped parsley

ADVANCE PREPARATION:

Trim the stems of the mushrooms and wash the mushrooms briefly in cold water. Dry immediately between paper towels. Using the vegetable slicer, force the mushrooms through the tube of a food processor; or slice them vertically by hand. Place them in a shallow glass or ceramic serving dish.

Mix the remaining ingredients except for the parsley, whisking until well mixed. Pour over the mushrooms. Cover and chill in the refrigerator.

Let stand at least two hours, stirring occasionally.

TO SERVE:

Give the mushrooms a final stirring and sprinkle them with chopped parsley.

Chopped Chicken Livers and Ham

1 pound chicken livers
½ bay leaf
1 small onion, sliced
1 teaspoon salt
⅛ teaspoon white pepper
½ cup (1 stick) sweet butter

1 teaspoon dry mustard
2 tablespoons cognac
1 slice boiled ham cut ¼ inch
    thick
Lettuce leaves

Put the livers in a saucepan and barely cover with cold water. Add the bay leaf. Bring to a simmer. Cover and cook very gently for 15 minutes. Drain the livers and pat dry with paper toweling.

Place the livers in a food processor or blender (the latter would necessitate dividing the livers in thirds). Add the onion and spin until finely chopped. Add the salt, pepper, butter, mustard, and cognac and spin until thoroughly mixed.

Dice the ham in ¼-inch cubes and mix with the chicken liver mixture by hand. Taste for seasoning.

TO SERVE:

Line a small dish with crisp lettuce leaves and shape the mixture on top, giving it a decorative touch with the tines of a fork.

Italian Meat Platter

This is not a recipe. It is a suggestion for a change from the usual meat platter. If you have access to an Italian market or even the delicatessen section of a supermarket, ask for an assortment of Italian cold cuts—mortadella, prosciutto, head cheese, etc. Buy some Provalone cheese which the store will slice for you. Everything should be sliced very thin.

Arrange the meat and cheese around a platter. In the center, place a tumbler containing well-trimmed and washed scallions and fennel sticks cut from fennel bulbs (these have a strong anise flavor). Surround the base with Sicilian olives.

Vegetable Salad Russe

2 pounds potatoes
¾ cup vinaigrette *
1 cup chopped celery
4 tablespoons chopped onions
2 cups cooked or canned peas
1 clove garlic, pressed
    (optional)

2 cups shredded carrots
3 or 4 radishes, sliced
Mayonnaise *
Salt and pepper
Parsley

ADVANCE PREPARATION:

Peel the potatoes and cut them into ½-inch dice (there should be about 4 cups). Drop them into a large pan of boiling salted water. Boil 8 to 10 minutes or *just* until tender. Drain thoroughly and mix while hot with the vinaigrette.

Meanwhile, prepare all the other vegetables and add to the potatoes all except the shredded carrots and radishes. Mix well and cool thoroughly. The dressing should be entirely absorbed by the vegetables.

Mix with just enough mayonnaise to bind the vegetables (½ cup should suffice). Taste for seasoning.

Shape the salad on a small platter, giving it a depth of 2 inches and smoothing the top with a small spatula.

Coat the sides with the shredded carrots and sprinkle the top in lattice fashion so that some of the salad shows through. Garnish the top with radish slices and parsley flowerets. Keep in a cool place until serving time.

Lentils Vinaigrette

1 pound dried lentils
3 small onions
1 bay leaf
2 stalks celery (with leaves)

¾ cup vinaigrette*
2 tablespoons chopped parsley
Lettuce leaves

ADVANCE PREPARATION:

Soak the lentils overnight or for 12 hours. Discard any imperfect lentils that come to the surface. Rinse thoroughly, and place in a pan of cold water. Add 2 onions, the bay leaf, and the celery stalks broken in half. Bring to a boil. Cover and simmer ½ hour or until the lentils are tender but not mushy. Drain and discard the onions, bay leaf, and celery.

Season with vinaigrette and add more salt if necessary. Cover and let stand until cool. Refrigerate for several hours.

Slice the remaining onion very thin and soak in cold water.

TO SERVE:

Drain the lentils of any excess dressing.

Mound them on a platter. Cover the surface with onion rings and chopped parsley. Surround with lettuce leaves.

Assorted Fish Platter

This simple preparation is not a matter of cooking—just a matter of opening cans and presenting their contents in an appetizing and decorative way. Nearby should be a basket of thinly sliced French, pumpernickel, and rye bread, so that your guests can make open-faced sandwiches in Scandinavian fashion. Serve the fish on a divided hors d'oeuvre platter or in several small dishes on a single tray.

1 large can (12½ ounces) tuna
1 small jar tiny pickled onions
Parsley
Watercress
2 cans anchovy fillets
Sweet butter, whipped

Capers
2 cans small sardines
1 lemon
2 jars herring in sour cream
2 scallions (green onions),
  chopped

Drain the tuna and place it on a plate or in a platter division. Garnish the edge of the top and the base with a necklace of onions. Fill the top ring with chopped parsley and surround the base with watercress.

Drain the anchovies and place them neatly in another division or on a small plate. Pipe the whipped butter through a cannellated pastry tip in rosettes around the edge of the plate, putting a caper on every other one—some people like capers; some don't—but the combination of the butter with the anchovies is a great favorite.

Drain the sardines and turn them out from the can in a block. Surround with parsley flowerets and sprinkle with lemon juice.

Cut the herring in bite-sized pieces before arranging them. Cover with the sour cream and sprinkle with chopped scallions.

Cucumber, Red Onion and Sesame Seed Salad

2 or 3 cucumbers
Sea salt
1 large red onion
3 tablespoons sesame seeds
2 tablespoons red wine vinegar

6 tablespoons salad oil
Black pepper
2 tablespoons chopped dill or
  parsley

ADVANCE PREPARATION:

Peel the cucumbers only if the skins are waxed or old. Split the cucumbers in half and scoop out the seeds with a teaspoon. Slice very thin by hand or with a food processor. Place the cucumbers in a soup plate and sprinkle generously with sea salt. Cover with another soup plate and weight it down with some heavy object. Let stand 1 hour.

Peel the onion and slice it very thin, breaking the slices into rings. Place in a bowl of cool water for 1 hour.

Toast the sesame seeds in an unbuttered skillet, tossing the pan and watching to see that the seeds do not burn. This only takes a minute.

Drain the cucumbers and press out the water. Drain the onions. Place in a salad dish and mix with the vinegar, oil, black pepper, and the dill or parsley. The cucumbers will still be salty enough. Cover and refrigerate for several hours.

BEFORE SERVING:

Toss the salad again and sprinkle with the sesame seeds.

Chick Pea and Tahini Spread

This recipe is of Turkish origin and serves as both an appetizer and a salad. Spread on sturdy dark bread to match its robust flavor, it could easily make a whole meal.

1 can (16 ounces) chick peas
2 cloves garlic
¾ cup tahini (ground sesame
    seeds)
½ cup olive oil

¾ teaspoon salt
⅛ teaspoon black pepper
1 tablespoon lemon juice
1 small can pitted black olives

ADVANCE PREPARATION:

Drain the chick peas of all but one-third of their liquid. Place in a food processor or blender. Spin with the garlic until the peas are crushed. Add the tahini and continue spinning, adding the olive oil gradually. Add the salt, pepper, and lemon juice and continue to spin until the mixture is smooth and blended.

TO SERVE:

Mound the mixture on a small platter. Cover the mound with olive slices. Serve with firm whole wheat, pumpernickel, or rye bread.

Artichokes Martinique (Hot)

2 cans (16 ounces) artichoke
   hearts
½ pound mushrooms
1 tablespoon minced shallots
5 tablespoons butter
3 tablespoons unbleached white
   or whole wheat pastry flour
1½ cups chicken broth

½ cup diced roasted red Italian
   peppers (in jars)
2 teaspoons lemon juice
½ cup cream
1 cup Gruyère, Muenster, or
   Emmenthal cheese, grated
Salt and pepper

ADVANCE PREPARATION:

Drain the artichokes. Wash them briefly and slice them in thirds vertically.

Trim the stems of the mushrooms. Wash the mushrooms briefly and pat them dry with paper toweling. Chop coarsely in a food processor or by hand. Sauté with the shallots in 2 tablespoons of butter or margarine for 3 minutes in a covered skillet. Drain and reserve the liquid.

Heat the remaining butter or margarine in a saucepan. Stir in the flour and cook over very low heat for 2 minutes. Add the chicken broth and the mushroom liquid and stir until smooth and thickened. Remove from the heat and add the peppers, lemon juice, and cream. Season to taste.

Spread a layer of artichokes in a shallow oven-serving dish (nonmetal if using a microwave oven). Cover with half the mushrooms. Sprinkle with cheese and half the sauce. Repeat the process. Keep in a cool place.

BEFORE SERVING:

Bake 25 minutes at 350 degrees F. in a regular oven. In the micro-wave oven, cover with wax paper and heat 2 minutes. Give the dish a quarter turn and cook 2 minutes longer. (An inserted temperature probe should register 150 degrees F.) Let stand 2 minutes before serving.

Creamed Oysters in Patty Shells (Hot)

This recipe is designed for 8 patty shells but can be stretched to fill 12 with the addition of ½ pound of mushrooms. It is best made in advance and reheated just before serving.

8-12 frozen patty shells	3 tablespoons unbleached flour
1 pint small oysters	1 cup milk
½ to 1 pound mushrooms	1 cup cream
5 tablespoons butter or	Salt and freshly ground black
margarine	pepper
½ cup water	⅛ teaspoon nutmeg
2 teaspoons lemon juice	Chopped parsley

ADVANCE PREPARATION:

Bake the shells according to directions on the package. Using a sharp knife, remove the center tops and reserve. When the shells are cool, scoop out the soft centers with a small spoon. Place the shells and tops on a heatproof serving platter.

Place the oysters and their liquid in a small saucepan. Cover and simmer 5 minutes or until the oysters are plump. Drain and reserve the liquid in a small bowl. If only large oysters are available, cut them in pieces when they are cold.

Trim the stems of the mushrooms, wash briefly, and dry the mushrooms between toweling. Slice or chop coarsely in a food processor or prepare them by hand.

Combine 2 tablespoons of the butter or margarine, the water, and the lemon juice in a skillet. Bring to a boil. Add the mushrooms, cover, and simmer 5 minutes. Drain the liquid into the reserved oyster broth. Combine the mushrooms and oysters.

Heat the remaining butter or margarine in the small saucepan. Stir in the flour and cook 2 minutes over low heat. Whisk in the reserved liquids and the milk. Continue whisking over moderate heat until thickened and smooth. Remove from the heat and stir in the oysters, mushrooms, and cream. Season to taste with salt, ⅛ teaspoon of nutmeg, and plenty of black pepper.

TO SERVE:

Reheat the oyster filling in a double boiler or reheat in a nonmetal casserole for 8 to 10 minutes in a microwave oven, depending on how cold the mixture is before reheating. Turn the dish halfway after 4 minutes of cooking.

Reheat the patty shells 5 minutes in a 300-degree F. oven. Just before serving, fill the shells. Top with chopped parsley; cover with the pastry rounds. Place on a warming tray on buffet table.

Fish Mayonnaise

You don't have to use a whole fish to make a very presentable fish mayonnaise which is a decorative and highly prized buffet dish. Ask your dealer for the tail end of the fish. It is firm of flesh and high in flavor. This dish deserves homemade mayonnaise.

3-pound piece of fresh salmon or haddock	2 boxes frozen peas and carrots
2 cups dry white wine	½ cup vinaigrette*
Cold water	1 clove garlic, halved
1 small onion, sliced thin	Mayonnaise*
1 bay leaf	1 package (1 tablespoon) gelatin
¼ teaspoon dried thyme	¼ cup water
2 teaspoons salt	Watercress
	1 tin anchovy fillets

ADVANCE PREPARATION:

Place the fish in a skillet. Add the wine and enough cold water to almost cover the fish. Add the onion, bay leaf, thyme, and salt. Bring to a boil and simmer 20 to 25 minutes. Do not overcook. The flesh must be cooked but not "flaking." Transfer the fish with two spatulas to a platter. Cool and refrigerate.

Cook the peas and carrots until just tender in a very small amount of salted water. Drain and, while they are still warm, mix with the vinaigrette and the garlic. Keep in a cool place.

Make the mayonnaise by the method you prefer. After adding the oil, beat in the gelatin which has been softened in cold water and then dissolved over hot water.

Wash and pick over the watercress. Keep in the refrigerator.

TO SERVE:

Carefully skin the fish. Split open the belly side and lay it open to remove the backbone. Lay the halves side by side on a platter, and garnish diagonally with parallel strips of anchovy fillets.

Remove the garlic halves and drain most of the vinaigrette from the vegetables. Mix with ⅔ cup of mayonnaise. Surround the fish with the mixed vegetables.

Put the rest of the mayonnaise in a pastry bag fitted with a cannellated tip. Pipe it around the edges of the fish. Garnish the edge of the platter with the watercress.

Cheese Log

1 cup drained Italian tomatoes
1 package (8 ounces) cream
   cheese
2 cups grated cheddar cheese
½ cup butter, softened
½ cup chopped onion

2 cloves garlic, pressed
1 teaspoon salt
¼ teaspoon cayenne pepper
1 cup finely chopped walnuts
Parsley sprigs

Combine the tomatoes, cheeses, butter, onion, garlic, salt, and pepper and spin in a food processor or beat with an electric mixer until smooth. Place on a piece of waxed paper and roll it up to make a log. Place in the freezer for 1 hour.

Remove the paper and transfer to a long platter. Smooth the sides with a moistened spatula. Coat the log with the chopped nuts. Garnish with parsley sprigs.

This can be frozen in smaller logs and thawed before serving.

Finger Fruits

Finger fruits are ideal for "something sweet" at the end of an hors d'oeuvre meal. Put small plates near the fruit platter because your guests will enjoy taking an assortment. All seasonal fruits lend themselves to this arrangement, but they should be prepared so that they can be eaten without benefit of fork or spoon.

2 small pineapples	*1 box medium-to-large*
1 honeydew or Persian melon	*strawberries*
1 cantaloupe	*2 lemons*

ADVANCE PREPARATION:

Wash the pineapples and cut off the top ¼ inch of each with the leaves and the bottom ¼ inch. Slice vertically in thin wedges, removing the cores unless the pineapples are very ripe. Cut each wedge in half if the pineapples are not very small.

Halve the melons and remove the seeds. Cut each half in thin wedges and remove the rinds. Cut each wedge in half.

Wash the strawberries only if necessary. Do not hull them.

Cut the lemons in wedges.

Arrange the fruits decoratively on a large platter. Surround with lemon wedges. Cover with plastic wrap and keep in a cool place. If refrigerator space is limited, do not chill the fruit until all the prepared dishes have been removed from the refrigerator.

Bring the fruit to the table when guests have had their fill of hors d'oeuvres. A cold, slightly sweet white wine or champagne goes very well with the fruit.

Summer Lunch or Supper for Four

When the temperature soars, appetites flag and the menu must be cool to prepare and cool to eat. Serve on a porch or shady patio if possible, and take time to deck the table with fresh greenery. The photo on this book's jacket shows the soup served from a hollowed-out squash; the green placemats under the white plates are giant rhubarb leaves from the garden. This menu can easily be expanded to serve six since the soup and dessert are of generous proportions.

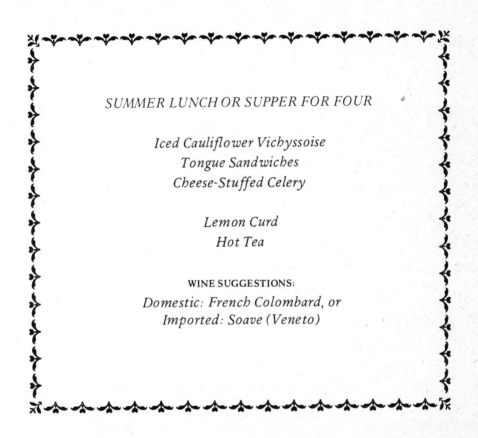

SUMMER LUNCH OR SUPPER FOR FOUR

Iced Cauliflower Vichyssoise
Tongue Sandwiches
Cheese-Stuffed Celery

Lemon Curd
Hot Tea

WINE SUGGESTIONS:
Domestic: French Colombard, or
Imported: Soave (Veneto)

SHOPPING LIST:
1 small cauliflower
2 or 3 leeks or 6 green onions
(scallions)
½ pint all-purpose cream
Celery hearts
4 ounces bleu cheese
1 package (3 ounces) cream
cheese

½ pound delicatessen tongue
1 loaf thin-sliced whole wheat
or rye bread
3 lemons
Potatoes
Parsley

Iced Cauliflower Vichyssoise

1 small cauliflower
2-3 leeks or 6 green onions
   (scallions)
2 tablespoons butter or
   margarine
3 medium potatoes

4 cups chicken broth
½ pint all-purpose cream
Salt
White pepper
Parsley

ADVANCE PREPARATION:

Trim the leaves and coarse stems from the cauliflower. Break into flowerets and soak 10 minutes in salted water to remove any unwelcome inhabitants. Steam or boil in a small amount of salted water for 12 minutes. Drain.

Trim and wash the leeks or onions and cut them into small pieces with a sharp knife or in the food processor. Sauté in the butter over moderate heat until soft.

Peel the potatoes and cut them into small chunks. Add them and the chicken broth to the onions. Cover and cook for 12 minutes or until the potatoes are very tender.

Spin the potato mixture and the cauliflower in a food processor or blender or force them through a food mill. Cool and stir in the cream. Season to taste with salt and pepper. Chill for several hours.

TO SERVE:

Serve from a tureen or other container. If the weather is very hot, do not hesitate to add a few ice cubes. Sprinkle with chopped parsley or parsley flowerets.

Tongue Sandwiches

Soft butter
Bahamian or Dijon mustard
1 loaf thin-sliced whole wheat
   or rye bread

½ pound delicatessen tongue,
   sliced ¼-inch thick

Mix the butter and mustard, allowing 1 teaspoon of mustard to every 2 tablespoons of butter.

Spread on bread slices.

Top half the slices with tongue and press the remaining slices firmly on top. Trim the crusts or not as desired. Cut the sandwiches diagonally. Place on a serving dish and cover tightly with plastic wrapping. Store in the refrigerator.

Cheese-Stuffed Celery

1 bunch celery hearts
4 ounces bleu cheese
1 small package cream cheese
2-3 tablespoons mayonnaise

1 teaspoon soy sauce
1 teaspoon scraped onion
Paprika

Wash the celery, leaving the small pieces with the leaves on and cutting the larger pieces into 2-inch lengths.

Blend the cheeses with 2 tablespoons of mayonnaise, the soy sauce, and the onion, using a food processor or a fork. Add more mayonnaise if necessary to give a smooth texture.

Place the mixture in a pastry bag fitted with a medium rosette tip. Force the mixture into the celery cavities and arrange on a serving dish. Sprinkle the filling lightly with paprika. Cover with plastic wrap and refrigerate until time to serve.

Lemon Curd

6 tablespoons sweet butter   1 cup sugar
3 medium-sized lemons   Garnish
3 large eggs

ADVANCE PREPARATION:

Heat the butter over simmering water in the top part of a double boiler. Grate 2 tablespoons of lemon rind and squeeze the juice from the lemons.

Beat the eggs with an electric beater or in a food processor. Continue beating, adding the sugar first and then the lemon rind and juice.

Pour the egg mixture into the double boiler and stir constantly until blended and thickened.

Pour into individual dessert dishes. Cover and refrigerate.

TO SERVE:

Garnish each dish of the curd with a fresh strawberry, slivered almonds, or a candied violet.

Winter Supper for Eight

Lasagne is the kind of hot and hearty entrée that delights chilled sports enthusiasts after outdoor events. Another plus: Lasagne isn't harmed by extra time in the oven or on the buffet table, waiting for guests who aren't quite ready when it is. This entire menu is easy to handle with just forks, so it is good for the very informal occasion when friends dine standing, walking around, or even sitting on the floor in front of the fireplace.

WINTER SUPPER FOR EIGHT

Baked Lasagne
Tossed Chinese Cabbage Salad
Italian Green Bean Sauté

Mocha Nut Refrigerator Cake or Honeydew Bowl*

Coffee

WINE SUGGESTIONS:
Domestic: Zinfandel, or
Imported: Valpolicella (Veneto)

SHOPPING LIST:

1 pound lasagne noodles
¾ pound Mozzarella cheese
1 pound ricotta or cottage
   cheese
1 pound ground beef
2 cans tomato paste
Grated Parmesan cheese
Italian green beans, fresh
   or frozen
Onion
Red wine

Parsley
Lemon
1 Chinese cabbage
2 carrots
1 red onion
1 green pepper
2 dozen ladyfingers
½ pint heavy cream
Walnuts
Baking chocolate
Rum (optional)

Baked Lasagne

1 pound lasagne noodles
1 tablespoon salt
1 tablespoon oil
4 eggs
¾ pound Mozzarella cheese
1 pound ricotta or cottage
   cheese
Grated Parmesan cheese

SAUCE:
1 large onion, chopped fine
1 clove garlic, minced

1½ tablespoons butter or
   margarine
1½ tablespoons olive oil
1 pound ground beef
1½ cans tomato paste
½ teaspoon powdered oregano
½ teaspoon sugar
1 teaspoon salt
⅛ teaspoon pepper
½ cup red wine (Burgundy)
4 cups water

ADVANCE PREPARATION:

To make the sauce: Sauté the onion and garlic in the butter or margarine and olive oil until tender. Stir in the beef and brown the meat well. Add the remaining ingredients and stir until the mixture boils. Reduce heat and simmer 45 minutes; the sauce should be quite thick. Cool the sauce.

To prepare the other ingredients: Fill a large kettle with water and bring it to a boil. Add the 1 tablespoon of salt and 1 tablespoon of oil. Add the long, wide strips of lasagne gradually so that the water does not stop boiling. Boil 12 minutes or until just tender. Drain in a colander and run cool water through the cooked noodles. Hard-cook, peel, and slice the eggs. Cut the Mozzarella cheese into thin slices.

To assemble: Butter or oil a rectangular baking dish. Line the dish lengthwise and breadthwise with a double layer of noodles, letting the ends come to the rim. Cover with a layer of meat sauce. Dot with egg slices and teaspoonfuls of ricotta or cottage cheese. Cover with a layer of Mozzarella and a thin layer of sauce. Place a layer of noodles over this and repeat the process until the dish is filled. For the top layer, basketweave the noodles and tuck the ends in at the sides. Brush the top with melted butter and sprinkle with Parmesan cheese.

Cover with aluminum foil and store in the refrigerator if more than an hour or two will elapse before baking.

BEFORE SERVING:

Bake 40 minutes at 300 degrees F. with the aluminum foil in place. Let stand 10 minutes before cutting into generous squares for serving.

Tossed Chinese Cabbage Salad

1 Chinese cabbage	3 tablespoons wine vinegar
½ cup shredded carrots	2 teaspoons sugar
½ green pepper	1 teaspoon salt
1 small red onion	⅛ teaspoon freshly ground black pepper

DRESSING:

3 tablespoons olive oil

ADVANCE PREPARATION:

Slice the cabbage into thin slices with a sharp knife or in the food processor.

Shred the carrots and green pepper by hand or in the food processor. Slice the onion into thin rings, using either method.

Combine these vegetables in the salad bowl, tossing them lightly by hand. Cover with wax paper and chill in the refrigerator.

Combine the ingredients for the dressing in a small bottle. Shake well.

BEFORE SERVING:

Give the dressing another shake and pour it over the salad. Toss thoroughly.

Italian Green Bean Sauté

2 pounds fresh Italian green
  beans or 3 boxes frozen
  Italian green beans
3 tablespoons butter or
  margarine

1 tablespoon olive oil
3 tablespoons chopped onion
2 tablespoons chopped parsley
1 teaspoon lemon juice
Salt and pepper

ADVANCE PREPARATION:

Wash the beans and remove the tips. Slice diagonally in ¾-inch
lengths. Boil them in a very little salted water for 15 minutes. Rinse
briefly in cold water and put into a strainer. If using the frozen beans,
cook according to package directions only until crisply tender.

Make the sauce by heating the butter or margarine and the olive oil
and cooking the onion and parsley in it for 2 minutes. Remove from the
stove and add the lemon juice.

BEFORE SERVING:

Lower the beans (in the strainer) into a pot of briskly boiling water
for not more than a minute. Drain and put into a heated vegetable dish.
Pour the reheated sauce over the beans and sprinkle with salt and
pepper.

Mocha Nut Refrigerator Cake

4 squares baking chocolate
⅔ cup sugar
⅛ teaspoon salt
1 tablespoon instant coffee
2 tablespoons water
2 teaspoons gelatin
2 tablespoons cold water
5 egg yolks

2 tablespoons rum or 1 teaspoon
   vanilla
5 egg whites, beaten stiff
½ pint heavy cream, whipped
½ cup chopped walnuts
2 dozen ladyfingers
Walnuts

ADVANCE PREPARATION:

Combine the chocolate, sugar, salt, coffee, and water in the top of a double boiler and cook over boiling water until the chocolate melts. Stir in the gelatin, softened in cold water, and cook for 2 minutes.

Beat the egg yolks with an electric beater for 1 minute and add the chocolate mixture gradually, beating until blended. Return the mixture to the double boiler and stir until the mixture begins to thicken—about 3 minutes. Pour the mixture into a bowl to cool. Add the rum or vanilla. Fold the egg whites into the partly cooled chocolate mixture and chill in the refrigerator until it starts to set. Fold in the whipped cream and chopped nuts.

Butter a deep cake tin or straight-sided mold very lightly. Line the sides with ladyfingers. Make a daisy of ladyfingers in the bottom of the pan, using a walnut half as a center. Cover with a thick layer of the mocha-nut mixture. Alternate layers of ladyfingers and mocha-nut mixture until the mold is filled. Finish with a layer of ladyfingers. Chill in the refrigerator overnight or for at least 8 hours.

BEFORE SERVING:

Unmold the dessert onto a round platter and garnish with additional walnut halves.

Luncheon for Female Friends

The ideal menu for an all-female party is something colorful, interesting, and delicious without being heavy. The quantities suggested here are for four—if you wish to invite friends enough to make two tables of bridge, double all the recipes except the dessert, which can serve eight. Start preparing the meal by making the dessert; it takes a little stirring which can be done while you are "beforehanding" the rest. You may have muffins in the freezer; if so, they will only need reheating.

LUNCHEON FOR FEMALE FRIENDS

Spring Pea Soup

Scallop Shells
Tarragon Tomato Baskets
Blueberry Muffins*

Fresh Pineapple Parfait

WINE SUGGESTIONS:
Domestic: Fumé Blanc or
Imported: Pouilly-Fumé (Loire).

SHOPPING LIST:

2 pounds fresh peas or 1 box
   frozen green peas
½ pint sour cream
1 pint scallops
4 tomatoes
1 cucumber
1 ripe pineapple
½ pint whipping cream

Cashews
Crackers (Ritz or similar)
Lettuce
Onion
Carrots
Lemon
Dry vermouth (optional)
White rum

Spring Pea Soup

1 small onion
1 carrot
2 cups freshly shelled peas or
   1 box (10 ounces) frozen
   peas

3 cups chicken broth
1 teaspoon salt
½ teaspoon white pepper
Sour cream

ADVANCE PREPARATION:

Shred the onion and the carrot or mince fine with a food processor or by hand. Place in a saucepan with the peas, chicken broth, salt, and white pepper. Bring to a boil. Cover, reduce the heat, and simmer for 30 minutes. Cool slightly. Spin in a blender or food processor or force through a food mill.

BEFORE SERVING:

Reheat 25 minutes in a double boiler or microwave 6 or 7 minutes in individual bowls, stirring once during the process. A temperature probe should be set for 160 degrees F.

TO SERVE:

The soup is served steaming hot with a dollop of sour cream.

Scallop Shells

This extraordinarily delicious though simple dish may be made from fresh or frozen scallops at your convenience and baked without supervision just before eating. If you don't have scallop shells, use individual baking dishes.

1 pint scallops
1 stack rich crackers (Ritz,
  Crax, etc.)
¼ pound butter or margarine
⅛ teaspoon paprika

1 teaspoon lemon juice
2 teaspoons dry vermouth
  (optional)
Salt and pepper
Parsley

ADVANCE PREPARATION:

Thaw the scallops if frozen. This can be done in a microwave oven by putting them in a covered glass dish for 4 to 5 minutes. Turn over and loosen scallops with a fork and microwave 4 minutes longer. If the scallops are large, cut them into bite-sized pieces.

Pulverize the crackers in a food processor or crush by hand. One stack will yield 1 cup of crumbs.

Heat the butter or margarine in a skillet until it bubbles. Stir in the crumbs. Add the paprika and continue cooking and stirring until lightly browned. Remove from the heat.

Stir the scallops into the crumb mixture until completely coated.

Divide among four scallop shells or baking dishes. Sprinkle with the lemon juice and vermouth, salt and pepper. Cool, cover, and refrigerate.

BEFORE SERVING:

Bake uncovered 20 minutes at 350 degrees F.

TO SERVE:

Garnish each shell with a sprig of parsley and serve on individual plates.

Tarragon Tomato Baskets

4 medium-sized tomatoes
1 cucumber
2 tablespoons tarragon vinegar
6 tablespoons salad oil

½ teaspoon salt
⅛ teaspoon white pepper
Tarragon leaves
1 small head garden lettuce

ADVANCE PREPARATION:

Choose tomatoes that are of uniform size. Wash them and dip them one by one into boiling water for 30 seconds. Slip off the skins and cut off the top ¼ inch. Scoop out the centers and sprinkle the interiors with a little salt. Turn upside down on a small trivet over a plate and place in the refrigerator.

Peel and split the cucumber and scoop out the seeds with a spoon. Cut tiny cucumber balls or cubes and place them in a small nonmetal bowl.

Mix the vinegar, oil, salt, and pepper and pour over the cucumber. Add 2 to 4 slightly crushed tarragon leaves. Cover and refrigerate.

Wash the lettuce, breaking it into large pieces. Crisp in the refrigerator.

TO SERVE:

Line four salad plates with the lettuce leaves. Place a tomato in the center of each plate. Fill with the cucumber balls and garnish with 3 or 4 tarragon leaves per plate. Serve very cold.

Fresh Pineapple Parfait

1 ripe pineapple   1 tablespoon lemon juice
1 cup sugar   ½ pint cream, whipped
¾ cup water   4 tablespoons white rum
1 teaspoon gelatin   Chopped cashew nuts (optional)

ADVANCE PREPARATION:

Cut the leaves from the pineapple. Holding the pineapple firmly with one hand on a wooden board, remove the peeling with a very sharp knife. Cut out the "eyes" with the point of an apple corer. Cut the pineapple into quarters and remove the core. Cut the fruit into large pieces and spin in a food processor or blender. Place the resulting pulp and juice in a bowl.

Measure out 1 cup of the pulp and juice into a saucepan. Add the sugar and water and bring to a boil. Boil 10 minutes. Remove from the heat and stir in the gelatin softened in 2 teaspoons of lemon juice.

Pour the mixture into a metal bowl and place in a larger bowl containing ice cubes. Stir until the syrup is cold and somewhat thickened.

Fold the mixture into the whipped cream and pour into a freezer tray. Freeze 30 minutes. Stir the mixture in the tray. Freeze 1 hour and beat with an electric mixer in a prechilled bowl. Return to the tray. Cover with foil and let freeze a minimum of 2 hours.

Meanwhile, to make the sauce, add the rum and remaining lemon juice to another cup of the pineapple. Cover and keep cool but do not chill.

TO SERVE:

Put a tablespoon of the sauce in the bottom of each glass. Fill three-fourths full with the cream mixture; top with more of the rum sauce. Sprinkle with cashew nuts and serve.

Lunch for a Male Foursome

This menu is designed to follow a foursome at golf, doubles in tennis, or any other occasion that happens to be stag. The dishes can all be prepared well in advance and retrieved from refrigerator or oven at almost any hour. No man likes to eat with a plate on his lap, so set up a table, possibly with checkered tablecloth, pottery plates, and mugs. There is no waiting on table because everything is placed on the table at once when the men sit down to eat.

LUNCH FOR A MALE FOURSOME

Protein Platter with Molded Potato Salad
or German Sauerkraut with Apple Cider Salad

Whole Wheat Bread, Pumpernickel, Rye Bread
Sweet Whipped Butter

WINE SUGGESTION:
Beer or Riesling Wine (California or Alsace)

Apricot Tarts
Coffee

SHOPPING LIST:

Choice: protein platter and potato salad or German sauerkraut and apple cider salad.

For the protein platter you will need 1 pound cold sliced meat and 1 pound cheese.

For the molded potato salad you will need potatoes, cucumber, 1 can anchovies, 4 tomatoes, lettuce and Kosher dill pickles.

For the German sauerkraut you will need 1½-2 pounds sauerkraut, 1 pound Polish or Italian sausage, 4-8 knockwurst, potatoes, tomatoes, Red Delicious apples, celery, ½ pint sour cream, rum, carrots and scallions.

For the dessert you will need 1 6-ounce jar apricot jam and 1 stick (¼ pound) sweet butter.

Protein Platter

Alternate slices of your choice of cold meat—beef, lamb, ham, salami, turkey, chicken, etc.—with slices of good aged cheeses—Gruyère, cheddar, Gouda, Monterey, Stilton, Provalone, etc.—around a platter. In the center, place a small glass of water containing a bouquet of fresh parsley.

Accompany the platter with mustard, horseradish, sweet butter, and plenty of pumpernickel and whole wheat bread.

Molded Potato Salad

4 large potatoes
4 eggs
1 cucumber
2 tablespoons wine vinegar
⅓ cup olive oil
1 clove garlic, minced or
  pressed

1 teaspoon salt
⅛ teaspoon black pepper
Mayonnaise*
4 tomatoes
1 head lettuce
1 can anchovies

ADVANCE PREPARATION:

Pare and cube the potatoes and boil them in salted water for 10 minutes or until tender. Drain immediately.

Cook the eggs in simmering water for 15 minutes. Plunge into cold water and crack the shells. Let cool.

Pare and split the cucumber and scoop out the seeds. Cube the cucumber.

While the potatoes are still hot, add the vinegar, oil, garlic, salt, and pepper and combine with the cubed cucumber in a bowl. When the vegetables are completely cool, mix in just enough mayonnaise (home-made or store-bought) to make them stick together.

Mound the potato salad on a round platter. Smooth the sides with a knife to make a four-sided pyramid. Place in the refrigerator while preparing the garnish.

Wash, peel, and halve the tomatoes. Scoop out small centers in each half. Wash the lettuce. Drain the oil from the anchovies. Slice the eggs.

To garnish: Outline the edges of the pyramid with anchovies. Cover the sides with egg slices and surround with lettuce leaves and tomato halves. Fill the centers of the tomatoes with mayonnaise. If you want to have fun, place some mayonnaise in a small pastry tube and decorate the pyramid. It's more fun than decorating a cake!

German Sauerkraut

Sauerkraut is a marvelous restorative after exercise. It is also most adaptable to any time schedule. It can be partially cooked at one's convenience and the final cooking can be done in 15 minutes, or even less in a microwave oven.

½ pound lean salt pork	12 peppercorns
1½-2 quarts bulk or canned	2 cups dry white wine
sauerkraut	8 medium potatoes
1 pound Polish or Italian	4-8 knockwurst
sausage	4 slices boiled ham
1 medium onion, sliced thin	

ADVANCE PREPARATION:

Rinse the salt pork in warm water. Place in a pan of cold water. Bring to a boil. Simmer 10 minutes. Drain and rinse in cold water. Cut in ½-inch slices without removing the rind.

Drain the sauerkraut and rinse in cold water. Drain, pressing out all the liquid possible.

On the bottom of a heavy casserole (nonmetal if using a microwave) place half of the salt pork. Cover with half the sauerkraut and the sausage cut into 4 pieces. Cover with the onion slices and 6 peppercorns. Spread the rest of the sauerkraut on top with 6 peppercorns and the rest of the salt pork slices. Pour on the white wine and add cold water to cover. Set aside.

Peel the potatoes and boil 20 to 25 minutes or until just tender. Do not overcook. Add the knockwurst to the potatoes for the final 10 minutes of cooking. Set aside.

BEFORE SERVING:

In a regular oven, bake the sauerkraut 2 to 3 hours at 300 degrees F. (Reduce the heat to 275 degrees F. if you are going to be gone 4 hours.) Twenty minutes before serving, remove the top layer of salt pork and bury the potatoes and knockwurst in the sauerkraut. Replace the pork and continue baking 15 minutes longer.

If you will be using a microwave oven to reheat, cook the sauerkraut as above, including the final heating of the knockwurst and potatoes. Keep in a cool place until almost ready to serve.

Place the casserole in the microwave for 10 minutes of reheating or until the temperature probe reaches 160 degrees F.

TO SERVE:

Place the sauerkraut in the center of a well-heated platter. Surround with pieces of salt pork, sausage, knockwurst, and potatoes. Cover with the boiled ham. Serve with hot mustard.

Apple Cider Salad

3 cups sweet cider

2 tablespoons cider vinegar

4 tablespoons rum

4 tablespoons brown sugar
  (optional)

2 tablespoons powdered gelatin

½ cup water

1 cup grated carrots

1 cup chopped apples

½ cup chopped celery

1 cup mayonnaise*

½ cup sour cream

4 tablespoons chopped scallions

1 clove garlic, pressed
  (optional)

ADVANCE PREPARATION:

Heat the cider, vinegar, rum, and brown sugar almost to the boiling point.

Soften the gelatin in the water and stir into the hot cider. Remove from the heat and set aside to cool.

Grate the carrots in a food processor or by hand.

Wash, quarter, and core the apples. Cut into small dice without peeling.

Chop the celery quite fine.

Stir the carrots, apples, and celery into the cooled cider.

Pour into a quart ring mold and cover. Refrigerate at least 3 hours.

Combine the mayonnaise, sour cream, scallions, and garlic. Cover and refrigerate.

TO SERVE:

Unmold the aspic on a round platter by running a knife around the interior and exterior sides. If it does not come out easily, dip the mold in hot water for 2 or 3 seconds. Fill the center with the dressing.

Apricot Tarts

These can be made from your own favorite pastry dough or from the packaged variety. I prefer the food processor pastry which anyone can make so well that it will banish pastry blues forever. The secret is having the butter stone cold. I keep some in the freezer for emergencies.

1½ cups unbleached all-purpose
   flour
½ teaspoon salt
1 stick cold butter

4 tablespoons ice water
½ jar apricot jam
1 tablespoon rum

Preheat the oven to 450 degrees F.

Spin the flour, the salt, and the butter (cut into 8 pieces) in a food processor for 8 to 10 seconds. Add the ice water through the tube and spin until the dough forms a ball on the blades.

Roll the dough out on a lightly floured surface to a thickness of ⅛ inch. Cut into eight 3-inch circles with a tumbler or a cookie cutter. Moisten the edges of half the circles with a little water.

Mix half a jar of apricot jam with the rum. Place a good teaspoon of the apricot jam in the center of 4 circles. Top with the remaining circles and place on an unbuttered baking sheet. Prick the tops well and bake 10 minutes.

Fish Fare

I t's a great occasion when fish caught personally or by a friend in lake or stream is brought into the kitchen. No home cook ever tries to compete with the taste of a fresh-caught fish cooked over a camp fire. It can't be done. However, there can be some compensatory additions when the fish is cooked at home.

A meal that features anything as special as trout or salmon deserves the undivided attention of the consumer and the cook. Eliminate a first course and make the fish do a solo, with nothing to accompany it except good French bread, in the case of trout; boiled potatoes, in the case of salmon; and a delicious white wine, in the case of either.

The rest of the meal is designed to complement the flavor of fish with foods that bespeak spring and summer.

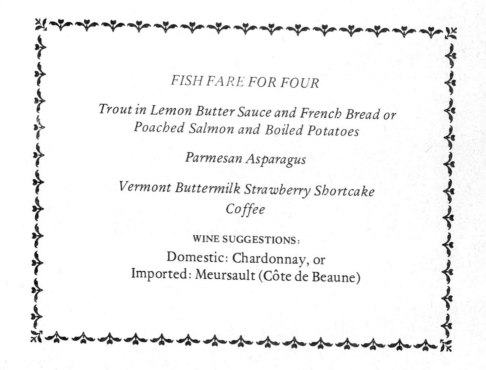

FISH FARE FOR FOUR

Trout in Lemon Butter Sauce and French Bread or
Poached Salmon and Boiled Potatoes

Parmesan Asparagus

Vermont Buttermilk Strawberry Shortcake
Coffee

WINE SUGGESTIONS:
Domestic: Chardonnay, or
Imported: Meursault (Côte de Beaune)

SHOPPING LIST:

¼ pound sweet butter
1 lemon
Parsley
Slivered almonds (optional)
2 pounds fresh asparagus

Buttermilk
1 quart strawberries
Maple sugar
½ pint heavy cream
Anchovy paste

Trout in Lemon Butter Sauce

4 8-ounce trout (fresh or
    thawed)
Salt and pepper
Flour
2 tablespoons salad oil
2 tablespoons butter or
    margarine

SAUCE:
½ cup sweet butter
1 tablespoon lemon juice
1 tablespoon chopped parsley
¼ cup slivered almonds
    (optional)

ADVANCE PREPARATION:

Wash the fish briefly and pat dry with toweling. Sprinkle inside and out with salt and pepper.

If you will be using a conventional range, dip each side of the fish lightly in flour. Place on wax paper on a plate, cover with wax paper, and refrigerate. Combine the ingredients for the sauce in a small saucepan.

With a microwave oven, prepare the fish as above but do not dip in flour. Place the fish in a rectangular glass or ceramic dish long enough to accommodate the fish arranged with tails in the center. Cover with wax paper and refrigerate. Combine the ingredients for the sauce in a heatproof pitcher.

BEFORE SERVING:

If you are using a conventional range, begin about 12 minutes before time to serve. Heat a stainless steel platter in the oven (it should be very hot). Warm the dinner plates.

Heat the salad oil, butter, or margarine in a large skillet on top of the range until it bubbles and then subsides. Do not let it brown. Sauté the fish 5 minutes on each side. At the same time, heat the sauce until it bubbles. Transfer the fish to the hot platter, pour the hot sauce over the fish, and carry sizzling to the table.

If you will be preparing the fish in a microwave oven that has a rack and time probe, insert the probe ½ inch into the thickest part of the fish. Place the covered fish on the rack and the sauce on the bottom of the oven. Microwave 5 minutes on "high." Remove the sauce. Continue to microwave for 4 minutes longer or until the probe has reached 145 degrees F. Remove the fish and let stand 5 minutes. Reheat the sauce for 30 seconds. Stir and pour over the fish. Serve immediately.

Poached Salmon with Anchovy Egg Sauce

1 small fresh salmon
2 cups dry white wine
1 onion, sliced
½ carrot, sliced
1 tablespoon salt
½ teaspoon peppercorns
4 tablespoons butter
   or margarine

4 tablespoons flour (unbleached
   or whole wheat pastry flour)
2 cups milk
2 teaspoons anchovy paste
Salt and white pepper
2 hard-cooked eggs
1 teaspoon lemon juice
Parsley

ADVANCE PREPARATION:

Wash the salmon inside and out under running water and place it in a piece of cheesecloth large enough so that you will have a 4-inch "handle" on each end. Tie the ends securely with kitchen twine.

Put the wine, onion, carrot, salt, pepper, and enough water to just cover the fish in a kettle. Bring to a boil. Cover and simmer 7 or 8 minutes per pound depending on the thickness of the fish. The fish will not be entirely cooked. Remove from the liquid and place the fish on a platter. Let cool for 10 minutes.

Meanwhile, heat the butter or margarine in the top part of a double boiler over direct heat. Add the flour and cook gently for 2 minutes. Add the milk and whisk until thick and smooth. Stir in the anchovy paste and season to taste with salt and pepper, remembering that the anchovy is salty. Remove from the heat and fold in the eggs cut in slices and the lemon juice. Cool and refrigerate.

BEFORE SERVING:

Reheat the sauce over simmering water. In a regular oven, cover the fish with a piece of buttered aluminum foil and bake 15 to 20 minutes at 350 degrees F. In a microwave oven, cover the fish with wax paper. Insert the temperature probe into the thickest part of the fish. Microwave for 5 minutes. Turn the dish, and continue baking for 5 minutes or until the probe measures 145 degrees F. Let stand 3 minutes.

TO SERVE:

Pour off any liquid from the serving platter. Outline a small "saddle" in the center of the piece of fish with parsley flowerets. Fill the center with a little sauce. Put the rest of the sauce in a gravy boat. Surround the fish with the potatoes.

Boiled Potatoes

Allow 2 medium-to-small potatoes per person unless that seems too little for your particular guests. Peel them in advance and keep them in cold salted water in the refrigerator.

About 20 minutes before serving time, boil the potatoes in well-salted water. Drain and keep warm in a saucepan if necessary, with the
cover ajar so that the steam can escape.

Parmesan Asparagus

If you are a real asparagus lover, you will pick the asparagus from your
garden or arrange to have it picked in late afternoon just before your
guests arrive; but this is a luxury limited to comparatively few and no
one but a connoisseur knows the difference. However, do get asparagus
as fresh as possible.

2 pounds fresh green asparagus	*½ cup butter*
4 slices homemade	*½ cup freshly grated Parmesan*
white or whole wheat bread	*Salt and pepper*

ADVANCE PREPARATION:

Cut off the tough lower part of the asparagus stalks so that all the
stalks are of equal length. It is not necessary to peel the stalks of green
asparagus as it is with white asparagus, but some French cooks insist
upon it. Wash the asparagus well because sand can lurk in the tips and
tiny leaves, but do not let the asparagus soak.

Tie the asparagus in 4 bunches. Refrigerate.

Trim the crusts from 4 half-inch slices of firm bread. Toast and wrap
in wax paper.

Have the butter ready to melt in a small saucepan (or glass pitcher if
using the microwave). Grate the cheese.

BEFORE SERVING:

Place the asparagus in a steaming basket. Lower into a kettle of
boiling salted (1 tablespoon salt to 2 quarts) water. The water should

come about three-quarters of the way up the stalks. Cook covered 12 to 15 minutes depending on the size of the spears. Drain thoroughly.

Heat the butter until it bubbles.

Place the toast on 4 heated salad plates. Lay a bunch of asparagus on each piece of toast and remove the string. Pour the hot butter over gently, leaving the whey in the bottom of the pan. Sprinkle lightly with salt and pepper and generously with the Parmesan. Serve immediately.

Vermont Buttermilk Strawberry Shortcake

2 cups unbleached all-purpose flour	¾ cup buttermilk
4 teaspoons baking powder	1 quart wild or garden strawberries
¾ teaspoon salt	Maple sugar
3 tablespoons cold butter, sliced	Butter or margarine
	½ pint heavy cream

ADVANCE PREPARATION:

Preheat the oven to 450 degrees F.

Combine the flour, baking powder, salt, and cold butter in a food processor or electric beater bowl. Spin or beat until the mixture becomes pebbly in texture. Add the buttermilk and continue to mix until you have a smooth dough. Turn out onto a lightly floured working surface and knead for 1 minute into a smooth ball.

Roll out to a thickness of ½ inch and cut into four 4-inch circles. Place the circles on a greased baking sheet and bake 12 minutes. Cool on a wire rack. Cut in half horizontally. Keep covered.

Pick or buy fully ripe berries because they are much sweeter than the unripe variety. Save out 4 berries for garnish and cut the rest into slices. Sprinkle with a little maple sugar. Cover and refrigerate.

TO SERVE:

Spread the biscuit halves with a little butter or margarine and reheat for 5 minutes in a regular 350-degree F. oven, or for 30 seconds in a microwave.

Place the lower halves on a dessert platter or on individual dessert plates. Cover with a thick layer of berries and sprinkle with more maple sugar if desired. Cover with the tops and add more strawberries. Spoon 2 tablespoons of heavy cream over each serving and garnish with a whole berry.

This recipe will serve four quite generously. For more modest appetites, make six 3-inch shortcakes and refrigerate the leftovers.

Hunters' Banquet

Try not to look dismayed when the returning hunter dumps a bag of game on the kitchen table with high expectation of a victor's meal. The cooking of game (presuming that it is properly prepared for cooking) is not difficult. But don't rush to the phone to line up the guests. Most birds—partridge, pheasant, and quail—are better if hung in a cool place for four days. Venison, unless very young, should be hung for two to three weeks and then marinated. It is a real and rare banquet when both a bird and venison can be served at the same meal. Either can be pridefully served alone. If there are two courses of game, eliminate the broth course.

Since the choice of game depends on the hunter as well as the cook, I offer no shopping list except a head of cabbage and a bottle of Grand Marnier. Check the recipes for anything else you may need.

HUNTERS' BANQUET FOR FOUR TO SIX

Sherry Beef Broth

Roast Partridge on Bordelaise Croutons
or Braised Pheasant in Madeira Sauce

Venison Pie or Venison Roast or Venison Steak

Cole Slaw with Boiled or Yogurt Dressing

Grand Marnier Soufflé
Coffee

WINE SUGGESTIONS:
With the partridge or pheasant—
Domestic: Cabernet Sauvignon, or
Imported: Château Clos Fourtet (St. Emilion)
With the venison—
Domestic: Petite Syroh, or
Imported: Côte Rôtie (Rhône)

Sherry Beef Broth

This is delicious made with home-brewed beef broth, but the sherry will improve the flavor of the canned variety. Sherry Beef Broth leads into game in a very pleasant fashion.

1 quart homemade beef broth or   ½ cup sherry
  2 10-ounce cans beef   1 tablespoon chopped parsley
  consommé

ADVANCE PREPARATION:

Put the broth or the consommé diluted with an equal quantity of water in the top of a covered double boiler.

BEFORE SERVING:

Heat the broth over simmering water. Add the sherry during the last few minutes of heating. Pour into individual soup cups and sprinkle with parsley.

Roast Partridge
on Bordelaise Croutons

2 or 3 partridge (with livers)   1 teaspoon lemon juice
½ pound salt pork, sliced   Salt and pepper
  paper thin   4 or 6 slices firm white or
¼ pound mushrooms   whole wheat bread
2 tablespoons olive oil   ½ cup chicken broth (optional)
2 teaspoons chopped onion   3 tablespoons Madeira
1 clove garlic, minced   Watercress
2 teaspoons chopped parsley
4 tablespoons butter or
  margarine

ADVANCE PREPARATION:

Split the cleaned birds and wipe inside and out with paper toweling. Place the birds on an open rack in a roasting pan. Cover the halves with salt pork slices which have been rinsed in warm water to remove excess salt. You may want to anchor the salt pork with toothpicks. Keep the birds at room temperature several hours before roasting.

Trim the stems of the mushrooms. Wash them briefly and pat dry with toweling. Chop them and the partridge livers very fine in a food processor or by hand. Heat the oil in a small skillet and sauté the mushrooms and livers for 2 minutes, stirring frequently. Add the onion, garlic, and parsley and cook 1 minute longer. Remove from the heat and stir in 2 tablespoons of butter or margarine. Add the lemon juice and season to taste with salt and pepper.

Trim the crusts from the bread. (Italian bread works very well for croutons.) Toast lightly on both sides and spread one side with the mushroom mixture. Place on a baking sheet for later reheating.

BEFORE SERVING:

Roast the partridge in a preheated 425-degree F. oven for 20 minutes. Remove from the oven and lift off the rack with the partridge. Keep the birds warm.

Pour off as much fat as possible from the pan. Add ½ cup of water or chicken broth and 3 tablespoons of Madeira to the pan. Bring to a rapid boil, scraping the juices in the pan with a fork. Remove from the heat and stir in the remaining butter or margarine.

Slip the croutons into the hot oven for 1 or 2 minutes. They should be just warm.

TO SERVE:

Place croutons on individual warm plates. Remove the salt pork from the birds and place one half on each crouton. Strain a little of the sauce over each one and garnish with watercress. Serve immediately.

Braised Pheasant in Madeira Sauce

This dish must be started a day in advance.

*1 large cock pheasant (including
neck, wing tips, and
giblets)
8 tablespoons butter or
margarine
2 tablespoons chopped onion
1 tablespoon chopped carrots
3 tablespoons flour (unbleached
or whole wheat pastry)
3 cups chicken broth*

*2 teaspoons tomato paste
Salt and pepper
2 tablespoons oil
½ cup Madeira
⅛ teaspoon allspice
6 juniper berries
½ pound noodles
½ pint sour cream
1 carrot, shredded*

ADVANCE PREPARATION:

To make brown sauce, cut the neck, wing tips, and giblets into small
pieces. Heat 3 tablespoons of butter or margarine in a saucepan and
sauté the pieces for 2 minutes. Add the chopped onion and carrots and
cook 2 minutes longer, stirring frequently. Sprinkle with the flour and
stir until the flour disappears. Add the chicken broth mixed with the
tomato paste. Bring to a boil. Reduce the heat and simmer for 1 hour,
removing any scum that comes to the surface. Taste for seasoning and
add salt and pepper as needed.

Preheat the oven to 325 degrees F.

Bind the wings and thighs to the body of the pheasant with kitchen
twine. Heat 3 tablespoons of butter or margarine and the oil in a heavy
heatproof casserole and brown the bird on both sides. Remove the bird
and remove all the cooking fat, wiping out the casserole with paper
toweling. Replace the pheasant and cover with the brown sauce,
Madeira, allspice, and juniper berries. The sauce should come halfway
up the sides of the bird. Bring to a simmer on top of the stove. Cover

and place in the oven. Cook 1½ hours. Test to be sure the pheasant is tender at the leg joint.

Remove the pheasant to a platter and boil down the sauce to approximately 2½ cups. Strain, cool, and chill overnight. Refrigerate the pheasant.

The next morning, remove the skin from the pheasant. Take off the wings and thighs and carve the breast meat in thin slices. Sever the thighs from the legs at the joints.

Arrange the meat in the center of a shallow heatproof platter (nonmetal if using a microwave oven). Defat the sauce and heat it. Taste for seasoning. Spoon the sauce over the meat. Keep in a cool place.

Boil the noodles for 6 minutes in a large pan of boiling salted water. Drain well and mix with 2 tablespoons of butter or margarine and the sour cream. Season with salt and pepper and place in the top part of a double boiler or in a glass dish.

Shred the carrot in a food processor or by hand. This will be used as a garnish.

BEFORE SERVING:

If using a conventional range, reheat the pheasant and sauce (covered with aluminum foil) in a 325-degree F. oven for 30 minutes. Reheat the noodles over simmering water for the same time.

With a microwave oven, cover the pheasant with wax paper and reheat for 10 minutes, turning the dish halfway after the first 5 minutes. Remove from the oven and let stand while reheating the noodles for 2 minutes. Stir the noodles and heat 2 minutes longer.

TO SERVE:

Surround the pheasant with the noodles and sprinkle the shredded carrot over the noodles.

Venison Pie

Meat for venison pie is usually cut from the shoulder or leg and needs to be marinated 12 to 24 hours. The pie is assembled the morning of the feast (or even the day before) and baked before and during the first course.

2½ or 3 pounds venison meat

MARINADE:
½ cup red Burgundy
½ cup wine or cider vinegar
1 bay leaf
¼ teaspoon powdered thyme
1 clove garlic, pressed
1 onion, sliced
½ teaspoon salt
6 peppercorns, bruised
6 juniper berries

2 cups potato balls
12 small onions
1 cup diced carrots
2 tablespoons butter or
margarine
2 tablespoons oil
4 tablespoons unbleached or
whole wheat pastry flour
Salt and pepper
1 recipe pie pastry
1 egg yolk

ADVANCE PREPARATION:

Cut the meat in large cubes and place in a glass or ceramic dish. Combine the ingredients for the marinade and pour over the meat. Let stand in a cool place for 12 to 24 hours, stirring occasionally.

Cut the potato balls from large white potatoes. Peel the onions if using fresh ones. Prepare the carrots and cut them into large dice. Boil the vegetables together in 2 cups of salted water for 10 minutes. Frozen onions will take less time and should be added later. Drain the vegetables, reserving the liquid.

Drain the venison, reserving the marinade. Discard the onion and other seasonings.

Pat the meat dry with paper toweling.

Heat the butter and oil in a heavy pan and brown the venison on all sides over high heat. Reduce the heat and sprinkle with the flour, stirring until the flour disappears. Add ½ cup of the marinade and the vegetable water. Continue stirring until thickened. Taste the sauce. It should be highly seasoned with salt and plenty of freshly ground black pepper. Remove from the heat and stir in the vegetables. Place in a deep 9- or 10-inch baking dish. Let cool.

Make the pie crust and roll into a circle about ¼ inch thick and 1 inch larger than the top of the baking dish. Trim evenly and roll the circle onto the rolling pin. Unroll over the top of the dish and fold the edges under to make a rim thick enough to hold the juices. Press the edges to the rim with the back of a fork and prick the pastry in several places. If you feel artistic, roll out the remaining pastry to a thickness of ⅛ inch and cut out leaves or something more complicated like an antlered stag. Moisten the underside and stick to the pastry top.

BEFORE SERVING:

Forty-five minutes before serving, paint the pastry with a mixture of the egg yolk slightly beaten and 1 tablespoon of water. Bake in a preheated 425-degree F. oven for 40 minutes. If guests linger over the first course, turn off the heat and keep the pie in the oven with the door open.

Venison Roast

5- to 7-pound leg or saddle of
  venison
¾ pound fat salt pork
Marinade (see preceding recipe)
2 tablespoons flour
2 tablespoons Madeira

1½ cups stock, consommé, or
  water
1 teaspoon chopped capers
  (optional)
Currant jelly

ADVANCE PREPARATION:

Wipe the venison with a damp cloth. Slice about ½ pound of the salt pork in thin slabs and the remaining pork in inch-long thin strips. Make small deep incisions all over the surface of the venison with a sharp pointed knife and poke the small strips of salt pork into them. Place the meat in a shallow platter and pour marinating sauce over it. Let it stand at room temperature for 12 to 24 hours, spooning the marinade over the meat from time to time.

BEFORE SERVING:

Preheat the oven to 450 degrees F. Place the meat in an open roasting pan. Cover with the slabs of salt pork. Roast the meat at the high temperature for 20 minutes. Reduce the heat to 375 degrees F. and continue roasting, allowing 20 minutes per pound unless you like venison rare.

TO SERVE:

Remove the pork from the venison and transfer the venison to a hot platter. Pour most of the fat from the pan. Sprinkle the drippings with flour and stir until blended. Add the Madeira and stock, consommé, or water. If you use water, fortify it with beef extract or bouillon cubes. Bring the mixture to a boil and strain into a heated sauce bowl, adding the capers if desired. Serve with a bowl of currant jelly.

Venison Steak

Venison steak is a much prized luxury; but unless the animal was killed at a very tender age, the steak is more enjoyable if tenderized for one or two days in a marinating sauce.

Venison steak
Marinade (see recipe for
   Venison Pie)

Butter or margarine
Salt and black pepper

ADVANCE PREPARATION:

Place the venison steak, wiped free of bone dust, in a shallow crockery dish. Spoon the marinating sauce over it and let it stay at room temperature. Spoon the sauce over the meat occasionally.

BEFORE SERVING:

Wipe the steak dry. Brush with melted butter and place on a well-greased broiling rack. Broil 2 inches from the flame, allowing 10 to 12 minutes on each side. Season with butter, salt, and freshly ground black pepper.

Cole Slaw, Boiled or Yogurt Dressing

6 cups shredded cabbage
½ cup chopped green pepper
¼ cup grated onion

BOILED DRESSING:
3 tablespoons unbleached or
   whole wheat pastry flour
2 teaspoons dry mustard
1 teaspoon salt
1 tablespoon sugar
2 eggs, slightly beaten

⅓ cup cider vinegar
¾ cup milk
4 tablespoons butter or
   margarine

YOGURT DRESSING:
½ cup plain yogurt
1 cup cottage cheese
2 teaspoons cider vinegar
1½ tablespoons honey
1 teaspoon caraway seeds

ADVANCE PREPARATION:

Shred and chop the cabbage, pepper, and onion in a food processor or by hand. Put the vegetables in a bowl and cover with water and a few ice cubes. Place in the refrigerator while making the preferred dressing.

Boiled Dressing: Combine all the ingredients in the top of a double boiler or in a heavy saucepan. Whisk constantly until the mixture is smooth and thick. Pour into a jar and cool completely before covering and chilling in the refrigerator.

Yogurt Dressing: Combine the ingredients, except the caraway seeds, in a food processor or blender and spin until smooth. Stir in the caraway seeds, pour into a jar, and cover. Keep in the refrigerator.

TO SERVE:

Drain the cabbage mixture thoroughly, patting dry with a paper towel. Mix with dressing and serve on individual plates.

Grand Marnier Soufflé

This is a favorite at countless restaurants all over the country but there is no reason why it cannot be made at home. It is a wonderful accolade to the successful hunter. The base is made 3 or 4 hours in advance. The flavoring and beaten egg whites are added just before the dinner and the soufflé souffles during dinner.

3 tablespoons butter
3 tablespoons unbleached
   flour
¾ cup milk
4 egg yolks
2 teaspoons vanilla extract
4 tablespoons Grand Marnier,
   Cointreau or Curaçao

5 egg whites
⅛ teaspoon salt
1 tablespoon grated orange
   rind
2 tablespoons sugar

ADVANCE PREPARATION:

Butter a 1½-quart soufflé dish on bottom and sides. Put a tablespoon of sugar in the dish and tilt it to coat all the interior. Shake out any excess.

Heat the 3 tablespoons butter in a saucepan and add the flour. Cook gently for 2 minutes. Add the milk and whisk vigorously until thick and smooth. Remove from the heat.

Place in an electric mixing bowl and add the egg yolks one by one, beating continuously. Put the egg whites (plus an extra) in another mixing bowl. Add the vanilla and orange liqueur to the egg yolk mixture and stir until blended. Cover both bowls and leave them at room temperature.

Spin the sugar and the rind (orange part only) in the food processor or blender, or grate the orange by hand and work in the sugar with the back of a spoon in a small bowl. Set aside.

BEFORE SERVING:

Just before sitting down to dinner, whip up the egg whites with ⅛ teaspoon of salt, starting slowly and increasing the speed until they are stiff but not dry.

Stir ⅓ of the whites into the yolk mixture thoroughly. Fold in the remaining whites with a kind of lifting motion so as to incorporate as much air as possible. Pour the mixture into the prepared soufflé dish.

If your oven is not free to bake the soufflé at that moment or your guests are lingering over cocktails, do not fret. Cover with the electric mixer cover or other enveloping cover to keep out the drafts. It will stand as long as an hour.

Just before putting the soufflé in the oven, sprinkle with the orange sugar. Time the dessert, allowing 35 minutes at 375 degrees F. for a soft souffle *à la française* or 40 to 45 minutes for a firmer variety.

A soufflé must be eaten immediately, so put it in the oven a little late rather than too early. It's better to let your guests wait a few minutes than to rush them nervously through the meal.

WEEKEND WITH GUESTS

Four to six guests for a weekend can be a lot of fun; but if the hosts are to enjoy it, it takes some thought and really "advance" preparation. Start thinking a week ahead. Read these menus, substituting favorites of your own when you wish, and figure out what can be prepared ahead of time on Wednesday, what on Thursday, and what on Friday. Presuming that the weekend starts with Saturday noon lunch, you will be serving four or five meals and all the advance preparation should be completed by Friday night or Saturday mid-morning. Check all your household supplies other than food—your table settings, your beverage supplies, ice, candles, etc.—early in the week. Make your entertaining as simple or as elegant as you like, but avoid last-minute crises by covering some areas early. Prepare such things as soup, cookies, and salad dressings (also bread and rolls that can be frozen and reheated when the time comes) on Wednesday. Do what you can on Thursday and Friday. If the guests are staying for Sunday night supper, cut up cheese for the Cheese Rarebit and put it in a plastic bag. With such preparation, you can start enjoying the weekend with the arrival of the first guest.

All recipes in this chapter are planned for eight persons.

Saturday Luncheon

With or without arriving guests, Saturday tends to become the busiest day of the week and Saturday noon is the time for an easy-to-serve meal planned around a hearty and satisfying soup. Here are suggestions for two such soups that can be prepared in advance and just reheated at the last minute. Both are a little out of the ordinary without being so strange that your guests might not like them; either could substitute for the main dish at any simple family meal.

SATURDAY LUNCHEON

Lentil Sausage Soup or Green Gumbo (Gumbo Z'Herbes)
Finger Salad
Dark Bread
Sweet Butter

Fruit Bowl*
Oatmeal Pecan Cookies

Lentil Sausage Soup

1 pound dry lentils
1 large onion, chopped
1 clove garlic, minced
½ cup chopped celery
½ cup chopped carrots
2 tablespoons bacon drippings
    or butter
1 teaspoon tomato paste

1 bay leaf
6 sprigs parsley
¼ teaspoon powdered thyme
Salt and pepper
1 pound Polish sausage,
    peeled, or all-beef
    frankfurters

ADVANCE PREPARATION:

Place the lentils in a strainer and rinse in cool water, removing any imperfect ones. Place in a large bowl and cover with 2 quarts of water. Let stand 6 to 12 hours.

Chop the vegetables by hand or in a food processor.

Heat the drippings or butter in a soup kettle and sauté the vegetables for 3 minutes, stirring constantly. Add the lentils and the tomato paste and stir until well mixed. Tie the bay leaf and parsley into a bouquet and add to the lentils along with the thyme and a good sprinkling of salt and freshly ground black pepper.

If necessary, add more water. The lentils should be covered by 2 inches. Bring to a boil and simmer 2 hours.

Remove the parsley bouquet and taste for seasoning. Some people prefer to serve the soup as is. I prefer to spin the soup in a food processor or blender. It is your choice.

BEFORE SERVING:

Reheat the soup and add the sausage or frankfurters cut into 1-inch pieces. Simmer the soup at least 30 minutes before serving.

Green Gumbo

This Creole dish, known in New Orleans as Gumbo Z'Herbes, should be made a day or two ahead and reheated just before serving. Plan to make it when you have a ham bone on hand. As with other regional dishes there are hundreds of versions of gumbo, but this one is unique in that it does not contain okra. You can add oysters, sausage, chicken, or stew meat; you can flavor it with allspice and cloves. It's all authentic, but this simple recipe seems to please everyone. Serve with boiled white or brown rice.

1 package frozen spinach
1 package frozen mustard
  greens
1 package frozen turnip
  greens
1 package frozen collard
  greens
4 cups shredded cabbage
4 bay leaves
8 sprigs Italian flat parsley
1 teaspoon powdered basil
½ teaspoon powdered thyme
2 medium onions, chopped

1 cup chopped green sweet
  peppers
1 cup chopped celery
4 cloves garlic, minced
1 large bunch green onions
  (scallions)
¼ pound butter or margarine
½ cup peanut oil
⅔ cup unbleached flour
Salt and pepper
Tabasco
1 ham bone
Rice (long-grain white or
  brown)

ADVANCE PREPARATION:

Place the frozen vegetables in a deep saucepan. Add 1 cup of water and bring to a boil, breaking the frozen blocks with a fork. As soon as the greens come to a boil, add the cabbage, the bay leaves and the parsley tied into a bouquet, the basil, and the thyme. Cover tightly and cook over moderate heat for 15 minutes.

Meanwhile, prepare the other vegetables, chopping them with a food processor or by hand. Sauté the chopped vegetables in butter or margarine until slightly tender. Stir frequently. Set aside.

Drain the greens, reserving the liquid carefully. Cut the greens coarsely with two sharp knives. Set aside.

Heat the oil in the bottom of a deep soup kettle. Stir in the flour and continue stirring until it becomes medium brown in color. Add the vegetable liquor gradually, stirring constantly until the mixture is smooth and thickened.

Add the greens and sautéed vegetables. Stir well while adding 2 quarts of cold water. Season with 1 teaspoon of salt and ½ teaspoon freshly ground black pepper and a few drops of Tabasco.

Put in the ham bone. Bring the mixture to a boil. Reduce the heat, cover, and simmer 1½ hours. Remove the ham bone and herb bouquet. Cool and refrigerate.

Allow 4 tablespoons of uncooked rice to a serving. If using white rice, allow 2 cups of cold water and 1 teaspoon of sea salt for each cup of uncooked rice. Bring to a rapid boil in a large heavy saucepan. Stir and cover tightly. Reduce the heat to low and cook 15 minutes. Remove to a glass or ceramic dish for later reheating. Fork-fluff with 1 teaspoon of butter or margarine. If using brown rice, allow 2½ cups of water and 1 teaspoon of sea salt for each cup of uncooked rice. Bring to a rapid boil. Cover, reduce the heat to low, and cook for 45 minutes or until all the water is absorbed. Transfer the rice to a glass or ceramic serving dish for later reheating.

BEFORE SERVING:

Reheat the soup for 30 minutes, adding oysters or cooked meat if desired. Taste for seasoning. Transfer to a heated soup tureen.

Reheat the rice in a 225-degree F. oven for 25 minutes or for 3 or 4 minutes in the microwave oven. The length of heating depends on the amount of rice.

TO SERVE:

Bring soup and rice to the table. For each guest, place a spoonful of rice in an individual soup plate and top with a generous serving of the gumbo.

Finger Salad

Prepare any or all of the following and arrange them on a platter around a small bowl of mayonnaise. Keep in the refrigerator until just before serving.

Celery sticks
Carrot sticks
Cucumber spears
Raw parsnip slivers
Radishes
Green or red pepper sticks
Broccoli flowerets

Cauliflower buds
Artichokes vinaigrette
    (store bought)
Kosher dill pickle spears
Cherry or yellow pear
    tomatoes

Oatmeal Pecan Cookies

These jiffy-made cookies are a joy to have on hand. If 4 dozen are not enough for the weekend, make a double batch.

¼ pound butter
1 egg
⅔ cup rolled oats
⅔ cup ground pecans
1 cup sugar

4 tablespoons unbleached
    white flour
⅓ teaspoon baking powder
2 teaspoons vanilla

Preheat the oven to 325 degrees F.

Melt the butter and set it aside to cool to lukewarm.

Beat the egg slightly in an electric mixing bowl or beat by hand in a deep bowl. Add the remaining ingredients and mix well. Pour in the melted butter and mix again.

Line a baking sheet with aluminum foil. Drop the mixture by teaspoonfuls onto the baking sheet. Allow room for the cookies to spread. Bake 10 to 12 minutes on the middle shelf, preparing another sheet in the meantime.

Allow the cookies to cool on the foil before removing them. Store in a covered container.

Saturday Night Supper

The supper suggested here is a simple but hearty meal, the kind that calls for casual wear and casual timing. It might, for example, follow an afternoon of football viewed either from stadium or living room. If the occasion seems to demand a more formal menu, consider substituting one of the Dinners for Eight described in an earlier chapter.

SATURDAY NIGHT SUPPER

Beef Carbonnades à la Paysanne or Oyster Pie
Fresh Corn on the Cob
or Corn Pudding
Spinach, Lettuce, and Mushroom Salad
French Bread

Sherry Chocolate Roll
Coffee

WINE SUGGESTIONS:
With the Beef Carbonnades—
Domestic: Zinfandel, or
Imported: Bandolino (Veneto)
With the Oyster Pie—
Domestic: Pinot Blanc, or
Imported: Muscadet (Loire)

Beef Carbonnades à la Paysanne

2½ to 3 pounds eye-of-the-round
  beef
¼ pound butter or margarine
¼ cup salad or peanut oil
5 medium to large onions,
  sliced thin
¼ teaspoon powdered bay leaf
¼ teaspoon powdered thyme
¼ teaspoon powdered sage

⅛ teaspoon cayenne
¼ teaspoon powdered basil
1 teaspoon salt
¼ teaspoon black pepper
12 ounces beer
1 cup canned bouillon
1 loaf French bread
Dijon mustard

ADVANCE PREPARATION:

Cut the eye-of-the-round into 6 to 8 ¾-inch steaks.

Heat 2 tablespoons of butter or margarine and 1 tablespoon of oil in a heavy skillet until it is smoking. Sear the steaks 15 seconds on each side and transfer temporarily to a platter. Discard the fat and wipe out the skillet with paper toweling.

Heat the remaining oil and butter or margarine in the same skillet over moderate heat and cook the onions until tender but not brown. Turn frequently with a spatula. Set aside.

Mix all the spices in a small bowl.

Spread half the onions in the bottom of a heavy casserole. Cover with the steaks and top with the remaining onions. Sprinkle with the herbs and pour the beer and bouillon over all.

Cut the bread in 6 to 8 1-inch slices and spread both sides with mustard. Place on top of the onions. Cover the casserole and bake 4 hours at 275 degrees F.

This can be baked a day in advance and reheated 30 minutes in a 350-degree F. oven—or 10 to 12 minutes in a microwave, turning the dish once or twice. Or it can be prepared in advance but baked the afternoon of the dinner.

TO SERVE:

Transfer the steaks to a well-heated platter. Cover with the sauce and serve with plenty of French bread.

Oyster Pie

6 large potatoes
1 cup hot milk
6 tablespoons butter or
  margarine
4 egg yolks
Salt and pepper
⅛ teaspoon nutmeg
½ cup fine bread crumbs
1 quart oysters, shucked

Milk
Butter or margarine
2 tablespoons chopped onion
4 tablespoons unbleached
  flour
1 cup heavy cream
2 tablespoons chopped parsley
1 egg yolk

ADVANCE PREPARATION:

Wash and peel the potatoes. Halve them and boil in salted water for 20 minutes or until tender. Or, pressure cook with ½ cup of water for 12 minutes. Drain the potatoes and return them to the pan. Dry over a low heat, tossing frequently until the potatoes are mealy on the outside.

Mash the potatoes by hand or with an electric beater, gradually adding the hot milk, butter, and egg yolks, one by one, while beating constantly. Season with salt, pepper, and nutmeg. Let cool for a few minutes.

Butter the bottom and sides of a 2-quart casserole. Spread the potato around the bottom and sides, reserving enough for the top crust. Sprinkle the potato lining with the fine bread crumbs. Roll out the reserved potato between two sheets of wax paper to the size and shape of the casserole. Place on a plate and put both the casserole and the top crust in the refrigerator.

Simmer the oysters in their own liquor just long enough for the edges to begin to curl. Drain, reserving the liquor in a 2-cup measure. If the oysters are large, cut them into halves or thirds. Add enough milk to the oyster liquor to measure 2 cups.

Heat the butter or margarine in a saucepan and sauté the onions just until tender. Stir in the flour and cook over moderate heat for 2 minutes. Add the oyster liquor-milk mixture and stir until smooth. Remove from the heat and stir in the cream. Season highly with salt and pepper and add 1 tablespoon of chopped parsley and the oysters. Cool before refrigerating.

BEFORE SERVING:

One hour before serving time preheat the oven to 350 degrees F.

Beat the egg yolk with 1 tablespoon of water in a small bowl.

Pour the oyster filling into the casserole. Peel off the top sheet of wax paper from the potato crust and turn upside-down on top of the casserole and remove the under sheet of paper.

Paint the surface with the egg yolk. Place the casserole on a baking sheet and bake for 50 minutes.

TO SERVE:

Transfer the pie to a round serving platter and sprinkle the surface with the remaining chopped parsley.

Fresh Corn on the Cob

To be really good, corn must be freshly picked. Real corn lovers advise having the water boiling on the stove before picking the corn. Allow 2 ears per person, assuming that some people will eat one and some will eat three.

Remove the husks and silk from the corn and rinse under cool water.

Throw the ears into a large kettle two-thirds full of rapidly boiling unsalted water. If the corn is not strictly fresh, add 2 tablespoons of sugar. Boil 5 to 10 minutes according to the size of the kernels.

Corn Pudding

Corn pudding can be made from fresh corn or from canned corn kernels. The addition of green chile peppers is optional. Both parts of the recipe can be prepared in advance and combined just before baking. The ingredients should be at room temperature.

2 cups fresh corn pulp or
  1 can (16 ounces) corn
  kernels
2 teaspoons salt
⅛ teaspoon white pepper
2 tablespoons chopped canned
  green chiles (optional)

1 tablespoon cornstarch
2 cups milk
3 tablespoons butter or
  margarine
3 eggs
2 tablespoons chopped parsley

ADVANCE PREPARATION:

If you are using fresh corn, remove the husks, silk, and wash briefly. With a sharp knife cut off the kernels to ⅔ of their depth. Then, scrape the rest of the kernels with the dull side of the knife, retaining as much of the pulp and liquid as possible.

If using canned corn, drain well.

Mix the corn with salt, pepper, chiles, and cornstarch. Set aside.

Heat the milk and butter just to the simmering point. Beat the eggs with an electric beater and continue to beat while adding the milk gradually.

BEFORE SERVING:

Allow 45 minutes for baking.

Preheat the oven to 350 degrees F.

Whisk the egg and milk mixture and combine with the corn mixture. Pour into a buttered 1½-quart casserole and sprinkle with the chopped parsley. Bake 45 minutes or until an inserted knife comes out clean.

Spinach, Lettuce and Mushroom Salad

1 pound fresh spinach
1 head Boston lettuce
1 pound mushrooms
2 tablespoons lemon juice
Pitted black olives (optional)

DRESSING:
2 tablespoons tarragon vinegar
4 tablespoons peanut oil
4 tablespoons olive oil
½ teaspoon salt
⅛ teaspoon freshly ground black pepper

ADVANCE PREPARATIONS:

Wash the spinach well, removing the stems. Dry in a lettuce spinner or basket, or between paper towels.

Wash the lettuce and dry well. Break into pieces.

Place both greens in a salad bowl. Cover and refrigerate.

Trim the stems of the mushrooms. Wash briefly and dry between paper towels. Mix with the lemon juice. Cover and refrigerate.

Combine the oils, vinegar, and seasonings.

TO SERVE:

Combine the mushrooms and the black olives, if desired, with the prepared greens. Add the dressing and toss well.

Sherry Chocolate Roll

CAKE:

6 egg yolks
1 cup sugar
1 teaspoon vanilla
¾ cup sifted cake flour
2 teaspoons baking powder
6 egg whites
¼ teaspoon salt

FROSTING AND FILLING:

2 squares baking chocolate
1 teaspoon instant coffee
1 tablespoon hot water
¼ cup sherry
1 cup sweet butter
2 cups confectioners' sugar,
   sifted
2 egg yolks, well beaten
Chocolate shot

ADVANCE PREPARATION:

Preheat the oven to 375 degrees F.

Beat the egg yolks for the cake for 3 minutes with an electric beater or in food processor, or longer if beating by hand. Add the sugar gradually and when the mixture is creamy, add the vanilla. Sift the dry ingredients and beat the egg whites with the salt until stiff. Add these two mixtures alternately to the egg yolks, folding them in gently but thoroughly.

Line a jelly-roll pan with foil, poking the foil into the corners so that the foil stands up about ½ inch taller than the rim on the long side. Allow 2 inches at both ends to serve as handles for rolling.

Pour the batter evenly into the pan, tipping or poking it into the corners. Bake 12 minutes.

Remove from the oven, lift the cake by the end handles of foil onto a counter top, and roll the cake up with the foil. The handles will be cool, the foiled cake very hot, so protect your hand if you need to touch the cake to form a good roll, or to flip the roll over onto the seam side to cool.

To prepare frosting and filling: Melt the chocolate in the top of a small double boiler over boiling water, or for 1 minute in a small glass or ceramic bowl in the microwave. Add the coffee dissolved in the water. Cool and add the sherry.

Cream the butter and sugar with electric beater or food processor or by hand, until light and smooth. Add the egg yolks and the chocolate mixture and beat until smooth.

Unroll the cooled cake and spread it with some of the frosting, having stripped off the foil wrapper. Reroll the cake with the seam side up and frost with the rest of the mixture. Sprinkle with chocolate shot. Place on a long serving tray and store in the refrigerator.

Sunday Breakfast

Sunday breakfast with guests must be a movable feast. Some like to lie abed for an extra hour or two; some like to jog a few miles before eating. Others feel neglected if they do not eat at a regular hour. The answer is to follow the example set by the British and to have a serve-yourself breakfast on the sideboard ready for the earliest and latest arrivals.

The host and hostess arrange with their guests a certain hour when the main hot dish will be served for those who want it. Otherwise, everything will be ready on the sideboard (or kitchen counter). Such gadgets as an automatic coffee maker, a warming tray, and a toaster make this possible.

A breakfast cloth is spread on the table but not set. Plates, glasses, cups, silverware, and napkins are placed on a side table. Everything that does not need to be kept cold is put on the sideboard or counter and covered with plastic film. Fruit juice, cream, and butter are prepared for serving and kept in the refrigerator. The first person down will flick a few switches, remove the plastic, and retrieve the perishables from the refrigerator.

also with pan filled with ice w/ juice, butter etc.

SUNDAY BREAKFAST

Fruit Juice Pitcher
Hi-Fi Cereal Sundae

Cinnamon Sherry Rolls
Health Muffins
Toast
Butter
Marmalade

English Sausage Pie
Coffee
Tea

Fruit Juice Pitcher

What goes into the fruit juice pitcher—orange juice (fresh or frozen), grapefruit juice (fresh or frozen), cranberry juice, or a combination of all three—is up to you. Pour it into a glass pitcher and cover it tightly. The next morning, put in a few ice cubes to keep it pleasantly chilled for late-comers.

Hi-Fi Cereal Sundae

A large number of men, women, and children start their days by eating high-fiber cereals as an aid to better health. A much loved doctor gave me his favorite recipe for morning cereal, which I serve for company breakfast. Lots of people ask for second helpings. Serve with skim or whole milk. The sweet nutty flavor requires no further sugar. Mix in a pretty bowl and let people help themselves.

6 cups Bran Buds
2 tablespoons Grapenuts
6 tablespoons unprocessed bran

2 tablespoons "natural"
    cereal (sweetened rolled
    oats and almonds)

Cinnamon Sherry Rolls

1 package dry yeast
¼ cup water
1 cup milk
¼ cup butter or margarine
1 tablespoon sugar
1 teaspoon salt
1 teaspoon cinnamon

2 eggs
3½-4 cups unbleached white
    flour
¼ pound butter or margarine
1½ cups brown sugar
½ cup chopped pecans
5 tablespoons sherry

Stir the yeast into the water and let stand.

Heat the milk, ¼ cup butter, sugar, salt, and cinnamon in a saucepan until the butter melts.

Beat the eggs lightly in a large mixing bowl and add the milk mixture. Beat until lukewarm and add the yeast, beating for 30 seconds.

Add half the flour and beat for 2 minutes. Add the remaining flour and beat 2 minutes more. The dough should be firm but not dry. Cover and let the dough rise 45 minutes. Knead down and place in the refrigerator for an hour.

Melt the ¼ pound butter and pour half of it into a round cake pan with 3-inch sides. Sprinkle generously with brown sugar, pecans, and 2 tablespoons of sherry.

Turn the dough onto a rolling surface lightly dusted with flour. Roll into a long rectangle with the long side near you. Spread with butter and brown sugar and roll up like a jelly roll. Paint the sides with a little butter and cut into pieces 1 inch thick. Place close together in the pan. Cover and let rise until doubled.

Bake 20 minutes at 375 degrees F. Turn out immediately onto a large plate and put back in the oven for a few moments to glaze. Sprinkle the surface with a little more sherry.

These may be eaten cold or reheated just before serving.

Health Muffins

There was a time when leftover cooked breakfast cereal went into bread or muffins. This was not only economical but marvelously nutritious. Leftover brown rice can be used in just the same way.

2 eggs
1 cup cold cooked rice
¾ cup milk
1¾ cups whole wheat flour

½ teaspoon sea salt
2 teaspoons baking powder
4 tablespoons butter or
    margarine, melted

Preheat the oven to 425 degrees F.

Grease the muffin tins with butter, margarine, or oil and dust lightly with flour, or spray with non-sticking oil.

Beat the eggs for 30 seconds. Add the rice and milk and mix well.

Combine the flour, salt, and baking powder in a measuring cup. Mix and add to the rice mixture, stirring just until blended. Pour in the melted butter and mix briefly.

Fill the muffin tins two-thirds full and bake 18 minutes.

English Sausage Pie

This dish, otherwise known as Toad-in-the-Hole, can be partially pre-pared a day in advance and baked just before serving. Both parts should be at room temperature before cooking.

2 pounds bulk sausage meat	*1 teaspoon salt*
4 eggs	*2 tablespoons melted butter or*
2 cups milk	*margarine*
1¾ cups unbleached flour	*½ teaspoon baking powder*

ADVANCE PREPARATION:

From the sausage, form 12 to 16 small patties approximately 2 inches in diameter and ½ inch thick. Sauté 3 minutes on each side in a hot skillet and drain on paper toweling. Cool.

Brush with sausage drippings the bottom of a shallow pan or cas-serole large enough to accommodate all the patties in a single layer. Arrange the patties. Keep the pan in a cool place.

Beat the eggs until light with an electric beater or in the food processor, and add the milk and flour mixed with salt. Stir just until blended. Add the melted butter and let stand overnight at room temperature. If the batter is made two days in advance, store in the refrigerator but remove the night before baking.

BEFORE SERVING:

Forty minutes before serving time, preheat the oven to 425 degrees F. Mix up the batter, stirring in the baking powder. Pour over the sausage and bake 30 minutes. Serve with butter or margarine.

Applesauce is a pleasant accompaniment.

Sunday Brunch

Sunday brunch is an American invention that is standing the test of time. The first course, during which drinks are served, is a stand-up affair while guests are gathering. I like to serve alcoholic and nonalcoholic drinks that look alike. When everyone is assembled, the main course can be served and savoured. Recipes given for eight persons can easily be doubled if outside guests are included in this part of the weekend activities.

SUNDAY BRUNCH

Grapefruit Juice on the Rocks or Frosted Daiquiris
Spiced Tomato Juice or Bloody Marys*
Avocado Toast
Smoked Salmon Canapés

Eggs Sardou or
Lamb Steaks Tarragon

Cucumber Sticks
Warm French Bread
Blueberry Muffins

Melon Platter
Café au Lait

Frosted Daiquiris

Daiquiris have to be served as soon as they are mixed, so have the ingredients ready and mix on demand. Here are two ways of making them.

Method I: For each serving, allow 1 tablespoon of lemon juice, 2 teaspoons of sugar, and 2 ounces of white rum. Spin in a blender with ice cubes until frothy.

Method II: Combine the contents of 1 can (6 ounces) frozen lemonade (unthawed) with 12 ounces of white rum. Spin until smooth. Serves 6 persons.

Spiced Tomato Juice

1 quart tomato juice
1 small onion, sliced
1 stalk celery (with leaves)
  cut in pieces
1 teaspoon sugar

1 small clove garlic, pressed
  (optional)
½ teaspoon oregano
1 bay leaf
2 teaspoons lemon juice
Salt and pepper

ADVANCE PREPARATION:

Bring the tomato juice to the simmering point with the onion, celery, sugar, and garlic (if desired). Add the oregano and bay leaf encased in a small tea ball. Cover and simmer very slowly for 30 minutes. Strain into a serving pitcher. Cool. Add the lemon juice and season to taste with salt and pepper. Cover tightly and chill well.

TO SERVE:

Stir well and serve in old-fashioned glasses.

Avocado Toast

1 large or 2 medium-sized
  avocados
1 large clove garlic, pressed
2½ teaspoons lemon juice
2-3 drops Tabasco

Salt and pepper
Thin-sliced whole wheat bread
Melba rounds
2 tablespoons chopped red
  pimiento

ADVANCE PREPARATION:

Split the avocados and remove the seeds. Reserve one shell. Scoop out the flesh and mash it by hand or in a food processor very briefly. Add the garlic, lemon juice, and Tabasco. Season to taste with salt and pepper. Place in a nonmetal bowl. Cover tightly and refrigerate.

BEFORE SERVING:

Cut the bread (toasted or untoasted) in 2-inch squares. Place them and the melba rounds around the edge of a platter.

Whip up the avocado mixture with a wooden fork and pile into the reserved shell. Surround the rim with the chopped pimiento. Serve with a couple of spreaders so that people will help themselves.

Smoked Salmon Canapés

(24 canapés)

1 package (8 ounces) thin-sliced
  rye rounds
1 package (8 ounces) cream
  cheese
6 tablespoons sweet butter

2 tablespoons chopped chives
6 ounces smoked salmon slices
Capers
1 tablespoon chopped parsley

ADVANCE PREPARATION:

Spread the rounds with a smoothly blended mixture of cream cheese, butter, and chives. Top each slice with a square of smoked salmon.

Put the remaining cheese mixture in a small pastry tip and pipe it around the edge and in the center of each canapé.

Dot each canapé with 4 or 5 capers and sprinkle with parsley. Cover and refrigerate.

TO SERVE:

Place on a round serving tray for your guests to help themselves.

Eggs Sardou

This dish is one that visitors to New Orleans savour and describe later to their friends. With a little prior planning and preparation you can make it for your own brunch. There are really four parts to the dish and you can ready three of them a day in advance. The fourth part—poached eggs—has to be prepared at the last minute and you will need an extra pair of hands for assembling and serving the dish.

SAUCE

4 egg yolks

¼ cup cream

4 teaspoons lemon juice

¼ pound butter

⅛ teaspoon cayenne

Salt and pepper

SPINACH BASE:

2 10-ounce packages
  frozen spinach

Milk

4 tablespoons butter or
  margarine

4 tablespoons flour

⅛ teaspoon nutmeg

Salt and pepper

2 cans artichoke bottoms or
  16 small artichokes

3 tablespoons butter or
  margarine

16 eggs

Cayenne

ADVANCE PREPARATION:

To prepare the sauce: Whisk the egg yolks and cream in a small saucepan over moderate heat until the mixture begins to thicken. Remove from the heat and stir in the lemon juice and 2 tablespoons of butter. Whisk over heat until the sauce starts to thicken again (a matter of seconds). Add the rest of the butter, 2 tablespoons at a time, whisking continuously until the butter is all incorporated and the sauce is thick. Season with ⅛ teaspoon cayenne and salt and pepper to taste. Pour into a glass measuring cup. Set aside.

To prepare the spinach base: Cook the spinach with ½ cup of water and ½ teaspoon of salt in a covered saucepan for 8 minutes. Drain the liquid into a 2-cup glass measure and put the spinach in a blender or food processor. Fill the measuring cup with milk and add along with butter or margarine, flour, and nutmeg to the spinach. Spin until pureed. Season to taste with salt and pepper and pour the spinach into the top of a double boiler or into a glass or ceramic dish if you have a microwave oven.

To prepare the artichokes: Drain the canned artichoke bottoms and rinse in cool water. Pat dry. Sauté them 1 minute on each side and place them stem side down on a platter, trimming the bottoms evenly if necessary. Cool, cover, and refrigerate.

If you live in artichoke country, boil fresh artichokes 40 minutes in salted water. Cool and trim off the leaves and choke. Fresh artichokes need not be sautéed.

BEFORE SERVING:

Reheat the sauce 1 minute on "simmer" in a microwave, or place the glass cup on a trivet in a pan of almost simmering water. If the sauce separates with reheating, spin it for a moment in the food processor or blender.

Reheat the spinach in the double boiler or, if using a microwave, cover with wax paper and reheat for 4 minutes.

Reheat the artichoke bottoms 10 minutes at 300 degrees F. in a conventional oven or cover and reheat for 2 minutes in the microwave.

Have ready 2 large skillets full of simmering water. Add 2 tablespoons of white vinegar and 1 teaspoon of salt to each skillet. Break 4 eggs into each skillet. Roll each one gently with a small spoon so that the white will adhere to the yolk. Poach 2 minutes.

TO SERVE:

Spread a layer of spinach on individual warm breakfast plates. Place 2 artichoke bottoms on the spinach. Fill the artichokes with the poached eggs and cover with the sauce. Sprinkle with a little cayenne. Serve immediately and repeat the process for the remaining 8 eggs.

Lamb Steaks Tarragon

Buy steaks cut 1 inch thick across the bone from a 5- to 7-pound leg of spring lamb. Allow ⅓ to ½ pound per person.

Lamb steaks   *1 teaspoon lemon juice*
Tarragon leaves   *Salt*
¼ pound butter   *Freshly ground black pepper*

ADVANCE PREPARATION:

To make the tarragon butter: Chop 2 dozen tarragon leaves in a wooden bowl or pulverize them in a blender or food processor. Work in ¼ pound of whipped or ordinary butter. Season with a teaspoon of lemon juice, salt, and freshly ground black pepper—lots of it.

Trim the steaks and cut them into serving portions.

BEFORE SERVING:

For oven broiling, place the steaks on a greased broiler rack in an aluminum foil-lined pan and set them about 2 inches from the heat under the broiler. For charcoal broiling, arrange the steaks on a greased grill. For pan broiling, place the steaks in a well-heated cast-iron or heavy aluminum skillet which has been generously sprinkled with table salt. For all methods of cooking, allow 5 to 6 minutes for each side. Transfer the steaks to a heated platter and spread with tarragon butter.

Cucumber Sticks

Pare small, freshly picked cucumbers. Quarter them lengthwise and soak them in ice water overnight.

Drain and serve very cold. If the day is hot, put a few small ice cubes in the bowl in which these are served.

Blueberry Muffins

(18 3-inch muffins)

These muffins can be made a day or two in advance and reheated before serving. For those who prefer it, whole wheat pastry flour may be substituted for the white flour.

1 cup blueberries
¼ cup all-purpose unbleached
  flour
¾ teaspoon salt
2 teaspoons baking powder
1½ cups all-purpose unbleached
  flour

2 eggs
¾ cup milk
4 tablespoons melted butter
  or margarine

ADVANCE PREPARATION:

Preheat the oven to 400 degrees F.

Dredge the berries in the ¼ cup of flour. Combine the salt, baking powder, and 1½ cups of flour in a measuring cup. Beat the eggs until frothy and add the milk and melted butter.

Stir the dry ingredients into the egg mixture quickly and briefly. The batter does not need to be smooth. The less stirring, the better the muffins. Fold in the berries.

Fill buttered muffin tins two-thirds full. Bake 20 minutes. Remove and cool on a wire rack.

BEFORE SERVING:

Place the muffins on a heatproof platter. Cover with aluminum foil and reheat 5 minutes at 425 degrees F. in a regular oven. For a microwave, cover with wax paper and heat 3 minutes. Let stand 2 minutes.

Melon Platter

ADVANCE PREPARATION:

This is a combination of two or more kinds of melon--cantaloupe, honeydew, casaba, Persian, and so on. Halve the melons, seed them, and slice into wedges. Pare the melon wedges and arrange them alternately by colors on a serving platter. Garnish with lemon slices and, if possible, with mint leaves. Cover tightly with wax paper before storing in the refrigerator.

TO SERVE:

Remove from the refrigerator 30 minutes before breakfast time. Melon loses flavor if it is too cold.

Sunday Dinners

Sunday dinner may or may not be part of a houseparty weekend, but in many families it is the one time in the week when all ages—family, friends, and relations—gather around the table. It doesn't have to be the huge midday meal of a generation ago but it should be expandable. If you will be serving more than eight, increase the vegetable and dessert recipes given here by half; the beef and turkey will serve ten or twelve.

Whether it is served at noon or in the evening or somewhere in-between, Sunday dinner should be a meal that children as well as grownups can enjoy. A first course makes the meal too long for most children, so, instead, plan one appetizing canapé to be served with a before-dinner drink.

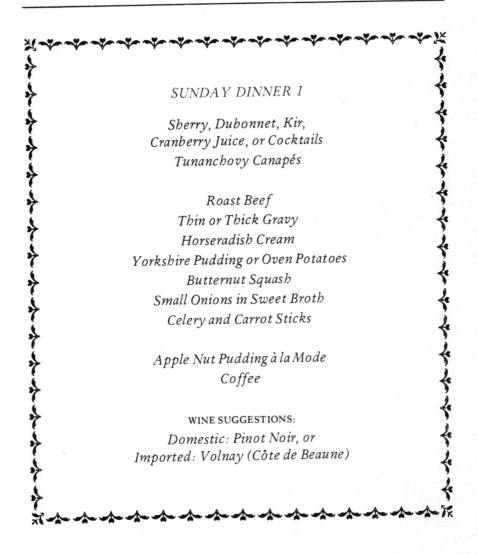

SUNDAY DINNER I

Sherry, Dubonnet, Kir,
Cranberry Juice, or Cocktails
Tunanchovy Canapés

Roast Beef
Thin or Thick Gravy
Horseradish Cream
Yorkshire Pudding or Oven Potatoes
Butternut Squash
Small Onions in Sweet Broth
Celery and Carrot Sticks

Apple Nut Pudding à la Mode
Coffee

WINE SUGGESTIONS:
Domestic: Pinot Noir, or
Imported: Volnay (Côte de Beaune)

Tunanchovy Canapés

1 can (6½ ounces) tuna fish
¼ pound sweet butter
2 teaspoons anchovy paste

Parsley
Melba toast or crackers

ADVANCE PREPARATION:

Drain the tuna and place it in a blender or food processor. Cut the butter in 8 small pieces and add along with the anchovy paste. Spin until smooth.

Lightly oil a small bowl or decorative mold. Place the mixture in the bowl, smoothing the surface evenly with a small spatula. Refrigerate.

TO SERVE:

Unmold on a serving platter. Garnish with parsley flowerets and surround with melba toast or crackers.

Roast Beef

Order a 6- to 8-pound standing rib roast or a 5- to 7-pound rolled rib roast, a face of the rump, or a sirloin roast. Do not season the roast with salt and black pepper until halfway through the cooking, as salt tends to draw out the juices too soon. Plan to have the cooked beef stand in a warm place for 20 minutes before serving.

If you will be using a regular oven, preheat to 300 degrees F. and place the roast fat side up on a rack in the middle of an open roasting pan. Insert a meat thermometer in the thickest part of the meat.

Timing and thermometer temperature:

18 minutes per pound for rare beef (140 degrees F.)

22 minutes per pound for medium (160 degrees F.)

25-30 minutes per pound for well-done (170 degrees F.) Allow 2 or 3 minutes extra time per pound for a rolled roast.

In a microwave oven, place the roast in a 2-quart glass baking dish with a microwave roasting rack. Follow directions that come with the oven for setting the first and second cooking times. Insert the temperature probe in the thickest part of the beef. Allow 5 minutes per pound on high for the first setting and 3 minutes per pound for the second cooking. The probe will be set for 125 degrees F. for rare, 145 degrees F. for medium, or 155 degrees F. for well done, since the meat continues to cook after the heat has turned off. Turn the meat over once during the cooking process, adding the salt and pepper when you do.

Remove the meat from the oven and cover tightly with foil for 10 minutes. This gives you time to reheat the vegetables.

Gravy

For thin gravy: Pour off the excess fat from the roasting pan. Pour 1½ cups of cool water into the pan. Place the pan over an open burner and bring the gravy to a boil, scraping the juices off the bottom of the pan. Season with salt and pepper. Reduce the heat and simmer 5 minutes. Strain the gravy into a heated sauce bowl. (Four tablespoons of Madeira and 1¼ cups of water make a pleasant variation to this gravy.

For thick gravy: Pour off all but approximately 4 tablespoons of fat from the pan. Add 4 tablespoons of flour to the fat and stir over high heat until it browns.

Add 1½ cups of cool water and stir until the mixture is smooth. Reduce the heat and simmer 5 minutes. Season with salt and pepper. If the gravy seems pale, add a little meat extract or caramel (Kitchen Bouquet). Strain into a heated sauce bowl.

Horseradish Cream

This can be made a day in advance and kept covered in the refrigerator.

½ cup cream, whipped
3 tablespoons grated
    horseradish

½ teaspoon salt
⅛ teaspoon white pepper

Combine the ingredients in a small serving bowl. Cover and chill until serving time.

Yorkshire Pudding

Yorkshire pudding can be a puff of glory, but more often is a sodden failure if cooked in the roasting pan. Baked in a separate dish, in a separate oven, it is a sure success. If you have just a single oven, the pudding can be baked while the roast is standing and brought into the dining room as soon as the beef is carved. In this case, the onions and squash will both have to be reheated in a double boiler.

3 eggs
1 cup milk
1 cup all-purpose unbleached
    flour

½ teaspoon salt
3 tablespoons beef drippings

ADVANCE PREPARATION:

Beat the eggs until frothy. Beat in the milk, flour, and salt just until completely blended. Cover and refrigerate. Plan to let the batter stand 2 to 3 hours at room temperature before baking.

BEFORE SERVING:

Preheat the oven to 425 degrees F.

Retrieve 3 tablespoons of drippings from the roasting pan, using a bulb baster or a spoon. Spread 2 tablespoons of the drippings on the bottom and sides of a straight-sided baking dish (1½ quarts). Stir the batter well, adding 1 tablespoon of drippings. Pour into the baking dish and bake 20 minutes or until golden brown and puffy.

Oven Potatoes

ADVANCE PREPARATION:

Scrub 12 medium-sized potatoes and boil them in their jackets for 15 minutes. Drain, cool, and peel.

BEFORE SERVING:

When the roast has cooked 30 minutes in a regular oven, place the potatoes directly into the fat around the roast. Turn the potatoes once or twice while the beef is cooking.

If you are cooking the beef in a microwave oven, cook the potatoes in a regular oven, basting them first with melted butter or margarine and then with drippings from the roast.

Butternut Squash

You may prefer another kind of squash, since there are several delicious varieties. However, this is the easiest kind to prepare because of its thin skin.

2 butternut squash or 3 boxes (10 ounces) frozen squash	6 tablespoons butter or margarine Salt and pepper

ADVANCE PREPARATION:

Pare the squash with a potato peeler. Cut off the bulbous end of each and split it to remove the seeds and fiber. Cut the squash in large pieces. Boil the squash in 1 cup of water until tender (15 to 20 minutes) or pressure-cook it for 6 minutes. If using frozen squash, follow directions on the package.

Drain thoroughly and mash with an electric beater or food processor, using the plastic blade. If the squash is still very moist, return it to the saucepan and stir over moderate heat to dry it a little. Place in a double boiler or in a glass or ceramic dish if you have a microwave oven.

BEFORE SERVING:

Reheat in the top of a double boiler or for 4 minutes in a microwave oven. Stir in the butter or margarine and season to taste with salt and pepper.

Small Onions in Sweet Broth

If you want to avoid a good cry, either peel the onions under cool water or take care to peel from the top, cutting off the root end last. The tear-making agent is in the root end.

2 pounds small onions ½ cup chicken broth or consommé 3 tablespoons butter	2 tablespoons light brown sugar Salt and pepper

ADVANCE PREPARATION:

Peel the onions and cook them in boiling salted water for 15 minutes. Drain well and place in a heatproof serving dish (nonmetal if you are using a microwave oven).

BEFORE SERVING:

Combine the broth, butter, sugar, ½ teaspoon of salt, and ⅛ teaspoon of pepper in a saucepan. Bring to a boil and pour over the onions. Bake 30 minutes at 325 degrees F. in a regular oven or 2 minutes in a microwave. If you are heating both the squash and onions in the microwave, you should count on 6 to 8 minutes.

Celery and Carrot Sticks

These may be the only vegetables some children will eat no matter what appears on the table. Sunday dinner is no place for arguing, so have a good supply of these and don't worry about it. Wash the celery and carrots well. Do not peel the carrots unless they are fairly old. Cut the celery and carrots into thin 4-inch sticks. Place in a bowl of cool water and refrigerate.

Drain thoroughly before serving on two easily reachable celery plates.

Apple Nut Pudding

8 tart apples
⅔ cup sugar
3 tablespoons unbleached
    flour or whole wheat
    pastry flour
1½ teaspoons cinnamon

¼ teaspoon salt
½ teaspoon nutmeg
½ cup chopped walnuts
2 tablespoons butter or
    margarine
1 pint vanilla ice cream

ADVANCE PREPARATION:

Preheat the oven to 375 degrees F.

Pare, core, and slice the apples in ⅛-inch slices. Arrange them in a buttered shallow baking-serving dish. Combine the dry ingredients and walnuts and sprinkle the mixture over the apples. Dot with butter or margarine and cover with a lid or aluminum foil.

Bake 35 minutes, taking the cover off for the last 10 minutes of cooking. Cool but do not refrigerate. This can be served at room temperature or warmed slightly.

TO SERVE:

Spoon into individual dessert dishes and top with the ice cream.

SUNDAY DINNER II

Roast Turkey
Old-Fashioned Stuffing and Thick Gravy
or Oyster Stuffing and Thin Gravy
Standby Mashed Potatoes
Brussels Sprouts in Parsley Butter
Sweet Turnip Chips

Coffee Butterscotch Pecan Sundae or
Fruit Compote *

WINE SUGGESTIONS:

Domestic: Cabernet Sauvignon, or
Imported: Château La Cabanne (Pomerol)

Roast Turkey with Old-Fashioned Stuffing and Thick Gravy

Making gravy is a stumbling block for many people, but it shouldn't be. If you feel hesitant about making gravy for guests, try following the directions given here and in the following recipe for thick gravy—good with old-fashioned American stuffing—and for the thinner gravy the French prefer.

10- to 12-pound turkey
2 cups water
1 bay leaf
Pinch of thyme
6 tablespoons butter or margarine
1 cup chopped celery
½ cup chopped onions

8 cups dried bread cubes
2 eggs, slightly beaten
1 tablespoon poultry seasoning
2 tablespoons chopped parsley
2 teaspoons salt
½ teaspoon black pepper

Take the liver from the giblets and cut it into small pieces.

Put the remaining giblets and the neck into a small pressure cooker with the water, bay leaf, and thyme. Add ½ teaspoon of salt and pressure-cook 12 minutes at 15 pounds pressure. To cook in the microwave, prick the giblets and put in a covered 1-quart glass dish with the seasonings and water for 10 minutes. Stir and cook 10 minutes longer. Or cook in a regular saucepan on the stove top for 1½ hours. When the giblets are cooked, strain the liquid into a measure and reserve. Discard the neck and bay leaf.

Chop the gizzard and heart quite fine by hand, or in the food processor.

Heat the butter or margarine in a skillet. Sauté the chopped onions and celery over moderate heat for 2 minutes, stirring frequently. Add the liver, cut in small pieces, and continue cooking for 2 minutes.

Put the mixture in a large bowl. Add the remaining ingredients, including the chopped giblets, and mix thoroughly. Place in a smaller bowl. Cover and refrigerate. If the bird is to be stuffed the evening before roasting, chill the stuffing very thoroughly before placing it in the very cold bird.

To stuff the turkey: Run cool water through the cavities of the bird and wipe it inside and out with paper toweling. Mix a tablespoon of salt with ¼ teaspoon of white pepper and rub the bird with the mixture inside and out. Fill the neck and body cavities with the stuffing of your choice, leaving room for the expansion that will occur during roasting. Close both openings with little skewers crisscrossed with kitchen twine.

To truss: Skewer the neck skin to the body. With the bird breast side up, run a large trussing needle threaded with kitchen twine through the center of one wing, through the body, and out the center of the other wing. Tie the thread securely over the back. In like manner, fasten the thighs to the body, running the needle through the center of one thigh, through the body, and out through the other thigh. Press the thighs close to the body and tie over the back. Tie the legs together, attaching them to the tail piece.

If this is done the evening before roasting, cover the bird and refrigerate. Remove from the refrigerator just 1 hour before roasting.

To roast: Sprinkle the roasting pan with ½ cup of flour. Spread the turkey all over with softened butter or margarine. Place breast side up on a rack and cover with a tent made of aluminum foil. Roast 15 minutes at 425 degrees F. Reduce the heat to 350 degrees F. and continue roasting, allowing 20 minutes per pound. Remove the foil for the last hour of roasting and baste every 15 minutes.

To make thick gravy: Twenty minutes before serving, transfer the turkey to a serving platter. Keep in a warm (not hot) oven. Pour off all but about ½ cup of the drippings. Mix well with the browned flour in the pan. Add 2½ cups of liquid, including the giblet broth, chicken stock, or water. Stir well, scraping the bottom of the pan with a fork. Simmer 3 minutes and strain into a heated gravy bowl.

Roast Turkey with Smoked Oyster Stuffing and Thin Gravy

10- to 12-pound turkey

STUFFING:
*1 can (3½ ounces) smoked
   oysters*
6 cups dried bread cubes
*¾ cup melted butter or
   margarine*
3 tablespoons chopped onion

2 tablespoons chopped parsley
*1½ teaspoons poultry
   seasoning*
1½ teaspoons salt
¼ teaspoon black pepper
1 tablespoon lemon juice

GRAVY:
2 cups giblet broth

Drain the oysters and cut them into large dice. Combine the oyster liquor and oysters in a medium-sized bowl with the remaining stuffing ingredients and mix thoroughly. Cover and chill in the refrigerator.

Make the giblet broth and stuff and truss the turkey as in the preceding recipe. Prick the skin of the turkey in several places and cover the breast and thighs with thin slices of salt pork (this eliminates the necessity of basting). Cover the bird and refrigerate.

Roast in 350-degree F. oven, allowing 22 minutes per pound. The last half hour remove the salt pork and let the turkey brown.

To make the gravy: Twenty minutes before serving, transfer the turkey to a platter. Keep warm in a warm (not hot) oven. Pour off all the fat from the pan. Add 2 cups of giblet broth to the pan. Mix well, scraping the juices from the bottom of the pan. Bring to a boil and strain into a heated gravy bowl.

Standby Mashed Potatoes

This way of cooking potatoes makes it possible to prepare the potatoes as much as 24 hours in advance and still have them creamy and delicious without any last-minute fuss and muss.

8-10 potatoes	*½ pint sour cream*
1 8-ounce package cream cheese	*Salt and white pepper*

ADVANCE PREPARATION:

Peel the potatoes and boil in salted water for 25 minutes or until tender. Drain thoroughly. Return to the heat to dry for a few moments, tossing the pan until the potatoes become mealy on the outside.

Mash the potatoes by hand or with an electric beater. Add the cream cheese blended with the sour cream. Season to taste with salt and pepper.

Place in a buttered 3-quart glass or ceramic casserole. Cover and refrigerate.

BEFORE SERVING:

Remove from the refrigerator 1½ hours before dinner time and let come to room temperature before baking 45 minutes at 350 degrees F. or 60 minutes at 325 degrees F.

Brussels Sprouts in Parsley Butter

1½ quarts Brussels sprouts	*2 tablespoons chopped*
or 3 boxes frozen sprouts	*parsley*
6 tablespoons butter or	*Salt and pepper*
margarine	

ADVANCE PREPARATION:

Wash the sprouts well and trim off the wilted leaves at the base. Cut a small slash in the bottom of each sprout. Cook in boiling salted water for 12 minutes. If using frozen sprouts, follow directions on the package. Cool immediately in cold water. Drain and place in an ovenproof vegetable dish. Refrigerate.

BEFORE SERVING:

Melt the butter or margarine. Add parsley, salt, and pepper. Pour over the sprouts and bake covered in the oven with the roast for 20 minutes, or for 3 minutes in the microwave oven, stirring gently once.

Sweet Turnip Chips

8 medium-sized white turnips
4 tablespoons butter or
  margarine
2 cups chicken broth

1 tablespoon sugar
½ teaspoon salt
⅛ teaspoon white pepper

ADVANCE PREPARATION:

Pare the turnips and cut them into ⅛-inch slices with a very sharp knife or with the food processor. Place them in a saucepan with the rest of the ingredients. The liquid should just cover the turnips. Cook the turnips over a high heat until almost all the liquid has disappeared. They should be tender but not mushy. Place the turnips in a shallow overproof vegetable dish (nonmetal if using microwave).

BEFORE SERVING:

Sprinkle the turnips with a little sugar and bake uncovered 30 minutes with the roast, or covered for 3 minutes in the microwave.

Coffee Butterscotch Pecan Sundae

ICE CREAM:
2 teaspoons instant coffee
⅔ cup water
2 teaspoons vanilla
1 cup sweetened condensed
    milk
1½ cups heavy cream, whipped

SAUCE:
2 egg yolks
½ cup butter
½ cup water
1⅓ cups light brown sugar
⅔ cup light corn syrup

TOPPING:
⅓ cup chopped pecans

ADVANCE PREPARATION:

Dissolve the coffee in ⅓ cup of very hot water. Add ⅓ cup of very cold water and blend well with vanilla and milk.

Chill the mixture in a freezing tray until it starts to freeze around the edge of the pan. Beat with an electric beater until smooth and fold in the whipped cream. Pour into 1 large or 2 small freezing trays and chill until half frozen. Beat in a chilled bowl until smooth but not melted. Return immediately to the tray and freeze 3 hours.

To make the sauce: Beat the egg yolks in the top of a double boiler. Add the remaining ingredients except the nuts and stir over boiling water until blended. Continue to stir frequently until the sauce is thick. This can be reheated over hot water.

TO SERVE:

Place the ice cream in individual dessert or parfait glasses. Top with the sauce and sprinkle with nuts.

Sunday Night Supper

Sunday night supper should be a light feast and a movable one. The makings are simple and all in the refrigerator. Such a supper can be served elegantly in the dining room or informally around the kitchen table, in front of the fireplace, or on the terrace. A lot will depend on the time of year and on the mood of the guests.

SUNDAY NIGHT SUPPER

Cheese Rarebit
Celery Sticks
Kosher Pickles
Beer

Fruit Bowls
Café Brûlot

Cheese Rarebit

Cooking rarebit takes a very few minutes. The important point is to have everyone eat it as soon as it is ready. It should be served on heated plates.

2 to 2½ pounds medium sharp	*¾ cup beer*
cheddar or Monterey	*1 tablespoon Dijon mustard*
Jack cheese	*1½ teaspoons salt*
12-16 thick slices bread	*½ teaspoon paprika*

ADVANCE PREPARATION:

Cut the cheese into cubes and place them in a plastic bag. Store in the refrigerator until an hour before cooking.

Trim the crusts from the bread and toast lightly on each side. Wrap in plastic film and keep in a closed container.

BEFORE SERVING:

Heat the beer in the top part of a chafing dish or double boiler over boiling water.

Reheat the toast in the same oven in which you heat the plates. Butter the toast if you prefer it that way.

Add the cheese to the hot beer and stir until it melts. Alert your guests. Add the seasonings and stir again. Serve immediately on toast, allowing 2 pieces per plate.

Serve with kosher pickles cut in sticks and a lavish supply of celery sticks.

Celery Sticks

Wash the celery and trim the ends. Place the stalks on a celery server. Wrap in plastic film and refrigerate. Have a good supply, because celery complements both the texture and flavor of rarebit.

Fruit Bowl

3 or 4 grapefruit
2 oranges

Cointreau or Grand Marnier
liqueur

ADVANCE PREPARATION:

Halve and seed the grapefruit. Spoon out the fruit sections and juice into a bowl.

Remove the white fibers from the grapefruit. The edges may be notched or scalloped if you want to take the time. Sprinkle the shells lightly with sugar. Place on a platter, cover with wax paper or plastic, and store in a cool place.

Spoon out the oranges in the same manner and save the peel of half an orange (to use in Café Brûlot).

Add 2 tablespoons of Cointreau or Grand Marnier to the combined fruit. Cover and chill in the refrigerator.

BEFORE SERVING:

Fill the grapefruit shells with the fruit and serve on individual plates.

Café Brûlot

Café Brûlot is a ceremony that calls for a chafing dish. All guests should be present for the excitement. Plan to make it when dessert is over. If possible, buy coffee with some chicory; it has more authority.

1¼ cups cognac
6 lumps sugar
10 cloves
½ cinnamon stick

Peel of ½ orange
Peel of ½ lemon
6 cups hot black coffee

ADVANCE PREPARATION:

Prepare a coffee tray with demitasse cups or little mugs. Provide yourself with a small ladle and a tea strainer.

Combine the cognac, sugar, cloves, and cinnamon stick in a small pitcher. Cover and keep at room temperature.

Cut the fruit peel into very thin slivers. Place on a small plate. Cover and refrigerate.

Prepare the coffee for brewing during dinner.

TO SERVE:

Heat the cognac combination with the peel in a chafing dish until very hot. Spoon up a ladleful and touch with a match. Slowly lower the ladle into the dish. While the flames are high, slowly add the hot coffee, thus quenching the flames. Stir with the ladle. When the last flame has died, ladle the mixture through a strainer into cups or mugs.

FOR LARGE GROUPS

Supper Receptions

Tea and Coffee

The Cocktail Party

Supper Receptions

I f you are planning a small wedding reception or would like to discharge social obligations grandly, yet fairly easily, here are two suggested menus which offer a wonderful chance to do some simple decorating. Instructions are given for dressing up both the mousse and the cake; though not necessary, it is lots of fun to do. For a wedding reception, wedding cake would replace the French pastry cake, of course.

The supper is served buffet and everything can be prepared the day before except the sandwiches and the coffee. Set up a long table and spread it with your finest cloth. The mousse, bedecked with fresh flowers, serves as a centerpiece and should have serving implements, plates, forks, and napkins nearby. The coffee and dessert are arranged at one end and the punch or champagne at the other. The plates of sandwiches can be placed on the same table or in convenient places in both living and dining rooms.

Make the coffee and place the food on the table before the party begins. Delegate one guest to help with the champagne or punch and ask another to supervise the coffee and dessert. The hostess should serve the mousse herself, if only to hear the praise she deserves.

SUPPER RECEPTION FOR 20 TO 25

Veal-Chicken Mousse Floribunda
Mushroom Sandwiches
Ham Rolls

French Pastry Cake
Champagne or White Wine Reception Punch
Coffee

SHOPPING LIST:

3 pounds veal knuckle
   with meat
5-pound roasting chicken
Unflavored gelatin
1 pint whipping cream
½ pound mushrooms
Parsley
Tarragon
Chives
2 loaves sandwich bread
4 dozen tiny rolls
Anchovy paste

½ pound boiled sliced ham
1¼ pounds sweet butter
Slivered almonds
Chopped walnuts
Onion
Lemon
Celery
Baking chocolate
Champagne or ingredients
   for the White Wine
   Reception Punch

Veal-Chicken Mousse Floribunda

Start this two days before the reception. Ask the butcher to saw the
knuckle into several pieces.

3 pounds veal knuckle   ¼ cup cold water
   with meat   6 egg yolks
1 large onion   2 cups milk
1 bay leaf   2 cups hot stock
1 sprig thyme   ½ cup slivered almonds
8 sprigs parsley   ¼ cup chopped parsley
1 stalk celery with leaves   2 hard-cooked eggs
2 teaspoons salt   Tarragon leaves, chives,
6 peppercorns   and green or red pepper
5-pound roasting chicken   1 pint heavy cream, whipped
1 tablespoon (1 package)   Salt and pepper
   unflavored gelatin

ADVANCE PREPARATION:

Wipe the knuckle pieces with a towel to remove the bone dust. Place
them in a large kettle and cover with 4 quarts of cold water. Bring to a
boil very slowly, skimming off the gray scum that will form on the
surface. When no more scum appears, add the onion (cut in pieces), the
herbs tied in a bouquet (or in a stainless steel tea ball), the celery, salt,
and peppercorns. Cover and simmer 1 hour.

Bind the legs and wings of the chicken, which has been cleaned and
dressed as though for roasting, to the body with a piece of kitchen
twine. Put the chicken in the kettle and simmer 1½ hours longer. The
liquid should never be allowed to boil hard.

Remove the veal and chicken from the kettle, and as soon as they are
cool enough to handle, cut off all the meat from the bones. Put the
bones, skin, and carcass back into the kettle and boil the stock down to

approximately 1½ quarts. Strain through a fine sieve and cool and refrigerate overnight.

The next day, remove every bit of fat which has formed on top of the jellied stock. If the stock is not quite firm, add the gelatin softened in water. Stir while bringing the stock to a boil and pour enough of it into a 14- by 10- by 3-inch roasting pan to measure ½ inch. Place in the refrigerator to set. Let the remaining stock stand at room temperature.

Beat the egg yolks with an electric beater 1 minute. Add the milk and 2 cups of hot stock and pour the mixture into the top part of a double boiler. Stir over boiling water until the sauce is thick and smooth. Season highly with salt and pepper. Pour the sauce into a bowl and cool.

Chop the veal and chicken into small pieces by hand or in the food processor. Add the almonds, the parsley, and the cooled sauce. Refrigerate for 30 minutes. Meanwhile, prepare the decoration.

To make the bouquet, cut tiny rounds of egg white with the end of a pastry tube. Sieve the egg yolks. Season them with salt and bind them with a little cream so that you can roll them into tiny balls. Using chives for stems, tarragon for leaves, and the egg yolks and whites for blossoms, fashion a bouquet in the jelly in the roasting pan. You can "tie" the bouquet with a strip of green or red pepper. Carefully spoon a little cooled stock over the bouquet and place the pan back in the refrigerator while it jellies, thus sealing in the bouquet.

Add the whipped cream to the chicken and veal mixture and taste again for seasoning. The mixture must not be bland. Fill the roasting pan with the mixture and smooth the top. Pour the remaining stock over the mousse. Set in the refrigerator for at least 6 hours.

TO SERVE:

Unmold the mousse onto a large rectangular silver tray or platter. Keep in the refrigerator until serving time, when you should surround it with fresh flowers—violets, sweetheart roses, lilies of the valley, or field daisies.

Mushroom Sandwiches

½ pound mushrooms
1 teaspoon scraped onion
4 tablespoons butter or
   margarine
2 tablespoons flour
1 cup milk

Salt and pepper
Juice of ½ lemon
1 tablespoon chopped parsley
1 loaf thin-sliced white
   or whole wheat bread
Soft butter or margarine

ADVANCE PREPARATION:

Trim off the stem ends of the mushrooms, wash briefly, and chop quite fine by hand or in the food processor. Sauté the mushrooms and onion in the butter or margarine over moderate heat for 3 minutes. Stir in the flour, and when that has disappeared, add the milk. Stir until the mixture is thick. Simmer for 10 minutes. Remove from the stove and season with salt, pepper, lemon juice, and parsley. Store in a covered glass jar in the refrigerator if it is made the day before the party.

BEFORE SERVING:

Have the mushroom mixture at room temperature and spread it between slices of lightly buttered bread. Cut the sandwiches in narrow lengths and arrange on plates. Cover with wax paper and keep in a cool place.

Ham Rolls

Tiny soft rolls
Anchovy paste

Sweet butter
Boiled sliced ham

Order the rolls or make them yourself (see recipe index). They should be 1½ inches in diameter.

Make a mixture of 1 part anchovy paste to 4 parts sweet butter. Split the rolls and spread both sides generously with the anchovy butter. Place a small piece of boiled ham between the halves and press together firmly. Cover with a damp towel and keep in a cool place until serving time.

French Pastry Cake

Make the cake two days in advance, frost it the following day, and store it in the refrigerator.

CAKE:
⅓ cup butter or margarine
6 egg yolks
1⅓ cups sugar
1¼ cups sifted cake flour
¼ teaspoon salt
6 egg whites, beaten stiff
1 teaspoon vanilla

FILLING:
2 squares baking chocolate
½ cup water
1¼ cups sugar

5 egg yolks
1 teaspoon vanilla
1 pound sweet butter

BITTERSWEET FROSTING:
2 squares baking chocolate
¼ cup butter or margarine
½ cup milk
1¾ cups sugar
1 tablespoon rum
  (optional)
Chopped walnuts

To make the cake: Preheat the oven to 350 degrees F. Butter two 10-inch layer cake tins and dust them with flour.

Melt the butter and let it cool while mixing the cake.

Beat the egg yolks for 5 minutes with an electric beater or longer if beating by hand. Add the sugar gradually and beat 5 minutes more.

Sift the flour and salt twice.

Beat the egg whites until stiff and fold them and the dry ingredients alternately into the yolks. When these are thoroughly mixed, add the melted butter and the vanilla. Pour the mixture into the pans and bake 35 minutes. Remove cakes from the pans to cool on a rack.

To make the filling: Melt the chocolate over hot water or place in a glass bowl in the microwave for 3 minutes. Let it cool slightly. Boil the water and sugar until it forms a thread. Beat the egg yolks with an electric beater for 1 minute. Start adding the hot syrup very slowly, beating continually. (I wouldn't be as enthusiastic as I am about this recipe if I didn't have an electric beater.) When all the syrup has been incorporated, add the vanilla and beat until just lukewarm. Add the butter, 2 tablespoons at a time, beating continuously. When the mixture is smooth, beat in the chocolate. If the filling is too liquid to spread, place it in the refrigerator for a few minutes.

Halve the 2 layers of cake horizontally to make 4 layers. Notch the edge at one point so that you can reassemble the cake accurately.

Spread 3 layers with the filling, leaving some for the sides. Re-form the cake, placing the unfrosted layer on top. Press down the top layer gently, and with a sharp long knife trim the sides to make them perfectly smooth. Cover the sides with the reserved filling.

To make the frosting: Melt the chocolate over hot water or in the microwave oven.

Combine the butter, milk, and sugar and boil gently for 15 minutes. Stir in the melted chocolate and remove from the heat. Beat until glossy and smooth. Add the rum if desired. Spread the frosting over the top of the cake, letting it run down the sides a little. Take small handfuls of chopped walnuts and slap them on the sides. They will stick very readily. The sides should be completely coated.

Transfer the cake with 2 large spatulas to a dessert platter.

To decorate: You can decorate by placing a stencil, cut to suit the occasion, on the hardened frosting. Sprinkle the stencil with powdered walnuts or confectioners' sugar. When you remove the stencil, the design will be left on the cake. Store the cake in the refrigerator. It is very rich and should be cut in thin wedges when served. You can easily serve 25 to 30 people with this cake. This cake freezes well.

White Wine Reception Punch

2½ cups sugar
3 pints lime juice
1 cup apricot brandy
3 quarts white rum
1½ teaspoons Angostura
   bitters

2 fifths chilled champagne
   or 1 bottle white
   Burgundy plus 1 bottle
   soda water

ADVANCE PREPARATION:

Stir the sugar and lime juice until the sugar dissolves. Add the brandy, rum, and bitters and pour the mixture into a jug. Cork well. Keep in a cool place for 12 to 24 hours.

TO SERVE:

Pour half the mixture over a large chunk of ice in a punch bowl and let it stand until chilled, ladling the punch over the ice from time to time. Add 1 bottle of champagne or its equivalent in wine and soda water.

Repeat the process when the bowl needs replenishing.

SUPPER RECEPTION FOR 25 TO 30

Capon Salad for a Grand Occasion
Herb Butter Sandwiches
Lobster Sandwiches

Chocolate-Layered Meringue
Coffee

SHOPPING LIST:

Capon, small turkey, or 2
   chickens
Calf's foot or veal knuckle
Potatoes
Frozen baby lima beans
Frozen green beans
Frozen peas
Frozen carrots
Celery
2 cups mayonnaise
½ pint heavy cream
½ pound boiled ham or tongue

8 ounces lobster meat
Garlic
Thyme
Parsley
Lemon
Onion
Watercress or parsley
Chives
Baking chocolate
Thin-sliced white and whole
   wheat bread

Capon Salad

This salad is started one or two days in advance, depending on whether you want to cook on the day of the occasion. Despite the length of the recipe, it is not difficult and the result is very attractive. A small turkey or 2 roasting chickens can substitute for the capon.

SALAD:

1 capon

1 calf's foot or ½ veal
    knuckle sawed in pieces

1 onion, stuck with 2 cloves

1 bay leaf

2 sprigs thyme

6 sprigs parsley

6 large potatoes

1 package small lima beans
    (frozen)

1 package frozen string beans

1 package frozen peas

1 package frozen diced carrots

2 cups diced celery

1 recipe vinaigrette *

2 cloves garlic

2 tablespoons gelatin

2 cups mayonnaise

½ pound boiled ham or tongue

Watercress or parsley

SAUCE:

2 tablespoons butter

2 tablespoons flour

2 cups broth

2 egg yolks

½ pint heavy cream

ADVANCE PREPARATION:

Place the capon, cleaned, dressed, and tied as though for roasting, in a kettle of cold water. Add the calf's foot or veal knuckle, the onion, and the herbs tied in a bouquet (or placed in a stainless steel tea ball). Cover and simmer 1½ to 2 hours or until tender. Let the capon cool in the broth.

Pare and dice the potatoes. Boil until tender. Cook the rest of the vegetables separately in a very little water and drain the vegetable waters into the capon kettle.

Combine all the vegetables except the celery and mix with the vinaigrette (about 1¼ cups). Halve and peel the garlic and poke the pieces down into the salad. They will be taken out later. Leave the vegetables in the dressing to marinate overnight in the refrigerator.

Combine the gelatin with ½ cup of cold water; bring to a boil. Stir the mixture into two cups of mayonnaise.

When the capon is cool, remove it from the kettle and boil down the broth to approximately 2 quarts. Strain through a very fine sieve and place both the broth and the capon in the refrigerator overnight.

The next day, skim off every bit of fat from the surface of the stock. Reheat, and if globules of fat are still visible, faintly brush the surface with a piece of paper toweling to absorb them. If the stock was not firmly jellied, add a tablespoon of gelatin dissolved in cold water. If the color is pale, add a drop or two of yellow vegetable coloring. Set aside 2 cups of broth; pour more in a pie plate to measure ½ inch. This is for decorating. Chill the rest in a bowl.

Retrieve the garlic from the vegetables and drain off the vinaigrette. Add the celery and the gelatinized mayonnaise and mix well. Pile the vegetable salad on the largest round or oval china or crockery platter that you can get into your refrigerator. Smooth into shape. It should be approximately 2 inches high.

Strip the skin from the capon and remove the wings and legs. Carve the breast meat in thin slices with a very sharp knife and cut the dark meat in as flat pieces as possible. Arrange the slices on top of the salad, completely covering it. Chill while making the sauce.

Start the sauce by heating the butter and stirring in the flour. Add the 2 cups of reserved stock and stir until the mixture boils. Reduce the heat and simmer 10 minutes, removing the skin that will form on the top. Beat the eggs yolks and cream lightly and, still beating, add the hot sauce very gradually. Pour into the top of a double boiler and stir over boiling water until the sauce thickens. Transfer the pan of sauce to a bowl of ice water and stir until the sauce cools. This is a matter of a very few minutes.

Spoon the sauce carefully over the capon slices, first in a thin layer and then in a thicker layer so that the surface is smooth. The sauce will stiffen as soon as it is spread.

Slice the ham or tongue ¼ inch thick and cut into thin strips. Fashion a design appropriate to the occasion, or the name of the guest of honor in block letters, with the meat strips on the jellied sauce.

From the hardened jelly in the pie pan, cut fancy shapes and place them around the salad. Garnish the whole thing with the rest of the jelly forced through a rose-tipped pastry bag.

Watercress or parsley sprigs around the base of the salad give a touch of color.

Herb Butter Sandwiches

(60 tea sandwiches)

The herb butter may be prepared 2 or 3 days in advance, but the sandwiches should be assembled the day of the party.

½ pound sweet butter
3 tablespoons chopped parsley
2 tablespoons chopped chives
1½ tablespoons lemon juice

Black pepper
2 loaves whole wheat bread,
  sliced very thin

Combine the softened butter with the herbs, lemon juice, and freshly ground black pepper. Taste and add salt if you wish. Store in a covered jar in the refrigerator if prepared ahead of time.

Trim crusts from the bread, which should be a day old. Work the butter to spreading consistency and spread between the slices of bread. Cut the sandwiches in halves diagonally and cover with a damp towel until serving time.

Lobster Sandwiches

(60 tea sandwiches)

Prepare the filling in advance, but spread the sandwiches the day of the party.

1 cup lobster meat (fresh, frozen, or canned)
½ cup soft butter or margarine
½ teaspoon chopped tarragon (optional)

½ teaspoon lemon juice
⅛ teaspoon white pepper
1-pound loaf firm white bread, sliced thin

Chop the lobster very fine and pound it in a wooden bowl with the butter or margarine until you have a smooth paste—or combine using the food processor. Add the tarragon and seasonings and mix well. Store in a covered jar in the refrigerator.

To make the sandwiches, spread the filling between the slices of bread and cut into small squares. Cover with a damp cloth and keep in a cool place until serving time.

Chocolate-Layered Meringue

This is best if it stands at least 24 hours before serving, so start this dessert two days in advance.

MERINGUE:
8 egg whites
¼ teaspoon salt
¼ teaspoon cream of tartar
2 cups sugar

FILLING:
3 squares baking chocolate
3 egg whites
¾ cup sugar
¾ pound sweet butter

Preheat the oven to 250 degrees F.

Beat the egg whites, salt, and cream of tartar with an electric beater until very stiff. Gradually add the sugar and continue beating 5 minutes or until the whites are glossy. Trace the circumference of a large (10-inch) pie plate 3 times on baking sheets lined with shelf paper or kitchen parchment. Fill these circles with a smooth layer of meringue about ½ inch thick. Bake 55 to 60 minutes.

Loosen the meringues with a spatula immediately. If they stick, moisten the back of the paper with a little water. Turn off the oven, but let the meringues continue to dry in it for an hour or more. Cool completely.

To make the filling: Melt the chocolate over hot water and let it cool a little. Beat the egg whites and sugar over boiling water with a rotary beater until the mixture is stiff and glossy. Remove from the stove and, with an electric beater or hand beater, beat in the chocolate and butter until smooth. Chill in the refrigerator for 1 hour.

To assemble: Spread the filling on all three layers, piling one on top of the other. Spread a smooth thick layer over the top and around the sides, reserving enough for decoration. Chill in the refrigerator 10 minutes. Put the rest of the filling in a pastry bag fitted with a small rose tip. Force it around the edge and base and fashion rosettes on the side. Chill.

When the frosting is hard, place a paper doily or stencil in the center. Cover it with powdered sugar. Lift off the doily, leaving a pretty design on the cake.

Serve in very thin wedges.

Tea and Coffee

There are occasions when you may be called upon to manage a large party in the afternoon or evening, either in your own home or in a club room, in connection with a meeting of a social or political nature. Such a party calls for both coffee and tea in large quantities and a variety of food.

A long table is a must for a party of this sort. Coffee will be served from one end and tea from the other. The center of the table is set for prettily arranged platters of sandwiches, breads, cakes, and cookies so that guests will help themselves. Extra platters are strategically placed elsewhere.

Arrange a coffee tray with coffee urn, large cream pitcher, large sugar bowl, and coffee spoons. Surround the tray with cups and saucers. (There are occasions for Styrofoam cups, but this is not one of them.) Napkins are placed on the edge of the table.

Set the tea tray at the end of the table nearest the kitchen or other source of supply. The tea tray will have a teapot, an urn or pot of hot water, a pitcher of room-temperature milk, and a sugar bowl filled with small lumps. Arrange thin lemon slices—some stuck with cloves—on a glass plate with a small fork and place within easy reach of the pourer. The cups, silver, and napkins are arranged the same way as for the coffee tray, but the hostess must always be on the alert to replenish the tea tray with fresh tea and hot water.

Preparing food for a large number has to be planned so that, when the day arrives, only the sandwiches have to be made. If freezer and refrigerator space is available, the breads, cookies, and cakes can all be made in advance. The sandwich fillings should be prepared a day in advance.

If bread is not homemade, buy only the best bread available: firm, made with unbleached white or whole grain flours. Nothing is as soggy as sandwiches made of most store-bought breads. The bread should be bought or made a day or two in advance of the party. The sandwiches can be made 4 to 6 hours in advance, wrapped in damp towels or plastic film, and kept in a cool place.

Before the guests arrive make or reheat the coffee. Boil the water for the tea and the hot-water jug. Arrange the sandwiches on the waiting platters. Place the cookies and cakes on plates or platters. Place the milk, cream, and lemon on the proper trays. Heat the teapot. Have everything on the table before the first guest arrives.

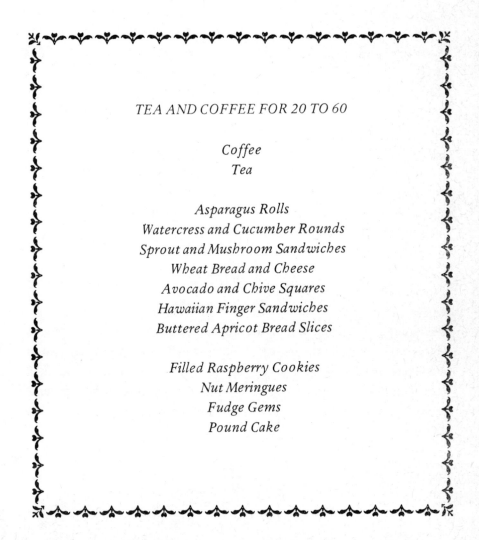

TEA AND COFFEE FOR 20 TO 60

Coffee
Tea

Asparagus Rolls
Watercress and Cucumber Rounds
Sprout and Mushroom Sandwiches
Wheat Bread and Cheese
Avocado and Chive Squares
Hawaiian Finger Sandwiches
Buttered Apricot Bread Slices

Filled Raspberry Cookies
Nut Meringues
Fudge Gems
Pound Cake

SHOPPING LIST:

Amounts vary according to the number of guests. Each loaf of bread will make 28 to 54 tea sandwiches, according to size and shape.

Thin-sliced white, rye,
  whole-wheat bread
  (homemade and/or bought)
Mayonnaise
Butter or margarine
Watercress
Cucumber
Asparagus
Avocado
1 small package cream
  cheese with chives
Canned or frozen shrimp
1 chicken breast
Mushrooms
Alfalfa sprouts

Green onions
¼ pound boiled ham
1 small can crushed
  pineapple
1 pound dried apricots
Chopped almonds and
  walnuts
Raspberry jam
Chives and parsley
Lemons, mint leaves, cream,
  milk
Tea and coffee
½ pound Gruyère cheese
  (optional)
Baking chocolate

Coffee

One pound of coffee will make 48 cups. There are some excellent coffee makers for large quantities, but if you do not have access to one start making your coffee early. Make it in the largest pot or pots that you have and transfer it to covered containers to store in the refrigerator. Reheated in enamel or glassware, it will not have a bitter taste.

Tea

Allow 1 teaspoon of tea to every cup of boiling water. However, in serving a large group, triple the strength and have plenty of boiling water on hand to weaken the tea according to individual tastes. Use fresh leaves for each successive pot. The method for making a pot of tea is to bring the water to a full rolling boil and pour it over the tea leaves in a china or ceramic pot which has been warmed by rinsing in hot water. The tea should steep for five minutes. If you have set up the tea tray with a silver pot, be sure that it is well heated before you transfer the steeped tea into it. And be certain that the hot water jug is kept filled with boiling water.

Asparagus Rolls

Make as many of these as you wish. Buy the slender stalks of asparagus and cook them for 4 to 5 minutes in salted water. They should not be overcooked.

Trim thin-sliced, firm white or wholewheat bread and roll out each slice until very thin. Spread each slice with mayonnaise seasoned with sharp mustard. Place an asparagus spear on the bread so that the tip protrudes over the edge of the bread. Trim the stem end even with the other edge. Roll up and fasten with half a toothpick. Lay seam side down on a platter. Repeat until all the asparagus has been used. Cover the sandwiches with a damp towel and refrigerate for at least 3 hours before serving.

Watercress and Cucumber Rounds

Count on 2 to 3 two-inch rounds from each slice of bread, depending on the size of loaf you buy or make. I give you the method rather than the amount since the number of guests is up to you.

Cream cheese with chives
Mayonnaise*
Watercress

Cucumbers (small in size to
avoid large seeds)

Mix each package of cream cheese with chives with 4 tablespoons of mayonnaise until thoroughly blended. Wash the watercress and remove the stems. Cut the bread rounds with a small cookie cutter.

Spread each round with a thin layer of the cheese mixture. Cover half of them with thin slices of cucumber and a few watercress leaves. Top and press together.

Sprout and Mushroom Sandwiches

If you can buy "party rye" bread, you will save a few minutes. Otherwise, cut large rye sandwiches into thirds.

½ pound mushrooms
6 tablespoons mayonnaise*
2 tablespoons green onion,
   finely chopped

Rye bread
1 cup alfalfa sprouts

Trim the stems of the mushrooms. Wash them briefly and pat dry with toweling. Slice very thin in a food processor or by hand. Place in a bowl. Cover and refrigerate.

Combine mayonnaise and chopped green onions, using only the green part.

Spread slices of rye bread with the onion and mayonnaise mixture. Spread half the slices with raw mushrooms and sprouts and top with the remaining slices.

Wheat Bread and Cheese

If you are fortunate enough to have a Vita Mix machine, follow the recipe for making the whole wheat bread (1 hour from wheat berry to plate), and while the bread is rising, make the cheese spread. This is not only delicious but a wonderful conversation piece. Make the bread and the spread a day in advance.

Vita Mix Whole Wheat Bread or
other firm whole wheat
bread

SPREAD:
½ pound Gruyère cheese
*4-5 tablespoons mayonnaise **
1 teaspoon Dijon mustard

ADVANCE PREPARATION:

Spin the cheese (cut in cubes), the mayonnaise, and the mustard for 10 seconds. Place in a bowl. Cover and refrigerate.

BEFORE SERVING:

Cut the bread in thin slices and spread with the cheese mixture. Serve the slices which are small in diameter whole, trimmed or untrimmed.

Avocado and Chive Squares

(32 sandwiches)

1 ripe avocado
2 tablespoons chives, chopped
  fine
2 teaspoons lemon juice
4 tablespoons mayonnaise *

Salt and pepper
Whole wheat bread
White bread
Butter or margarine

Pare and seed the avocado. Mash it with a silver fork or in a food processor and mix in the chives, lemon juice, and mayonnaise. Season with salt and pepper.

Spread slices of lightly buttered whole wheat bread with the mixture. Cover with lightly buttered slices of white bread. Cut in small squares.

Hawaiian Finger Sandwiches

(42 to 56 sandwiches)

1 small can crushed water-
  packed pineapple
1 large chicken breast
½ cup diced cooked ham
½ cup chopped almonds

2 tablespoons crushed pineapple
Mayonnaise *
Bread
Butter or margarine

Drain the pineapple as dry as possible. Put the juice and the chicken breast in a saucepan. Add ½ teaspoon of salt and just enough water to almost cover the breast. Bring to a boil. Reduce the heat and cook gently for 30 minutes. Drain and cool.

Dice the chicken meat very fine, using a food processor or a hand chopper. Mix with the diced ham, almonds, pineapple, and enough mayonnaise to bind. Season to taste.

Spread thinly sliced *firm* whole wheat or white bread with a film of mayonnaise, butter, or margarine. Spread half the slices with the filling. Top with the remaining slices, pressing them firmly. Cut each sandwich into 3 or 4 strips, using a very sharp knife.

Apricot Bread

2 cups dried apricots	2½ teaspoons baking powder
1¾ cups water	½ teaspoon salt
2 tablespoons butter or	1 egg, slightly beaten
margarine	1 teaspoon lemon or orange
1½ cups sugar	extract
2½ cups unbleached flour	

By hand or in the food processor, chop the apricots rather fine. Combine the water, butter or margarine, and sugar in a saucepan and bring to a boil. Boil 1 minute and pour over the apricots. Cool.

Combine and sift the flour, baking powder, and salt. When the apricots are almost cool, add the dry ingredients, egg, and flavoring. Stir until well mixed and pour into two small or one ordinary bread tin which has been buttered and dusted with flour. Let the batter stand 15 minutes and then bake for one hour in a preheated oven at 350 degrees F. Turn out immediately on a rack to cool. Serve thin slices spread with softened butter.

Filled Raspberry Cookies
(3 to 4 dozen)

1 cup butter or margarine	2 teaspoons baking powder
1 cup sugar	½ teaspoon salt
2 eggs	2½ teaspoons cinnamon
3 cups unbleached white flour	Raspberry jam

Cream the butter or margarine with the sugar, using an electric beater or food processor, until light and fluffy. Add the unbeaten eggs, one at a time, beating continuously.

Sift and add the dry ingredients. Beat until blended.

Chill the dough 30 minutes in the refrigerator.

Roll out ⅛ inch thick on a floured surface with a well-floured rolling pin. Cut into small circles or squares. Place a little jam on half the squares and cover with the other half. Press the edges together.

Bake the cookies 10 minutes at 400 degrees F.

Nut Meringues
(4 dozen)

2 egg whites	1½ cups chopped walnuts
½ teaspoon salt	1 teaspoon vanilla
1 pound (2 cups) light brown sugar	Confectioners' sugar

Preheat the oven to 350 degrees F.

Beat the egg whites and salt until very stiff with an electric beater. Add the sugar gradually and continue beating. Reduce the speed of the beater and fold in the finely chopped walnuts and vanilla.

Place the mixture in a pastry bag fitted with a medium-sized rose tip, and drop the batter in small rosettes on a buttered and floured baking sheet. Or, drop the mixture from the end of a teaspoon.

Powder with sifted confectioners' sugar and bake 8 minutes.

Fudge Gems

(2 dozen cakes)

3 squares baking chocolate
¼ cup boiling water
2 cups cake flour
1¼ cups sugar
1 teaspoon baking soda
1 teaspoon salt
½ cup melted butter or
  margarine
1 cup rich milk
1 teaspoon vinegar
3 eggs, well beaten

1 teaspoon vanilla

FROSTING:
2 cups sugar
1 cup water
2 tablespoons light corn syrup
2 squares baking chocolate
2 tablespoons butter or
  margarine
1 teaspoon vanilla

Preheat the oven to 375 degrees F.

Bring the chocolate and water to a boil, stirring constantly. When the chocolate is melted, set it aside to cool.

Sift the dry ingredients into a mixing bowl. Add the butter, milk, and vinegar and beat with an electric beater until smooth and creamy. This should take 2 to 3 minutes. Add the beaten eggs, vanilla, and chocolate and continue beating until smooth.

Butter tiny muffin pans and dust them with flour. Fill the tins only half full of the mixture and bake 15 to 20 minutes. Let the cakes stand in the tins 5 minutes before turning them out on a rack to cool.

To make frosting: Stir all the ingredients for the frosting except butter and vanilla over a gentle heat until the mixture boils. Cook slowly for about 15 minutes or until the syrup forms a ball when a little is dropped in cold water (238 degrees F.). Add the butter and cool. Add the vanilla and beat until the frosting is of spreading consistency. Frost each cake and smooth with a moistened knife.

Pound Cake

This is best made a day or two in advance.

1 cup butter or margarine	*¾ teaspoon baking powder*
1⅔ cups sugar	*2 cups cake flour*
5 eggs	*¼ teaspoon salt*

Preheat the oven to 300 degrees F. Butter and flour a bread tin.

Cream the butter and sugar with an electric beater or food processor, adding the sugar gradually. Add the eggs one by one, beating hard after each addition.

Combine and sift the dry ingredients and fold them in gently but thoroughly. Pour the batter into the bread tin and bake 1¼ hours.

The Cocktail Party

There are two kinds of cocktail parties. A small cocktail party is one where all the guests can be comfortably seated. Talk is more general and the atmosphere relaxed. A large party is one planned for any number exceeding eight. Everyone remains standing and changes conversational partners or groups occasionally in a kind of unrehearsed dance pattern. Conversation is often more spirited but frequently interrupted (and sometimes inaudible). Both kinds of parties have their special social virtues.

For either kind of party, it is a good idea to make a supply of the mixed drinks (martinis, manhattans, etc.). If the weather is warm, add daiquiris to the list. They should be put into well-labeled pitchers or decanters. Many a party has gotten out of hand when the martini pitcher was mistaken for water. Long drinks and special drinks like old-fashioneds are made on demand. While it is courteous for the host or hostess to offer the first drink, it is good sense and good form to trust your guests to serve themselves after that. Be sure to have nonalcoholic drinks available. White wine, either plain or served in a drink called kir, is gaining popularity as a preprandial drink. There should also be some fortified wine—sherry, port, Dubonnet, etc.—for those who prefer it.

For those mixtures requiring sweetening, make a sugar syrup by boiling equal parts of sugar and water for 5 minutes.

For some large parties, it is more convenient to offer a punch. These punches, if they are to substitute for cocktails or long drinks, must be authoritative and not too sweet. I give you three recipes that fit these requirements.

Unlike a predinner party cocktail hour, where only the simplest of nibbles and raw vegetables should be served, the cocktail party should have interesting canapés. For small parties, plan to have canapés strategically and conveniently placed so that the guests can remain seated. For large parties, small manageable canapés are best since one hand is usually holding a glass.

The small cocktail party is a boon to the host and hostess and their friends. There is no pleasanter time of day, and no nicer way to catch up on gossip. It is designed for relaxation and general conversation. Invite only as many guests as you can seat comfortably and arrange your eatables so that there will be a minimum of jumping up and down to pass and refill. Individual cocktails are ideal for serving at the small party, and it's good to have an ample supply of "nibbles" (chips, raw vegetables, nuts) within everyone's easy reach, as well as two or three kinds of canapés—hot and cold. Good choices would be Red Caviar on Rye and Savory Stuffed Eggs for the cold canapés, plus Hot Sausage Patties and/or Smoky Cheese Canapés for something hot.

When you are giving a large cocktail party, it is well to limit the number of different eatables you will prepare and serve. I give you several to choose from, but three cold canapés and two hot, plus a variety of "nibbles" conveniently placed, are all that is necessary. Plan to pass the hot canapés at intervals during the party. It is a good way to get a chance to chat with your guests. Small sandwiches such as those suggested for the tea party make delicious cold canapés.

Dry Martinis

6 parts gin
1 part dry French vermouth

GARNISH:
*Olive, lemon twist, or pearl
 onion*

More gin and less vermouth makes a drier cocktail

Sweet Martinis

5 or 6 parts gin
1 part sweet Italian vermouth

GARNISH:
Twist of orange peel

Manhattans

3 parts whisky (rye, bourbon,   Dash of Angostura bitters
  or Scotch)
1 part sweet Italian vermouth   GARNISH:
                                     Maraschino cherry (optional)

Dry Manhattans (Bronx)

3 parts whisky (rye, bourbon,   GARNISH:
  or Scotch)   Twist of lemon peel
1 part dry French vermouth

Daiquiris

1 part lime juice   4 parts rum
1 part sugar syrup

Stir the lime juice and sugar until the sugar dissolves. Add rum and shaved ice. Shake vigorously or mix in a blender. Serve in chilled stemmed glasses.

Frosted Daiquiris

1 part lime juice   4 parts rum
1 part sugar syrup   Ice

Stir the lime juice and sugar until the sugar dissolves. Add the rum. Pulverize the ice in an electric blender and add the mixture. Blend until frosted.

Dubonnet Cocktails

2 parts Dubonnet   1 part gin

Combine with cracked ice and shake hard. Strain into stemmed cocktail glasses.

Whisky Sours

4 parts whisky (rye, bourbon,   Sweetening to taste
    or Scotch)
1 part lemon juice   GARNISH:
1 part orange juice   Orange peel, maraschino cherry,
                                   lemon peel (optional)

Old-Fashioneds

Whisky (rye, bourbon, or   GARNISH:
    Scotch)   Cherries, lemon slices, orange
Sugar   strips, pineapple wedges,
Angostura bitters or cherry   or twisted lemon peel
    juice
Ice cubes

Place ½ teaspoon (more or less) sugar in each glass. Moisten with a dash of bitters or a little cherry juice. Add the ice cubes and pour 1½ to 2 jiggers of whisky over the ice. Add the garnish or just twist lemon peel over the whisky without dropping it in. Give each guest a muddler to stir his own drink.

"On the Rocks"

The simplest and easiest of all cocktail drinks to serve. Place 3 or 4 ice cubes in an old-fashioned glass. Pour over 1½ to 3 jiggers of any desired liquor. Some guests will prefer to have a little water added.

"In a Mist"

Crack the ice very fine and fill old-fashioned glasses ⅔ full of ice. Fill the glasses with any desired liquor and serve with small straws.

Bloody Marys

This tomato juice base for bloody Marys or the one on page 157 can serve for both alcoholic and nonalcoholic cocktails—straight up or "on the rocks." Have the base premixed and well chilled in a glass pitcher. For those who want it, allow 1 to 1½ ounces of vodka or gin to 4 ounces of the tomato base. Serve in old-fashioned glasses.

1 quart unseasoned tomato
  juice
1 tablespoon lemon juice
¼ teaspoon celery salt
¼ teaspoon garlic salt
½ teaspoon sugar

¼ teaspoon Tabasco
1 teaspoon Worcestershire
½ teaspoon salt
⅛ teaspoon fresh ground black
  pepper
Gin, vodka

ADVANCE PREPARATION:

Combine all the ingredients except the alcohol. Mix well. Cover and chill.

TO SERVE:

Place the pitcher on a tray of glasses flanked with a bottle of gin and a bottle of vodka.

Aperitifs

A fine dry sherry is the most universally popular aperitif. Sherry may be served at room temperature, slightly chilled, or iced.

Dubonnet or Italian vermouth, poured over shaved ice and garnished with a twist of lemon peel, makes a very pleasant warm weather drink.

Kir

This light and refreshing drink has recently become popular as a before-dinner offering. One of its virtues is that it is pretty to look at.

6 parts chilled dry white
  wine or champagne

1 part cassis (black currant
  brandy)

Make in individual glasses, a glass pitcher, or a punch bowl. Serve icy cold.

Light Guard Punch for 50

6 bottles of champagne
6 bottles California semillon
  or other dry white wine
1 fifth brandy
1 fifth rum

1 pint Curacao (preferably
  white)

GARNISH (optional):
  Fresh strawberries, cherries,
    or lime slices

This punch recipe is presented with a bow to the Somerset Club of Boston. There is no advance preparation that can be made except chilling the champagne and white wine and providing yourself with a large chunk of ice.

There is a lovely feeling of lavishness that both you and your guests will enjoy when you mix the punch just before serving. Set up a tray with a punch bowl, bottles, and ladle. Surround the tray with glasses.

To mix, pour half of each bottle of brandy, rum, and Curaçao over the ice and 3 bottles each of champagne and white wine. Add the fruit, if desired, and ladle the punch into the glasses.

Replenish when necessary.

Reception Punch
(25 to 30 people)

2½ cups sugar
3 pints lime juice
1 cup apricot brandy
3 quarts rum

1½ teaspoons Angostura bitters
2 fifths chilled champagne or
  1 bottle white Burgundy
  plus 1 bottle soda water

Stir the sugar and lime juice until the sugar dissolves. Add the brandy, rum, and bitters and pour the mixture into a jug. Cork well. Keep in a cool place for 12 to 24 hours.

To serve, pour half the mixture over a large chunk of ice in a punch bowl and let it stand until chilled, ladling the punch over the ice. Add 1 bottle of champagne or its equivalent in wine and soda water. Repeat the process when the bowl needs replenishing.

Rum Punch for 50

This punch can be prepared a day or two in advance. For each half gallon of the rum mixture poured over ice cubes, add 1 quart of soda.

*2 12-ounce cans frozen orange
   juice
2 46-ounce cans unsweetened
   pineapple juice*

*½-¾ cup fresh lemon juice
3 quarts white rum
1 quart dark rum
2 quarts soda*

Mix in advance all the ingredients except the soda. The amount of lemon juice is a matter of taste since there is no sugar added to this recipe. Pour the mixture into ½-gallon jugs for easy storing. Chill.

At serving time, pour over a chunk of ice in the punch bowl and add the soda.

Asparagus and Dip

Pick or buy the asparagus the day of the party. The dip can be made in advance.

2 bunches fresh thin asparagus

DIP:
1½ cups mayonnaise *

1 tablespoon Madras curry
  powder
1 teaspoon Worcestershire
1 teaspoon soy sauce
2 tablespoons chopped parsley

ADVANCE PREPARATION:

Cut off 3½ inches from the tip of each spear of asparagus. (Save the rest to make soup.)

Wash the tips very carefully. Place them in a strainer, 8 at a time, and dip them in rapidly boiling salted water for just 60 seconds. Plunge immediately into cold water. Drain well. Repeat until all the asparagus is cooked. Wrap in plastic film or foil and chill in the refrigerator.

Mix the dip ingredients in a small bowl.

TO SERVE:

Place the bowl of dip in the center of a round platter and arrange the asparagus spokelike with the tips pointing in.

Stuffed Cherry Tomatoes

1 quart cherry tomatoes
  (approximately 30)
Vinaigrette *

Cocktail onions
Small pitted black olives
Parsley

Wash the tomatoes and scoop out a small hole in the stem end of each one. Put a drop or two of vinaigrette in each one. (An eyedropper is very useful for this operation.) Place the tomatoes on a serving platter and stuff them alternately with cocktail onions and black olive halves. Garnish each with a speck of parsley. Serve very cold.

Eggs with Chicken Livers

18 hard-cooked eggs
½ pound chicken livers
2 tablespoons butter or
  margarine
1 teaspoon scraped onion

4 tablespoons soft butter
  or margarine
Salt and pepper
Parsley

Peel and split the eggs lengthwise. Remove the egg yolks and sieve them into a mixing bowl.

Sauté the chicken livers in 2 tablespoons of butter or margarine just long enough to brown them on both sides. Add the scraped onion and sauté 3 minutes. Force the liver mixture through a sieve into the mixing bowl with the egg yolks. Add the 4 tablespoons of soft butter or margarine and work the mixture together. Season with salt and pepper. Fill the egg whites with the mixture and garnish with parsley. Keep in the refrigerator until ready to serve.

Smoked-Oyster Blinis

BATTER:
1 cup unbleached flour,
  sifted
½ teaspoon salt
1 cup milk
2 eggs, slightly beaten

FILLING:
1 can smoked oysters
Sour cream
1 teaspoon soy sauce
½ clove garlic, minced
Salt and black pepper

ADVANCE PREPARATION:

Beat the flour, salt, and milk until smooth with an electric beater or in the food processor. Add the beaten eggs and let the mixture stand 1 hour while making the filling.

Drain the oysters. Chop them very fine and add enough sour cream to make a spreading paste. Season with soy sauce, garlic, salt, and black pepper. Mix well.

Heat 2 skillets and brush them with a little oil. Drop small portions of batter, each about the size of a 50-cent piece, on the hot skillets. Brown on both sides and transfer the cooked rounds to a working surface. Continue this until all the batter is used. Spread the filling on the rounds and roll them up. Place them seam side down on buttered pie plates. They should be pressed close together. Putting them on several plates will let you reheat them in relays so that they may be served hot at several times during the party. Keep them in a cool place until ready to heat.

BEFORE SERVING:

If your oven is at 425 degrees F., the blinis will heat in 5 minutes or less. Allow 1 or 2 minutes in the microwave, depending on the number of blinis.

Anchovy Straws

1 recipe pie dough *   1 egg yolk
1 can anchovies   1 tablespoon water

Roll the dough out in a thin long strip. Trim the edges and cut into rectangles, 4 inches long and 2 inches wide. Moisten the edges and place a strip of anchovy on one half of the rectangle. Fold over to make the edges meet and press them together. Place the straws on a baking sheet and paint each one twice with the egg yolk beaten slightly with water. Keep in the refrigerator and bake just before serving (5 minutes at 450 degrees F.) or bake in advance and reheat in the warming oven before serving.

Toasted Brazil Nuts

½ pound Brazil nuts   2 tablespoons butter or
                                        margarine

   Boil the shelled nuts for 5 minutes. While they are still hot, slice
them very thin with a sharp knife. Place on a baking sheet and brush
with 2 tablespoons of melted butter or margarine. Brown under the
broiler. Drain and place in a copper or earthenware dish which can be
kept on a candle warmer. Salt well. If your party is really large, double
the recipe and replenish the supply when necessary.

Avocado Balls

The avocados must be ripe but not soft. The large imported avocados
are perfect for this.

¼ cup peanut oil   ⅛ teaspoon freshly ground
¼ cup olive oil   pepper
1 large clove garlic, minced   2 tablespoons lemon juice
½ teaspoon salt   2 large avocados
Cayenne   1 tablespoon chopped parsley

ADVANCE PREPARATION:
   Combine all the ingredients except the avocados and parsley in a
shallow nonmetal bowl. Mix well.
   Split the avocados and remove the seed. Using a potato ball cutter
cut the flesh into balls and drop them into the marinade. Make sure that
each ball has been coated on all sides. Cover with foil and refrigerate.

BEFORE SERVING:

Drain off the marinade. Place in a bowl. Sprinkle with the parsley and serve with toothpicks.

Roe and Ham Canapés

Melba rounds
Butter or margarine

Canadian bacon or lean
   boiled ham, sliced very thin
1 can shad roe

Brush melba rounds with melted butter and cover with a small piece of bacon or ham. Place the canapés on a baking sheet. Cover with a piece of fish roe which has been browned in butter. Before serving, place under the broiler for 2 or 3 minutes.

Hot Stuffed Mushroom Caps

The hardest part of this recipe is picking out 30 mushroom caps of about the same size and shape. Some shops package them in uniform sizes, which is helpful.

30 mushroom caps (1½ pounds)
4 tablespoons butter or
   margarine
Salt and pepper
1 small can water chestnuts

¼ pound crab meat
Mayonnaise * (homemade or
   bought)
1 teaspoon lemon juice

ADVANCE PREPARATION:

Remove the stems and reserve for another use.

Divide the butter or margarine between 2 skillets. Heat until it ceases to bubble and sauté the mushrooms, 2 minutes on each side, starting with the rounded side down and turning them so that all the moisture will disappear. Transfer the mushrooms, cup side up, to an oven-serving platter (nonmetal if using a microwave). Sprinkle with salt and pepper. Cool.

Slice the water chestnuts quite thin and cut into pieces to fit inside the mushrooms.

Combine the crab meat with just enough mayonnaise to bind it. Season with salt, pepper, and lemon juice.

Place a piece of water chestnut in each cap. Cover with crab meat and top with a tiny dab of mayonnaise. Refrigerate.

BEFORE SERVING:

Remove from the refrigerator so that the mushrooms will be at room temperature. Just before serving, heat 3 minutes at 400 degrees F., or 1 minute in the microwave on "roast." These may be served plain or with thin slices of French bread or melba rounds.

Savory Shrimp

(approximately 64 pieces)

1 pound fresh medium-sized shrimp	2 slices onion
	4 sprigs parsley
1 quart water	4 tablespoons butter or
2 teaspoons salt	margarine
1 cup dry white wine	2 teaspoons anchovy paste
¼ lemon	1 teaspoon lemon juice
1 bay leaf	

ADVANCE PREPARATION:

Rinse the shrimp briefly and set aside.

Combine the remaining ingredients except the butter, anchovy paste, and lemon juice in a saucepan. Bring to a boil. Cover and simmer 10 minutes. Add the shrimp and simmer for 5 minutes or until bright pink. Drain and cool.

Mix the butter or margarine with the anchovy paste and lemon juice until smooth and creamy.

Remove the shells from the shrimp; with a sharp-pointed knife make a ¼-inch incision down the rounded side of the shrimp, removing the black intestinal strip when necessary.

Using a pastry bag fitted with the smallest rosette tube available, pipe the anchovy butter the length of the incision. Chill in the refrigerator.

TO SERVE:

Line 1 large or 2 smaller bowls with lettuce leaves and cover with ice cubes. Hang the shrimp around the rim of the bowl so the guests can easily help themselves.

Ginger Cheese Balls

1 large package (8 ounces)
cream cheese
1 tablespoon scraped onion
2 teaspoons soy sauce

1½ teaspoons finely chopped
candied ginger
½ cup finely chopped almonds

Work the cheese, onion, soy sauce, and ginger together by hand, electric beater, or food processor. Add a tablespoon of milk if necessary, but the mixture must be stiff.

Toast the almonds under the broiler for a moment in a pie plate.

Shape the cheese mixture into tiny balls and roll them lightly in the nuts. Keep in the refrigerator until ready to serve.

Cheese Crescents

1 recipe pie dough *   Butter or margarine
Grated Parmesan cheese

ADVANCE PREPARATION:

As you roll out your dough, sprinkle it with grated cheese as you would flour. Roll the dough into a long rectangular strip and cut into parallel strips 2½ inches wide. Cut them into triangles with 2½-inch bases. Spread each triangle with a little butter or margarine and sprinkle with cheese. Roll up tightly toward the tip and place tip side down on a baking sheet. Bend the ends in to form a crescent. Keep in the refrigerator.

BEFORE SERVING:

Bake 5 to 6 minutes at 450 degrees F. Serve in a napkin-lined dish.

Stuffed Artichoke Canapés

2 7½-ounce cans artichoke   2 tablespoons flour
   bottoms   ½ cup cream
1 teaspoon lemon juice   2 tablespoons grated sharp
¼ pound mushrooms   cheese
2 tablespoons butter or   Melba rounds
   margarine

ADVANCE PREPARATION:

Drain the artichoke bottoms and place them on a buttered baking sheet. Brush them with lemon juice.

Wash, trim, and chop the mushrooms very fine. Sauté them in butter or margarine for 3 minutes. Sprinkle with flour, and when that has disappeared, stir in the cream and grated cheese. Stir until the cheese melts. Season with salt and pepper.

Fill the artichoke bottoms with the mixture. Keep in a cool place.

TO SERVE:

Heat the artichoke bottoms in a very hot (450 degrees F.) oven for 5 minutes. Place on melba rounds and serve immediately.

Red Caviar on Rye

Rye bread, sliced thin
1 jar red caviar (4 ounces)
1 teaspoon scraped onion

1 tablespoon chopped parsley
½ teaspoon lemon juice

Use party rye bread or cut small rounds from larger slices. Spread them with butter.

Place the caviar in a small strainer and let cool water run through it for a moment to remove the brine.

Combine the caviar with the scraped onion, parsley, and lemon juice. Mix well, adding a dash of freshly ground black pepper. The caviar can be placed in a small dish and surrounded on a platter by rounds of bread so that guests will serve themselves, or you can spread the rounds just before the guests arrive.

Hot Sausage Pasties

½ pound sausage meat
Salt and pepper

½ teaspoon poultry seasoning
1 recipe pie dough*

ADVANCE PREPARATION:

Season the meat with a little salt, pepper, and the poultry seasoning. Make tiny balls of the spicy sausage meat and fry them in a hot skillet for 3 minutes, turning constantly. Drain on paper toweling. Cool.

Roll out pie dough to a thickness of ⅛ inch. Cut out small circles with a cookie cutter or the rim of a fruit juice glass. Moisten the edges of half the circles with cool water. Place a sausage ball on the moistened circles and cover with the remaining circles. Press the edges together and place the pasties on a baking sheet. Prick the tops and paint each one twice with an egg yolk beaten slightly with a little water. Keep in the refrigerator until baking time.

BEFORE SERVING:

Preheat the oven to 425 degrees F. Bake 8 minutes or until golden brown.

Scandinavian Stuffed Eggs

8 to 10 hard-cooked eggs
4 tablespoons butter
¼ pound liverwurst

1½ teaspoons anchovy paste
Chopped chives or parsley

Peel and split the eggs. Sieve the egg yolks into a mixing bowl. Work the butter, liverwurst, and anchovy paste with them until smooth. Stuff the egg whites with the mixture and dust the top with finely chopped chives or parsley.

Smoky Cheese Canapés

1 6-ounce roll smoky
  cheese
6 tablespoons butter or
  margarine

⅔ cup unbleached flour
2 slices Canadian bacon

ADVANCE PREPARATION:

Work the cheese and butter together with an electric beater, by hand, or in the food processor. Add the flour and the Canadian bacon which has been very finely diced. Mix well. Roll on a floured surface into a long thin roll. Wrap in wax paper and place in the refrigerator for 2 or 3 hours.

Slice the chilled dough in ¼-inch slices and place on a baking sheet. Cover and keep cold until baking time.

BEFORE SERVING:

Bake 4 or 5 minutes at 425 degrees F. or until the edges are browned. Transfer to a platter and serve warm.

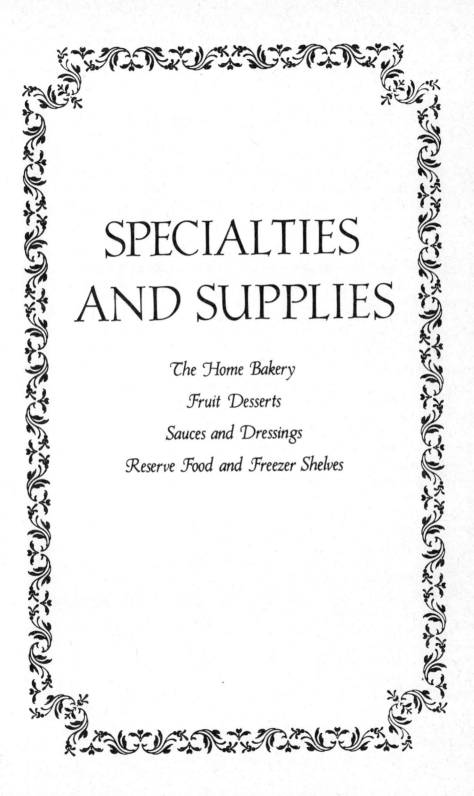

SPECIALTIES
AND SUPPLIES

The Home Bakery

Fruit Desserts

Sauces and Dressings

Reserve Food and Freezer Shelves

The Home Bakery

B aking bread at home can bring immense satisfaction to both the cook and those who eat the products. There is something very reassuring in knowing just what ingredients go into bread and in avoiding all the preservatives and additives that go into most store-bought bread, for which shelf life is so important. For those really interested in baking pure, pure bread we recommend the Vita Mix 3600 machine or an electric grinder which will allow you to make your own flour.

As with other cooking, there is a time for bread making, and it is not during the last stages of preparing a festive meal. I recommend keeping bread in the freezer. There is the bake-and-serve French bread which can be bought in many stores, and if, when you bake your own bread, you feed some of it to the freezer you can always have bread and rolls ready for rapid reheating.

Other baked goods such as rolls, muffins, sweet breads, and pie pastry are all included in this chapter to help you plan ahead.

Refrigerator Yeast Rolls

(3 to 4 dozen rolls, depending on size)

This recipe can be made a day or two in advance. Once the dough has risen, it can be kneaded down and kept in a covered bowl in the refrigerator for several days. Thus, a variety of rolls can be made for two or three successive occasions. It is possible to shape rolls in the morning and keep them covered on a baking tin in the refrigerator until 45 minutes before baking time. They rise somewhat in the refrigerator. The standard procedure is to shape the rolls about 1½ hours before baking and let them rise at room temperature until doubled.

2 cups milk
½ cup butter or margarine
¼ cup sugar
2 teaspoons salt
2 eggs, slightly beaten

1 package fresh or dry
    yeast blended with ¼
    cup lukewarm water
5½ cups unbleached flour

TO MIX:

Scald the milk and add the butter or margarine, sugar, and salt. Stir until the butter melts and pour into a bowl to cool until lukewarm. Add the eggs, yeast, and half the flour. Beat 3 minutes with an electric beater or longer by hand. Add the remaining flour gradually, working it in with your hands until you have a very soft, but not sticky, dough. Cover with a damp cloth and let the dough rise until tripled in bulk. Punch the dough down and knead it well in the bowl. Transfer the dough to a well-buttered bowl and turn the dough around in it to grease all sides. Cover well and place in the refrigerator. Punch it down if it rises.

TO SHAPE:

Take the amount of dough necessary for the desired number of rolls. A third of the dough will give approximately 1 dozen rolls. Knead the portion on a floured surface and roll it out to a thickness of ½ inch. Dust the surface lightly with flour and cut and shape in any of the three ways suggested below.

For Parker House Rolls: Cut the rolls with a small round cookie cutter or with one end of a frozen-juice can. Let the circles stand while melting ½ cup butter or margarine and greasing a baking sheet. Dip a table knife in flour and use the back edge of the blade to make an indentation across each circle, dividing it into two halves. Paint the surface with melted butter. Stretch each circle slightly and fold one half over the other, letting the lower half extend out about ½ inch. Press the halves together gently. Arrange the rolls on the baking sheet, leaving space between them.

For Cloverleaf Rolls: Flour the palms of your hands and roll out small balls of dough until all the dough is used. Butter muffin tins and place 3 balls in each cup.

For Finger Rolls: Flour the palms of your hands and roll out small portions of dough on a floured surface to make small bread sticks. Flatten the center part lightly and taper the ends. Place the rolls on a buttered baking sheet.

Cover the rolls with a damp cloth and let rise until doubled. Bake 12 to 15 minutes at 425 degrees F. Or, shape the rolls in the morning and keep them in the refrigerator until 45 minutes before time to bake them.

Crusty Water Rolls

(18 to 24 rolls)

2 egg whites
¾ cup hot water
1 tablespoon sugar
1 teaspoon salt
2 tablespoons butter or
　margarine

1 package dry or fresh
　yeast blended with
¼ cup lukewarm water
4 cups unbleached flour
Fine cornmeal

TO MIX:

Beat the egg whites until very stiff. In another bowl, but using the same beater, combine the water, sugar, salt, and butter. Beat until the butter melts and the mixture is lukewarm. Add the blended yeast and half the flour. Beat 3 minutes with an electric beater or longer by hand. Fold in the egg whites and enough of the remaining flour to make a soft, elastic dough. Turn the dough onto a floured surface and knead it until it is shiny and smooth. Place the dough in a greased bowl. Cover with a damp towel and let rise for 2 hours at room temperature. Punch it down and let it rise for another hour.

TO SHAPE:

Turn the dough onto a floured surface and knead it slightly. Divide the dough into 18 to 24 pieces. Let them rest while you wash the bowl and grease a baking sheet. Sprinkle the baking sheet with fine cornmeal. Shape the pieces into round or rectangular rolls. Place them on the baking sheet, leaving space between each one. Cover and let rise 45 minutes.

TO BAKE:

Preheat the oven to 450 degrees F. While the oven is preheating, place a roasting pan of hot water on the lowest rack. This will fill the oven with steam. Have boiling water to replenish the pan if necessary. Bake the rolls 15 to 20 minutes, or until golden brown and crusty.

French Herb Loaf

½ cup butter or margarine
2 teaspoons chopped parsley
or 2 teaspoons mixed
fresh herbs (tarragon,
basil, thyme, parsley)

1 clove garlic (optional)
1 long loaf French bread

Melt the butter or margarine and add the herbs and the garlic, pressed or finely chopped. Let the mixture stand in a warm place for at least 30 minutes. Slice the bread in ¾-inch slices but do not cut all the way through. Paint each slice with the butter and place the loaf in a very slow oven or a warming oven to heat through.

Sweet Rolls and Coffee Rings

(3 to 4 dozen rolls or 2 large coffee rings)

1 cup milk
¼ cup sugar
½ cup butter or margarine
1½ teaspoons salt

1 package fresh or dry
 yeast blended with
 ¼ cup lukewarm water
2 eggs, slightly beaten
4 to 4½ cups unbleached flour

TO MIX:

Heat the milk to lukewarm. Add the sugar, butter, and salt and stir until the butter melts. Pour the mixture into a large bowl and, when it is cooled to lukewarm, add the blended yeast and eggs. Mix well and add half the flour. Beat 3 minutes with an electric beater or longer by hand. Add the rest of the flour gradually, using just enough to give a soft, elastic dough. In a well-greased bowl, turn the dough so that it is well greased on all sides. Cover with a damp cloth and let rise 2 hours or until tripled in bulk.

TO SHAPE:

Punch down the dough and place it on a floured surface. Divide in half and let the portions rest for 3 minutes. Take one portion, dust the top lightly with flour, and roll it out with a floured rolling pin to a rectangle ½ inch thick. This will make a large coffee ring or 18 to 24 rolls, depending on the size. The other half can be made like the first one or into one of the following recipes.

For Cinnamon Rolls: Paint the surface with melted butter. Combine ½ cup of sugar with 1 tablespoon of cinnamon and sprinkle the mixture over the rectangle. Roll loosely like a jelly roll and paint the roll with melted butter. Cut the roll in ½-inch slices and place them on a buttered baking sheet. Cover and let rise for 1 hour. Bake 25 to 30 minutes at 375 degrees F.

For Butterscotch Pecan Rolls: Paint the surface with melted butter and sprinkle generously with brown sugar. Roll loosely like a jelly roll. Butter muffin tins liberally and place ½ teaspoon brown sugar and some chopped pecans in each cup. Slice the rolls ½ inch thick and place a slice in each muffin cup. Cover and let rise for 1 hour. Bake 25 to 30 minutes at 375 degrees F. Remove from the pans to a rack to cool, or serve at once.

For Spiced Fruit Coffee Ring: Paint the rectangle with melted butter. Combine 1 small can (3 ounces) of candied fruit peels, ½ cup raisins, ½ cup chopped walnuts, 1 tablespoon cinnamon, ½ teaspoon powdered cloves, and ¼ teaspoon nutmeg with ½ cup sugar. Sprinkle the mixture over the rectangle and roll like a jelly roll. Shape the roll into a ring and place on a buttered baking sheet. Paint with melted butter and place a large jelly glass in the center to keep the shape of the ring. Cut the ring at the outer edge at 2-inch intervals and about 2½ inches deep, leaving the inner circle intact. Cover and let rise for 1 hour. Bake 35 minutes at 375 degrees F. When the ring is removed from the oven, transfer it to a rack; and when the ring is almost cool, spread with confectioners' frosting. (Make the frosting by combining 1 cup confectioners' sugar with ½ teaspoon vanilla and enough light cream to make a frosting that will spread easily.)

Whole Wheat Bread and Rolls

(1 loaf and 12 rolls)

¾ cup milk
5 tablespoons brown sugar
½ cup butter or margarine
1 tablespoon salt
1½ cups lukewarm water

2 packages dry yeast
5 cups whole wheat flour
2½ cups unbleached flour
1 egg

Bring the milk to a boil in a small saucepan. Remove from the heat. Add the sugar and butter or margarine and salt. Stir until the butter or margarine melts. Pour into a bowl to cool until lukewarm.

Rinse the mixing bowl in hot water. Pour in the lukewarm water and sprinkle with the yeast. Stir. Cover and let stand 15 minutes. Combine the two liquid mixtures.

Add 2 cups of whole wheat flour to the combined mixtures and beat well for 3 minutes. Add the remaining whole wheat flour, still beating, and 1 cup of unbleached white flour.

Turn onto a floured surface and knead hard for 10 minutes, adding and kneading in enough additional white flour to form a firm, elastic dough. Place the dough in a well-greased bowl, turning the dough to coat it on all sides. Cover and let rise in a warm place for 60 to 90 minutes. It should be slightly more than doubled.

Knead down the bread and divide it in half. Shape one half into a loaf and place it in a well-buttered or -sprayed loaf tin. Shape the remaining half into 12 balls and place them on a greased baking sheet, allowing 2 inches between rolls. Cover both the bread and rolls and let rise until doubled.

Preheat the oven to 400 degrees F. Bake 10 minutes. Brush the surfaces with egg beaten with 1 tablespoon of water. Bake 15 minutes longer.

Remove the bread from the tin and the rolls from the baking sheet and cool on a wire rack.

White Bread and Rolls

Here is a recipe that will make a lovely loaf and a dozen rolls. Start making the bread before breakfast and in a few hours your kitchen will smell like the finest French bakery. Both bread loaf and rolls will freeze well for future use. It's a comfort to have them on hand.

1½ cups lukewarm water

2 packages dry yeast

7 cups unbleached all-purpose
  flour

2 tablespoons sugar

1 cup milk

1 tablespoon salt

4 tablespoons butter or
  margarine

1 egg

Rinse out the electric mixing bowl with hot water. Pour in the lukewarm water and sprinkle with the yeast. Stir just enough to moisten the yeast. Cover with the mixer cover or with a towel and let stand 15 minutes.

Add 1½ cups of the flour mixed with the sugar. Beat until well blended. Cover again and let stand 30 minutes.

At the same time, heat the milk to the boiling point. Stir in the salt and butter or margarine. Pour into a bowl and let cool to lukewarm (about 30 minutes). Stir into the yeast mixture.

Add 2 cups of flour and beat hard for 3 minutes. Gradually add more flour, still beating, until the dough is soft but firm.

Turn onto a floured surface and start kneading, adding enough flour to keep the dough from sticking. Knead it, bang it, pound it, and throw it onto the surface with all your strength. Continue this therapeutic process for 10 minutes.

Place the dough in a greased bowl, turning the dough so that it will be coated on all sides. Cover and let rise until a little more than doubled. Do not hurry the process. It may take 45 to 90 minutes depending on room temperature. Knead the bread down and divide it in half.

Shape one half into a loaf and place in a well-buttered or -sprayed loaf pan. Cover and let rise until doubled (30 to 45 minutes).

Divide the remaining dough into 12 portions and shape them into smooth balls. Place them on a greased baking sheet 2 inches apart. Cover and let rise until doubled. Preheat the oven to 400 degrees F.

Put the loaf and the rolls on an upper middle rack. Bake 10 minutes. Brush the surfaces with an egg beaten with 1 tablespoon of water. Bake the rolls and the bread 15 minutes longer. Turn the bread out from the loaf tin and remove the rolls from the baking tin.

Pie Dough

(1 covered pie, 2 shells, or 12 tart shells)

Pie-makers have varied theories about the best shortening to use for making crusts. Some swear by lard, some by vegetable shortening combined with butter, and so on. Whatever you prefer, use only the highest quality shortening—this is no place to economize.

For some, making pie crust seems very difficult. The beginner may find it helpful to roll out the dough between two sheets of wax paper. Work quickly with a light hand, and chill the dough before rolling it if at all possible. For best results, the ingredients and the utensils should all be cold. On a very hot day, wrap a towel around some ice cubes and run this over the working surface to chill it.

2½ cups all-purpose flour	*¾ cup cold shortening*
¾ teaspoon salt	*½ cup ice water*

Sift the flour and salt in a bowl and add the cold shortening. Cut the shortening into the flour with a pastry blender, two knives, or an electric beater, until the mixture is like a lot of small peas. Add the ice water gradually and continue cutting until the dough sticks together when lightly pressed. Let the dough rest in the refrigerator for at least 15 minutes.

To Make a Covered Pie: Place the dough on a lightly floured surface. Cut it in half. Roll one half lightly over the surface to form a ball floured lightly on all sides. Working with a chilled and slightly floured rolling pin, roll the dough out from the center, turning it frequently to insure an even circle. Do not roll over the edges. Pick up the circle once or twice to dust underneath with a little flour. When the circle is 1½ inches larger than the pie plate, roll it up on the pin and unroll it over the plate. Fit the dough into the plate loosely. Place in the refrigerator while rolling out the top crust in the same manner. When the pie is filled, unroll the top crust over the pie. Trim the extra dough around the rim and press the edges together with fingers or with the moistened tines of a fork. Baking time will depend on the filling.

To Make a Pie Shell: For a 9-inch shell, make ½ recipe of dough; but if you are making a large meringue pie, make a whole recipe and bake in a 10- to 12-inch pie plate. Roll out the dough 1½ inches larger than the size of the pie plate. If the pie is to be served in the plate, line the inside of the pie plate with the dough. Prick thoroughly with a fork and flute the edge between thumb and forefinger. If the pie shell is to be served unsheathed, invert the pie plate and drape the dough over the back and prick all over. Support the pie plate on a tin cup or other prop so that the fluted edges will not break. Place it on a baking sheet for easier handling. Bake 12 minutes at 450 degrees F.

To Make Tart Shells: Roll out the dough as you would for a pie. Cut in 4-inch circles with a round cookie cutter and drape the circles over the backs of muffin cups. Press the dough in place lightly to give the tarts a good form. Prick well and bake 12 minutes at 450 degrees F. Small tarts are made and baked the same way, using small muffin cups.

Rich Pie Dough Made from a Mix

(1 covered pie or 2 shells)

1 package prepared pie-crust   *4 tablespoons light cream*
mix

Mix the ingredients with an electric beater, food processor, or a pastry blender just until the dough sticks together. Roll into a ball and chill in the refrigerator for 15 minutes.

Roll and bake as in the preceding recipe.

Food Processor Pie Dough

(2 crusts)

You will serve pies and tarts more often if you have this kind of machine just because mixing the dough is so very easy. To be ready to make pie crust in a hurry at any time, keep a stick of butter (not margarine) in your freezer.

1½ cups all-purpose
  unbleached flour
1 stick frozen butter
½ to 1 teaspoon salt

1 tablespoon sugar (for
  sweet pies and tarts)
4 tablespoons ice water

Put the flour in the food processor. Cut the butter into 8 pieces. Add the salt, using more if the butter is unsalted. Add sugar if desired. Spin for 5 seconds or until the mixture has the texture of meal. Still spinning, add the ice water through the tube and continue spinning for about 40 seconds. The dough will ball up on the blades.

Use the dough immediately or wrap and keep in the refrigerator until you need it.

Fruit Desserts

A fruit dessert is the best alternative to high calorie sweets. Individual fresh ripe fruits—apples, pears, grapefruit, oranges, peaches, nectarines, apricots, grapes, strawberries, raspberries, melons, pineapples, papayas, kiwis, bananas—are all delicious served plain, with just a touch of lemon or lime juice, perhaps a pinch of salt, and maybe a little sugar. The riper the fruit, the less it has to be sweetened. Never hesitate to serve fruit rather than pastry at your most elegant meal, and if you want to try a fruit dessert that is a little different, choose one from the suggestions that follow.

Fruit Bowls

The fruit bowl serves as both a centerpiece and dessert on certain occasions. The fruits should be fresh and seasonal and arranged on a tray, on a pedestaled cake plate, or in a pretty bowl. Have fruit knives available for those who want them. One favorite combination of mine is a mixture of yellow fruits—a grapefruit and lemons for the color, and Yellow Delicious apples, perfect bananas, and ripe Bartlett pears for eating. A few green leaves and some kumquats give a slight color accent. Another favorite: an assortment of several varieties of grapes, broken into small clusters and piled high. But anyone can invent his own Still Life of Fruits!

Fresh Fruit Compote

(8 servings)

Almost any combination of fresh fruits is delicious. Allow ¾ to 1 cup of prepared fruit per person. Get in the habit of cutting the fruit over the serving bowl whenever possible; this is to catch the juices that might otherwise be wasted.

1 can (6 ounces) frozen
  lemonade
1 pint strawberries
2 apples

2 pears
2 seedless oranges
1 small cantaloupe
2 bananas

ADVANCE PREPARATION:

Thaw the lemonade and pour it undiluted into a large dessert bowl.

Wash the strawberries very briefly. Remove the hulls and cut the strawberries directly into the bowl. Save out a few small ones for garnish.

Wash the apples well. Quarter and core them and cut them into small chunks directly into the bowl. Do not peel.

Pare the pears. Quarter and core. Slice into the bowl.

Peel the oranges and divide into sections and remove all the white fibers possible. Cut each section in half.

Halve the melon and remove the seeds. Cut into small wedges for easy paring, then in cubes. Peel and slice the bananas. When all fruit is in the bowl stir gently. Cover and refrigerate.

TO SERVE:

Bring the bowl to the table garnished with small strawberries and mint leaves if available. Serve in individual dessert bowls.

Hot Fruit Compote

(8 servings)

Having the ingredients for this dessert on your reserve shelves means that you are never at a loss for a good dessert.

1 can (16 ounces) apricots or peaches	*1 package frozen sliced strawberries (just thawed)*
1 can (16 ounces) pears	*2-4 tablespoons brown sugar*
1 can (11 ounces) mandarin oranges	*2-4 tablespoons dark rum (optional)*
1 can (16 ounces) grapefruit	*Sour cream*

ADVANCE PREPARATION:

Drain the canned fruits completely. Combine in an ovenproof serving dish. If the fruit pieces are large, cut them into bite-sized pieces. Stir in the strawberries, adding the sugar and rum as desired.

BEFORE SERVING:

During the meal, heat 30 minutes at 300 degrees F. in a regular oven or 5 to 6 minutes in the microwave. Serve lukewarm, topped with sour cream.

Cherries Sambuca

(8 servings)

The Italian liqueur Sambuca Romana has a special flavor that goes well with fruits. Its anisette flavor is somehow gentler than its French or Greek counterparts. Cherries Sambuca can be eaten plain, over ice cream, or over pound cake.

1 can (21 ounces) red pie cherries
1 tablespoon orange peel
4 tablespoons.red currant jelly

3 tablespoons Sambuca Romana
2 tablespoons lemon juice
2 tablespoons orange liqueur
Vanilla ice cream or 8 slices pound cake (optional)

ADVANCE PREPARATION:

Combine the cherries, orange peel, and currant jelly with 1 tablespoon of Sambuca in a saucepan and heat just to the simmering point, stirring constantly. Add the lemon juice and set aside.

BEFORE SERVING:

Place the cherries in a chafing dish or in a small nonmetal serving bowl. Heat 10 minutes in a moderate oven or 3 minutes in the microwave on "high."

Combine 2 tablespoons of the Sambuca with the orange liqueur and heat 1 minute in a saucepan or 15 seconds in a glass pitcher in the microwave oven. Pour over the cherries and ignite with a match. Serve as desired.

Cheese-Stuffed Pears

(8 servings)

These can serve as a combination salad-dessert course.

4 large pears	2 tablespoons milk
½ lemon	1 teaspoon scraped onion juice
1 package (8 ounces) cream cheese	4 tablespoons chopped walnuts
	Lettuce leaves
2 teaspoons chopped candied ginger	Currant jelly

ADVANCE PREPARATION:

Peel the pears and rub the outsides with the cut side of the lemon. Cut in half and remove the cores with a sharp knife. Rub the insides with the lemon and squeeze the lemon for juice.

Combine the cream cheese with the chopped ginger, milk, onion juice, chopped walnuts and the lemon juice. Fill the pear cavities with the mixture, using a spoon or a pastry bag fitted with a plain tip. Chill in the refrigerator.

TO SERVE:

Line individual dessert plates with a lettuce leaf. Place the pear on the leaf and top with a little currant jelly. Serve with saltine crackers.

Guava Shell Sorbet

(6 servings)

Guava shells are sold in 18-ounce cans in Chinese food shops and other gourmet specialty stores.

1 can guava shells

2 teaspoons lemon juice or
   2 tablespoons kirsch

1 pint pineapple sherbet

ADVANCE PREPARATION:

Drain the guava shells and chill them. Boil down the syrup to half its volume. Remove from the stove. Stir in the lemon juice or kirsch and cool.

TO SERVE:

Put 2 shells in each of 6 dessert glasses. Cover with a scoop of pineapple sherbet and top with a little syrup.

Baked Bananas Flambé

(4 servings)

3 large, slightly underripe
   bananas
4 tablespoons butter
½ cup brown sugar
½ cup dark rum

1 teaspoon lemon juice
1 tablespoon grated orange
   peel
Vanilla ice cream (optional)

ADVANCE PREPARATION:

Peel the bananas. Slice them in half lengthwise and cut each half into two equal parts.

If you will be using a conventional oven, spread half the butter in a nonmetal casserole and put in the banana pieces. Sprinkle with the sugar and half the rum mixed with the lemon juice. Stir gently to make sure the bananas are coated on all surfaces. Sprinkle with the orange peel.

With a microwave, combine the butter, sugar, and half the rum in a 2-quart glass casserole and place in the oven on "high" for 4 minutes. Remove from the oven and cool to lukewarm. Add the banana pieces and turn them to coat all surfaces. Sprinkle with the lemon juice and the orange peel.

BEFORE SERVING:

Bake in a conventional oven 20 minutes at 325 degrees F., or in a microwave for 90 seconds. Heat the remaining rum 1 minute on top of the stove or 15 seconds in the microwave. Pour over the bananas and light with a match. Serve immediately, with or without vanilla ice cream.

Caribbean Avocado Balls

(4 servings)

2 ripe avocados	*4 tablespoons white rum*
2 tablespoons lemon juice	*4 tablespoons chopped pecans*
2 tablespoons honey	

Cut the avocados in halves and remove the seeds. Using a small melon ball cutter, scoop out the flesh. Put in a bowl containing the lemon juice, honey, and rum, which have been stirred until well blended. Stir until well coated. Cover and refrigerate.

(Scoop out any remaining avocado flesh—and give yourself the treat of Avocado Toast*.) Wipe the shells dry and set aside.

TO SERVE:

Serve the avocado shells filled with the avocado balls on individual dessert dishes. Spoon the syrup over the balls and sprinkle with chopped pecans.

Honeydew Bowl
(6 to 8 servings)

1 pound seedless white grapes	1 tablespoon lemon juice
1 egg white	½ cup dry white wine
¾ cup granulated sugar	Mint leaves
1 ripe honeydew melon	

ADVANCE PREPARATION:

Remove the grapes from the stems.

Beat the egg white stiff and stir in the grapes so that each one is coated.

Sprinkle a baking sheet with ¼ cup of sugar. Spread the grapes on the sugar so that they do not touch each other. Sprinkle with another ¼ cup of sugar so that each grape is covered. Place in the refrigerator for several hours.

Slice a thin sliver from the bottom of one end of the melon so that it will sit evenly on a dessert platter. Remove the top third of the melon. Scoop out the seeds and cut out the interior flesh into balls with a small melon cutter, placing the balls in a bowl. Sprinkle the balls with the remaining sugar, the lemon juice, and wine. Sawtooth the rim of the empty melon and chill it as well as the balls.

TO SERVE:

Place the melon balls in the melon bowl and top with frosted grapes. Garnish with mint leaves.

Strawberries Melba

(6 to 8 servings)

This dessert is delicious with or without ice cream. If you think your guests may be divided in preference, serve the ice cream in a separate bowl.

1 quart very ripe strawberries
1 pint fresh raspberries or
   1 box (8 ounces) frozen
   raspberries
½ cup sugar

1 teaspoon lemon juice
Vanilla or strawberry ice
   cream (optional)
1 package (3 ounces) slivered
   almonds

ADVANCE PREPARATION:

Wash the strawberries. Hull them and store in a covered bowl in the refrigerator.

Spin the raspberries, sugar, and lemon juice in a food processor or blender for 30 seconds. Strain to remove the seeds. Store in a covered jar.

TO SERVE:

Serve the strawberries plain or on top of ice cream as desired. Cover with the raspberry puree and sprinkle with slivered almonds.

Blueberry Parfait

(8 servings)

1 quart blueberries
1 cup dark brown sugar

½ pint heavy cream
½ pint sour cream

ADVANCE PREPARATION:

Wash the berries and spread them on a baking sheet to dry. Chill.

Alternate tablespoonfuls of blueberries and brown sugar in parfait glasses. Keep in the refrigerator.

TO SERVE:

Serve the glasses on individual dessert plates. Pass the two kinds of cream in small bowls for each person to choose.

Tropical Pineapple

(4 servings)

This will take about 15 minutes to prepare, but it can be done in advance and kept in the refrigerator for several hours.

1 ripe pineapple	*4 glacé cherries*
2 bananas	*4 mint leaves (if available)*
2 tablespoons lemon juice	*Grand Marnier, kirsch, and rum*
2 tablespoons sugar (raw sugar,	
if available)	

ADVANCE PREPARATION:

Put the pineapple on its side and cut with a large sharp knife, beginning at the bottom end and cutting right through the leaves. Cut each half in two. Using a small, very sharp knife, cut off the core on top of each piece. Cut the flesh into ¼-inch slices. Run the knife under the slices, parallel to the pineapple shell. Remove every third slice and set aside.

Peel and cut the bananas into ¼-inch slices. Place the slices in a small bowl containing the lemon juice and 1 tablespoon of the sugar. Raw sugar is recommended because of its crunchy quality. Stir to cover all the slices with lemon juice. Insert the banana slices in between the pineapple slices.

Cut the reserved pineapple into fan-shaped pieces and insert them on either side of the banana slices. Sprinkle with the remaining sugar.

Place the quarters on a tray. Garnish with the cherries and mint leaves.

TO SERVE:

Serve the pineapple quarters on individual dessert dishes. Serve with a tray of liqueurs, which each person can sprinkle on the pineapple if desired or enjoy in a liqueur glass while eating the pineapple.

Orange Quince Compote

(4 to 6 servings)

Quinces are usually reserved for jelly, but they are a delicious fruit when baked. They are not easy to pare and core, but they are worth the effort.

4 quinces	*Boiling water*
1 orange	*½ cup sugar*
½ lemon	

Peel the quinces. Cut them into quarters and remove the core. Cut into eighths. Cut the orange and half lemon into thin slices and remove the seeds. Arrange the quince pieces in a 2-quart nonmetal casserole.

If you will be using a conventional oven, pour boiling water over the quince pieces to a depth of ½ inch. Sprinkle with the sugar and cover with the orange and lemon slices. Cover the casserole and bake at 350 degrees F. 2 hours or until tender.

If using a microwave, pour ½ cup boiling water over the quince pieces. Top with the sugar, orange slices, and lemon slices and microwave on "high" 35 minutes or until tender.

Cool, then chill in the refrigerator. Serve cold in individual dessert glasses.

Gourmet Applesauce
(4 servings)

2 cups (1 pound) applesauce (homemade or bought)
2 tablespoons candied ginger, diced fine
2 tablespoons grated orange peel
½ cup chopped pecans

¾ cup vanilla cookie crumbs
2 tablespoons butter or margarine
2 tablespoons rum
2 teaspoons vanilla
¼ teaspoon salt
½ pint sour cream

ADVANCE PREPARATION:

Combine everything except the sour cream in a saucepan. Heat just to the simmering point, stirring constantly. Remove from the stove and transfer to a nonmetal bowl that is heatproof. Taste for sweetness. If necessary, add 2 or 3 tablespoons of brown sugar.

BEFORE SERVING:

Bake for 10 minutes at 375 degrees F. in a regular oven or 3 minutes in the microwave. Serve lukewarm topped with the sour cream.

Sauces and Dressings

Sauces are an important part of many dishes and they require the special attention of the cook. Fortunately, most sauces can be prepared in advance and kept ready to be added at the appropriate time. Thanks to the food processor and the blender, today sauces like Hollandaise and Béarnaise that used to be considered tricky can be made successfully by even the brand new cook, without worry or fuss. In this book we are presenting both the classical and modern methods for making sauces and salad dressings; you can try both and decide which you prefer.

White Sauce

White sauce is the basis for many dishes. For a thin sauce, halve the amount of butter and flour. For a thick sauce increase by half the same ingredients. Whole wheat flour gives the sauce a good nutty flavor. The recipe given will yield 2 cups of sauce.

4 tablespoons butter or
   margarine
4 tablespoons unbleached white
   or whole wheat pastry flour

2 cups milk
Salt and white pepper

Heat the butter or margarine in a saucepan. Add the flour and stir over moderate heat for 2 minutes. Add the cold milk all at once and whisk vigorously until the sauce thickens. Season to taste with salt and pepper.

Brown Sauce

Good brown sauce is hard to make well, but there are tricks to the trade. The problem with making good brown sauce is to brown the flour without scorching it. If you brown the flour first, you will have no problem. This can be done at your convenience and the flour kept covered in the refrigerator. Spread 2 cups of unbleached white all-purpose flour in an iron skillet or roasting pan; the flour should be about ½ inch deep. Brown in a 250-degree F. oven for 30 to 40 minutes, stirring occasionally. Cool. Place in a covered jar and store in the refrigerator.

4 tablespoons butter or
   margarine
4 tablespoons browned flour
½ teaspoon tomato paste

2 cups meat stock or canned
   bouillon
Salt and black pepper

Heat the butter or margarine in a small pan. Stir in the flour and cook for 1 minute. Add the tomato paste and meat stock or bouillon. Whisk vigorously until smooth and thick. Season to taste with salt and pepper.

Maître d'Hôtel Butter

¼ pound soft butter or
   margarine
1½ teaspoons wine vinegar or
   lemon juice

2 teaspoons chopped parsley
Freshly ground black pepper

Combine the ingredients, using plenty of black pepper. If possible, let the mixture stand an hour before using. Spread on fish or steaks just before serving.

Hollandaise Sauce I

Hollandaise is a favorite sauce with almost everyone and there are many ways of preparing it. This recipe is for the kind you make in the morning and reheat later. The second recipe is for sauce made with a food processor or blender, and the third is for the occasions when you want just enough Hollandaise for one or two people or when it is to be used as an accent, not an over-all sauce.

4 egg yolks	Salt and white pepper
¼ cup butter or margarine	Dash of cayenne
1 tablespoon lemon juice	2 tablespoons heavy cream

The best utensil is a small double boiler with an earthenware or stainless steel top part that can serve as a sauce bowl. The water in the lower half must be kept just below the boiling point and must never actually touch the upper part.

Beat the egg yolks slightly with a wire whisk in the top part of the double boiler. Add about a third of the butter and whisk over the simmering water until it melts. Add another third and whisk until that melts. Add the remaining third and whisk until the sauce is smooth and thick. Remove the top part from the lower part of the double boiler and whisk hard for a few minutes. Add the lemon juice, salt, pepper, and cayenne. Cool, cover, and place in the refrigerator.

BEFORE SERVING:

Before the guests arrive, reheat the sauce over simmering water, stirring frequently. Add the cream to keep the sauce from separating. Remove the double boiler from the heat but keep the sauce over the hot water. Hollandaise is served warm, not hot. It will keep warm enough over the hot water for a fairly long time, but you can reheat it quickly, if necessary, at the last minute.

Hollandaise Sauce II

4 egg yolks
2½ tablespoons lemon juice
½ teaspoon salt

⅛ teaspoon cayenne
12 tablespoons butter or
margarine, melted

ADVANCE PREPARATION:

Put the egg yolks, lemon juice, salt, and cayenne in a food processor or blender. Give it a spin for 2 seconds and cover.

Measure the butter into a saucepan and let stand at room temperature.

BEFORE SERVING:

Heat the butter until bubbly. Start the food processor or blender and, while it is spinning, add the butter slowly. The sauce will thicken quickly.

Hollandaise Sauce III

1 egg yolk
1 tablespoon cream
1 teaspoon lemon juice
¼ teaspoon salt

Pinch of cayenne
2 tablespoons butter or
margarine

Whisk the egg yolk and cream over moderate heat for 30 to 60 seconds or until the mixture starts to thicken. Withdraw from the heat. Add the lemon juice, salt, cayenne, and 1 tablespoon of butter while whisking constantly for 30 seconds. Add the remaining butter or margarine and place on the heat, whisking until the butter is incorporated. Serve immediately or pour into a glass container. Before serving, reheat by placing the glass container in a bowl of hot (not boiling) water or in the microwave, uncovered, for 30 seconds at "simmer."

Béarnaise Sauce

This delicious sauce is made in the same way as Hollandaise. It is served with steak, chops, roasts, and fish.

3 tablespoons white wine
   vinegar
2 teaspoons chopped chives
1 teaspoon fresh tarragon,
   chopped, or ½ teaspoon
   dried tarragon

4 egg yolks
12 tablespoons butter or
   margarine
½ teaspoon salt
¼ teaspoon black pepper
1 tablespoon chopped parsley

Put the vinegar, chives, and tarragon in a small saucepan. Boil down to approximately 1 tablespoon.

Beat the eggs and vinegar mixture together and prepare as for Hollandaise I or II, substituting the black pepper for cayenne and adding the chopped parsley just before serving.

Mousseline Sauce

If you want to add a special touch to fish, chicken, asparagus, broccoli, and other vegetables, add 6 tablespoons of cream, whipped to peaks but not stiff, to a cup of Hollandaise sauce.

Hard Sauce

Hard sauce is a must with Indian Pudding, which is one of my suggestions for the Reserve Shelf. It is also good with so many other desserts that I recommend having a small jar of it always in the freezer.

½ cup soft sweet butter
1½-2 cups confectioners' sugar
⅛ teaspoon nutmeg

¼ teaspoon salt
2 teaspoons rum or brandy

ADVANCE PREPARATION:

Beat the butter and 1 cup of sugar in a food processor or with an electric mixer. Add the nutmeg, salt, liquor, and enough sugar to make a thick paste. Transfer to a small container for storage in refrigerator or freezer. If frozen, remove from the freezer and let stand at room temperature until thawed but still firm before serving.

Tossed Salad and Dressings

A good green salad is an important item in many of the menus suggested in this book, so it seems best to give a general outline for salads and let you choose your own combinations.

Basically, a tossed salad consists of fresh salad greens and a well-seasoned dressing. One may vary the basic salad by combining different greens and adding cooked vegetables, raw vegetables, and salad herbs. It is a good idea to wash the greens as soon as they come from the garden or the store and keep them in the refrigerator crisper until just before the guests arrive. The salad dressing can be mixed in advance, stored in a bottle or decanter, and brought to the dining room for a final shaking and mixing just before serving. The dressing should be at room temperature. Make sure that the greens are cool, very clean, dry, and crisp.

SOME SUGGESTIONS:

Salad Greens: Lettuce (several varieties), escarole, romaine, chicory, endive, tiny beet greens, fresh dandelion greens, Chinese cabbage, small spinach leaves, watercress.

Salad Vegetables: Scallions, raw carrots, tomatoes, radishes, avocados, celery, onion rings, shredded cabbage, sprouts; thin slices of kohlrabi, turnip, parsnip; cooked peas, string beans, carrots.

Salad Herbs: Chives, parsley, basil, tarragon, dill, fennel, borage, chervil, rosemary, or thyme. You can use a pinch of the dried variety or a mild blend of the fresh—but go lightly. Fresh herbs should be chopped and added at the last minute.

Vinaigrette

¼ cup red wine or cider vinegar
½ teaspoon salt
⅛ teaspoon freshly ground
   black pepper
½ cup olive oil
½ cup corn or peanut oil

½ clove garlic, pressed or
   minced
2 teaspoons chopped chives
1 teaspoon chopped tarragon
1 tablespoon crumbled bleu
   cheese
2 teaspoons chopped anchovies

OPTIONAL ADDITIONS :
½ teaspoon prepared mustard

Combine the vinegar, salt, and pepper and mix well. Add the oil and shake hard just before adding to the salad. For variations, add any of the optional ingredients or a combination of them.

The dressing can be made in advance. Store in the refrigerator in a stoppered bottle, but remove in time to have at room temperature at time of use. When ready to toss the salad, shake the dressing hard and add just enough dressing to coat the leaves.

Charlotte's Salad Dressing

(About 1 quart)

This is a very useful dressing for a large party and it will keep a long time in the refrigerator.

1 teaspoon prepared mustard	½ teaspoon powdered oregano
1 cup wine vinegar	1 teaspoon onion powder
⅓ cup catsup	½ teaspoon garlic powder
1 tablespoon sugar	1½ cups corn oil
1 tablespoon salt	1½ cups olive oil
½ teaspoon black pepper	1 tablespoon soy sauce

Mix all the ingredients except the oils and stir or whisk until the sugar dissolves. Add the oils and store in a large covered jar. Shake very hard before using.

Mayonnaise I

3 egg yolks	2 tablespoons wine vinegar or
1 teaspoon salt	3 tablespoons lemon juice
Dash of cayenne	1 cup olive oil
1 teaspoon dry mustard	1 cup salad oil

Place the egg yolks and the dry ingredients in a mixing bowl. Beat the mixture slightly with an electric beater or whisk and add half the vinegar or lemon juice. Beating continually, start adding the oil drop by drop. As soon as the mayonnaise begins to thicken, the oil may be added more rapidly. If the dressing should curdle, place ¼ cup of boiling water in a mixing bowl and add the dressing drop by drop until it thickens. From time to time, add a little more vinegar or lemon juice. The dressing is finished when all the oil and vinegar or lemon juice has been absorbed.

Mayonnaise II

This mayonnaise is made in a food processor or blender; it has a creamier consistency than Mayonnaise I.

2 whole eggs	*1 pinch cayenne*
1 teaspoon dry mustard	*½ cup olive oil plus*
½ teaspoon salt	*½ cup peanut oil or 1 cup*
2 tablespoons lemon juice or	*salad oil*
white wine vinegar	

Put the eggs, mustard, salt, cayenne, 1 tablespoon of lemon juice or vinegar, and 4 tablespoons of oil in a food processor or blender. Spin 5 seconds. While it is still spinning, add half of the remaining oil in a very thin stream. Add the remaining lemon juice or vinegar and continue pouring in the oil until the sauce is smooth and thick.

Store in a covered glass jar in the refrigerator.

Pesto

This northern Italian sauce is delicious served on pasta or as a condiment for vegetables. Make it in a blender or food processor. Serve, or store it in small 4-ounce containers in the freezer.

1 cup (tightly packed) small
   fresh basil leaves
4 large cloves garlic
½ teaspoon salt
⅛ teaspoon freshly ground
   black pepper

½ cup grated Provalone cheese
½ cup grated fresh Parmesan
2 tablespoons chopped walnuts
   or pine nuts
½ pint olive oil

Put the basil, garlic, salt, pepper, cheese, walnuts, and 4 tablespoons of oil in the food processor or blender. Spin until pureed. Add the rest of the oil gradually until all is incorporated.

Reserve Food and Freezer Shelves

The Reserve Shelf suggested here is not intended to include basic staples, though it is a good idea to have a secret cache of such basics as coffee, butter, and margarine in your freezer. The supplies on the Reserve Shelf are for those occasions when unexpected guests need nourishment, or when there just isn't time to shop for the family meal. You may wish to add some of your favorite items to the list, or omit some items I have suggested, but, for ease of mind as well as ease of entertaining, keep your Reserve Shelf well stocked.

RESERVE SHELF:

2 cans beef consommé
2 cans chicken broth
Bouillon cubes
2 cans shrimp or lobster
   bisque
2 20-ounce cans artichoke
   hearts
1 7½-ounce can artichoke
   bottoms
2 4½-ounce cans cleaned shrimp
2 cans sardines
1 can crab meat
2 cans smoked oysters
2 cans minced clams
1 canned cooked ham (2 pounds)
1 tube anchovy paste
1 can anchovy fillets
1 8¾-ounce can shelled beans
2 3-ounce cans mushroom caps
4 1-pound cans potato balls
1 15-ounce can small green beans
1 can diced celery
2 pounds spaghettini or
   linguini
1 jar Parmesan cheese (for
   emergency use only; the
   fresh is better)
Melba rounds
Cocktail crackers and nibbles
1 bottle lemon juice
1 large and 1 small can sliced
   pineapple

1 can peaches
2 packages chopped
   walnuts
2 packages chopped pecans
1 package slivered almonds
1 can grapefruit sections
1 can mandarin oranges
1 can apricots
White and brown rice
1 or 2 cans Indian pudding or
   babas au rhum
1 or 2 cans evaporated milk
Kaluah, kirsch, Cointreau

RESERVE FREEZER SHELF:

1 pound coffee
1 pound butter
1 pound margarine
2 packages frozen beans
3 packages frozen spinach or
   broccoli
Pesto *
Tomato Paste *
1 pint chocolate ice cream
1 pint coffee ice cream
1 quart vanilla ice cream
2 loaves French bread
1 quiche shell
1 package frozen strawberries
1 package frozen raspberries
½ pound Gruyère or
   cheddar cheese

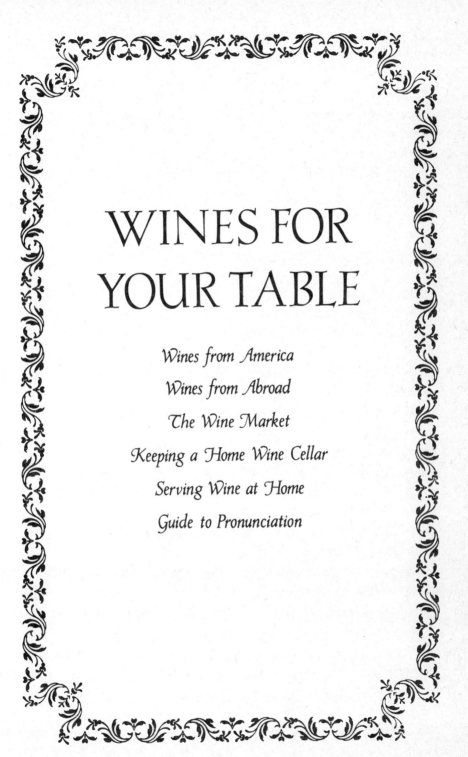

WINES FOR YOUR TABLE

Wines from America

Wines from Abroad

The Wine Market

Keeping a Home Wine Cellar

Serving Wine at Home

Guide to Pronunciation

Almost as important to successful home entertaining as good food and a relaxed host or hostess is a beverage selected to suit the occasion. For more and more Americans, that beverage is wine.

Anyone who doubts wine's new popularity in the United States need only check the dramatic ascent in its sales figures over the past decade and the corresponding dip in consumption of hard liquor. We appear to be in the midst of a major shift in our national preferences with respect to alcoholic beverages, and the pattern that is emerging in this country is much closer to the norm in other Western nations. The younger segment of our population is leading the way in this small but important cultural revolution, but all age groups and sections of the country are involved in varying degrees.

This shift toward wine is a positive development from virtually any standpoint. In the first place, wine is affordable. Some prestigious, limited-production wines are, of course, quite expensive; but the great majority of the world's wine output can be purchased at reasonable prices. Secondly, wine is healthful in comparison to other alcoholic beverages. Ounce for ounce, it contains only about one-fourth the alcohol in distilled spirits and its effect is further moderated by the fact that it is almost invariably consumed with food. Third, food tastes better with wine because its mildly astringent character helps to cleanse and refresh the palate as the meal proceeds. Finally, this same characteristic helps to break down the fatty substances in our food, thus making wine an aid to digestion.

All of these practical advantages are as nothing, however, compared to the heightened pleasure which people take in a meal which includes wine. Having an appropriate wine, however simple in character, makes any such occasion seem more festive; and that, after all, is what entertaining is all about. Or, to put it another way, wine is the ideal accompaniment for those happy occasions when good food, family, and friends come together—precisely the kinds of situations for which the meals in this book were created.

No one need become a wine "expert" to choose or enjoy some of the hundreds of different varieties of this very special beverage. Some basic knowledge is helpful, however, in making selections, and the surer you are about your choices the greater confidence and satisfaction you will take in offering them to your guests. As Americans become increasingly familiar with wine, the vintages served on any occasion very often become a topic of conversation. Again, knowing a bit about wines will be helpful in your role as host or hostess when these situations arise.

What follows, therefore, is an overview of the major sources of wine, a brief description of today's wine market, and some tips on how you can purchase wines most economically. Thereafter, you will find a discussion of how to establish and maintain a modest home wine cellar—a less ambitious undertaking than you might expect. Finally, we'll outline a proper but unfussy approach to wine service, including bottle preparation, appropriate glassware, and pouring etiquette.

As you may have discovered already, many of the menus included in this book offer suggestions for appropriate wines at different price levels. These suggestions are traditional in the sense that they represent the wines most informed people have chosen to go with particular types of food for many hundreds of years. As your own experience with and love for wine grows, you may find that you would prefer alternative combinations. The next few pages are intended to start you on a road to wine knowledge which will give you both pleasure and a sense of assurance in making such selections.

Wines from America

Most of what America drinks comes from our own vineyards. Surprising as this may seem to those who have concentrated on imported vintages, the fact is that more than three-fourths of all the wine sold in the United States is of domestic origin. It may also surprise some to learn how important America has become among the world's wine-producing nations. Today we stand sixth in total output, and commercial wineries exist in more than two-thirds of the fifty states.

The latter point requires some slight elaboration, however. In America, there are basically two sources of wine: California, first and foremost; and then all the rest of the states combined. This is so because America's first vintners discovered that California's benign environment offered a natural haven for the cultivation of the classic wine grapes of Europe—something no other state could manage, at least on a comparable scale. Consequently, vintners in our other states have had to rely almost entirely on fruit from native American grape varieties. Because these grapes are fundamentally different from those raised in California or Europe, they result in wines which represent exceptions in the mainstream of world wine production.

It is not our place here to argue the merits of Californian versus other American wines. It is important to understand, however, when you are choosing a domestic wine to accompany one of the meals in this book, that the California and New York versions of a wine with the same name will be very different indeed. New developments in crossbreeding the classic grape varieties with native American stock are beginning to yield a new breed of Eastern American wines much closer to the world standard. These wines deserve your interest because they represent increasingly good quality and value, but for your next dinner party you may find it safer to make a selection from a California vineyard.

Such a selection should pose no hardship since over four-fifths of all American wine comes from the Golden State and its products receive the widest national distribution. That being so, you may find it helpful to know a bit more about the places where California wine is made, the basic divisions from the standpoint of quality, and the nomenclature you will encounter on California wine labels.

The vast majority of California wine comes from the great inland valley which runs nearly 300 miles from Sacramento to Bakersfield; there vineyards can extend from horizon to horizon. The climate is too hot and dry for the most sophisticated grape varieties and the approach.

to wine making is distinctly industrial, but out of this unlikely setting flows a mighty river of what many experts have come to regard as the best *vin ordinaire* in the world. Honestly made, consistently satisfying, and fairly priced, it reaffirms the American knack for achieving surprisingly good quality through mass production and constitutes a unique contribution to the science and art of wine making. The producers of these simple but admirable vintages can fairly be referred to as California's "standard" wine makers; representative firms include Gallo, Guild, Petri, Roma, and Winemasters.

From a purely qualitative standpoint, however, these inland-grown, bulk-produced wines are overshadowed by those which come from several small valleys clustered around San Francisco Bay. Collectively, they are known as the wines of the North Coast counties, but consumers are increasingly familiar with the names of the individual and highly picturesque valleys in which they are made. Going clockwise around the Bay from north to south, the best known include Sonoma, Napa, Livermore, Santa Clara, and Monterey. Although their output amounts to only about 15 percent of the state's total, they produce the wines on which California's sharply escalating reputation for high quality primarily rests.

These small coastal valleys are uniquely suited to the cultivation of the best grape varieties because the extensive sunshine they receive is moderated by cool, moist air from the Pacific. The vineyards are much smaller than in the great central valley, though still somewhat larger than plots of comparable distinction in Europe. The wine-making equipment available to these North Coast vintners is generally equal to or better than the best in France or Germany. Such a heavy investment in the most advanced equipment is made possible by an extensive state government research program and the recent dramatic upturn in the fortunes of the California wine industry. It is necessary because its vintners must make use of the best technology to overcome the fact that, although their grape-growing conditions are the best in America, they are still not equal to those of northern Europe.

Basically, there are two types of wine makers at work in these North

Coast valleys. Those longest established and controlling most of the land are usually referred to as the state's "premium" wine producers. Representative firms include Almadén, Paul Masson, Mirassou, Wente, Louis Martini, Beaulieu Vineyards, Inglenook, Christian Brothers, Charles Krug, Sebastiani, Sonoma, and Simi. These are firms which grow or purchase high-grade grapes to make a wide range of the world's best-known types of wines. Their goal is to offer the public a complete "line" of fine vintages under one label in the hope that consumers will come to depend on an individual producer for all their wine needs.

These vineyards were all started as small, family-owned enterprises, but in the past decade many have been sold to large corporations with the capital for vineyard expansion and winery equipment made necessary by the American public's new demand for large volumes of better quality wine. Many industry observers believed that these corporate takeovers would result in a decline in standards or at least a diminution of the individual character of each winery's products. For the most part, however, this has not occurred because the original owners have stayed on as operators and are making inspired use of the new land and equipment. Indeed, it is possible to say that never before have these North Coast wineries so richly deserved to be described as "premium."

Overarching even their achievements, however, is a new breed of wine makers—the other type at work in these favored coastal valleys. They may be referred to as the "superpremium" vintners of California and, in fact, of the entire country. Most have been established only in the past few years and their combined output is minuscule compared to that of the standard and premium wine producers. Nevertheless, they have already achieved international recognition, and the inclusion of one or more of their vintages at your next dinner party is sure to provide a topic of conversation as well as a handsome accompaniment to the food.

Among the most respected of this new breed of vintners are Hanzell, Joseph Phelps, Château St. Jean, Schramsberg, Stony Hill, Mayacamas, Freemark Abbey, Robert Mondavi, Joe Heitz, Chappellet, David

Bruce, Ridge, and Chalone. Generally, these firms own only small parcels of land scattered among longer established vineyards. Their sites have been chosen with care, however, to afford near-perfect growing conditions for particular grape varieties. Some of these producers had to purchase grapes from others until their own vines began to bear, but most are now able to make their wines only from fruit which they have nurtured on their own land. After the grapes are harvested, their fermentation, maturation in special wood casks, and extended bottle aging are characterized by a standard of care not found elsewhere in the industry.

Aside from the handcrafted approach of these vintners to their work, the most significant difference between them and the premium growers is specialization. Instead of attempting to make a full line of products, these small firms have decided to concentrate only on those few wines for which their land is best suited and whose innate quality is such that it is most likely to be enhanced by painstaking care in the wine-making process. In employing this approach, they have moved American viticulture one step closer to the ultimate specialization practiced in Europe, where each vineyard produces only a single kind of wine.

Now for a word about some of the nomenclature you are likely to encounter on the labels of American wines. In addition to the name of the producing firm—and in some cases its geographic location—the name of the kind of wine in the bottle is always prominently displayed. Some producers still use "proprietary" names, i.e. names peculiar to that particular firm, like "Ripple" or "Rhinecastle." Mercifully, however, these are few in number and the great majority share a common, bi-level system for naming their products which is both logical and easy to remember.

Most American wines go to market bearing what are called "generic" names. These are names borrowed from the best-known wine-producing regions of Europe (e.g. Chablis, Rhine, Burgundy, and Chianti) and are meant to suggest that the contents of the bottle so labeled will generally resemble those classic wine types. The resemblance is often only faint because industry regulations do not require the producer to use the grapes which made the original wine of that name famous; in fact, he is free to use any grape or combination of grapes he chooses. This does not necessarily mean that the wine will be inferior—only that it is unlikely to be a close replica of its namesake. The most extensive use of such generic names is made by the standard wine makers of California's central valley.

A smaller percentage—perhaps a quarter—of America's wine production is sold under what are called "varietal" names. These are names borrowed not from places in Europe but from the principal variety of grape with which the wine was made, e.g. cabernet sauvignon, pinot noir, chardonnay, Johannisberg riesling, and barbera. The names are less familiar than the generics and initially a little more challenging to pronounce, but they are meant to alert you to the fact that the producer considers these his very best wines. Varietal labeling is used extensively by the premium wine makers in California's North Coast counties, though they also market a large volume of generically named wines—many of which are purchased in bulk from growers in the central valley. Varietal labeling is employed almost exclusively by the superpremium small vintners along the North Coast.

Wines from Abroad

Wherever the climate permits, man makes wine. Viticultural activity is concentrated, however, within two bands circling the globe in both the northern and southern hemispheres where the average annual temperature is between about 50 degrees F. and 65 degrees F. Included in the ranks of major wine-producing nations are the Soviet Union, Algeria, South Africa, Argentina, and Australia.

For our purposes, however, there is only one source of foreign wine that really matters: Europe. It has provided the model on which our own wine industry has been built and it supplies virtually all the imported wines you are likely to encounter in an American wine shop. Several European countries deserve attention even in so brief a survey as this, but paramount among them is France. More than any other nation, she has defined the language, science, art, and legal regulation of wine making; and everyone who produces or enjoys wine stands to some degree in her debt. Libraries could be filled with what has been written about French viticulture; but again we will confine ourselves here to identifying the principal wine sources, delineating the basic levels of quality, and deciphering some of the key words found on French wine labels.

France

If one were to start from Paris and begin a clockwise journey around the most important wine regions of France, he would start—most fortunately—at Champagne. Located about 90 miles northeast of the capital, this world-famous wine-producing area is centered around the ancient city of Reims. Many nations have pirated the name of this venerable province but none have quite equaled the excellence of the magical sparkling wine it produces. This excellence is attributable in part to the top-quality pinot noir and chardonnay grapes which can be cultivated so effectively in this, France's northernmost vineyard area. But it is also due to the strictly regulated, labor-intensive *méthode champenoise* with which the wine is made. This demanding process involves fermentation of the wine inside the bottle in which it will be sold (instead of in large tanks), the introduction of additional sugar into the still wine to start a secondary fermentation that will make it sparkle, and, finally, the removal of sediment and the addition of a final dose of sugar and brandy—all without losing the effervescence that makes this wine so special!

In selecting champagnes to accompany a dinner, it is important to understand that they are made in several styles appropriate to different stages of the meal. The driest usually available is labeled *brut* and is at its best when used as an aperitif. Next comes *extra sec*, which, though it has a trifle more sugar, is certainly not sweet and can go well with a number of first courses or entrées. *Sec* has another percentage point of sugar and borders on being too sweet for mid-meal dishes unless they involve perhaps a combination of fruit with meat, fish, or fowl. Finally, there is *demi-sec*, which is really quite sweet and to be used with dessert or as an after-dinner drink. Really there is nothing quite so elegant as using one of these *demi-sec* champagnes to ring down the curtain on a great dinner party.

Continuing clockwise around the country, we come next to Alsace, that idyllic but tragic province which has so often been the scene of conflict between French and German armies. The wines made here are almost all white and are produced from many of the same grapes used across the border in Germany: riesling, sylvaner, and gewurztraminer. The French love for dry wines, however, and their expectation that they will be a foil for food make the Alsatian vintages quite different from those produced along the Rhine. Always refreshing, never cloying, they are a first-rate choice to accompany chicken and pork, hot-weather fare, and that occasional dish in which the spices call for a white wine with extra zest. Alsatian wines are relatively inexpensive and constitute one of the few exceptions to the general French practice of naming wines after the places in which they were grown. In this region, the same system is used as that for California's best wines, i.e. naming the wines after the variety of grapes from which they are made.

The next region is possibly even more famous than Champagne and certainly more complex: Burgundy. First the Romans, then the feudal nobility and various monastic orders, next the postrevolutionary peasantry, and now some of the world's most sophisticated vintners have tilled this remarkable territory which the French have good reason to believe was divinely predestined for viticulture. Actually, it is not a single region but six individual districts arranged on a north-south axis, and it is useful to recognize the quite different role which each plays.

The three northernmost districts are usually treated as a group and produce the highest quality wines. At the top is Chablis, the tiniest of all and that unique place where a cool climate combines with a soil rich in fossil sea life to make some of the world's driest white wines from the chardonnay grape. Long thought of as the quintessential accompaniment to oysters, the wines of Chablis work well with all sorts of fish dishes, and a really good one makes a spectacular aperitif. The name of this special district has been stolen to identify a host of lesser wines in other countries but once you have sampled the real article you'll have a new respect for the word. True Chablis is made in four quality grades: *grand cru, premier cru*, plain *Chablis* and last of all, *petit Chablis.* The *grand cru* designation is reserved for only eight tiny vineyards: Blanchots, Bougros, Grenouilles, La Moutonne, Les Clos, Les Preuses, Valmur, and Vaudésir.

Next comes the Côte de Nuits district, which produces the lion's share of the most prestigious red wines of Burgundy. Here is where the world-renowned vineyards of Chambertin, Le Musigny, Clos de Vougeot, Richebourg, La Romanée-Conti, and La Tâche are located. All wines are made from the pinot noir grape on a nondescript slope which faces east toward the Saône River plain. In addition to the famous individual vineyard wines—which are quality-rated as either Grand Cru or Premier Cru—much of the wine from lesser properties is combined and sold under the names of the well-known villages of the Côte such as Gevrey-Chambertin, Chambolle-Musigny, Vosne-Romanée, and Nuits-Saint-Georges. You will quickly recognize that the town fathers have been astute enough to tack the names of the best vineyards to the original names of their villages. The great reds of the Côte de Nuits are superlative companions to beef, fowl, game, and indeed any richly flavored or sumptuously sauced meat dish. They can also be glorious with some of France's finest soft and semisoft cheeses.

Last in northern Burgundy is the Côte de Beaune, but it would be hard to argue that it is in any way inferior to the two more northerly districts. Beaune makes both whites and reds of world-class quality, again from the chardonnay and pinot noir grapes. Foremost among its *grand cru* vineyards are Le Corton, Corton-Charlemagne, and Le Montrachet, but there are also scores of *premier cru* wines and an even greater volume sold under village names. The red-wine townships include Aloxe-Corton, Savigny-les-Beaune, Pommard, and Volnay; and those best known for whites include Meursault, Puligny-Montrachet, and Chassagne-Montrachet. The reds of the Côte work well with the same foods as those suggested for the Côte de Nuits but are perhaps a bit lighter in character. The whites can be dazzling companions for chicken, veal, and all sorts of fish dishes.

When one passes into southern Burgundy, it is quickly apparent that viticulture is even more widespread but that the quality of wines is somewhat less awesome. This is attributable in part to a warmer climate, a flatter landscape, larger vineyards, and, in the southernmost district, a complete change both in the type of soil and in the grapes that are cultivated. The first district is the Côte Chalonnaise which, like the Côte de Beaune just to the north, produces both white and red wines from the chardonnay and pinot noir grapes. Their quality is very good, but relatively little is imported to the United States. Next in line to the south comes the Côte Maconnais, best known for its simple, but highly satisfying, chardonnay-based white called Macon Blanc. The most coveted Macon is Pouilly-Fuissé, but the laws of supply and demand have made this wine much overpriced.

The southernmost district of Burgundy is Beaujolais—a name familiar to every wine lover. This wine is made from the gamay grape in granitic soil, rather than in the limestone soil which underlies the rest of the region. Beaujolais is sold in four quality grades: simple *Beaujolais, Beaujolais Supérieur, Beaujolais-Villages*, and then a top rank whose

labels bear the names of the nine foremost townships of the district:
Moulin-à-Vent, Chénas, Juliénas, Saint-Amour, Fleurie, Chiroubles,
Morgon, Brouilly, and Côte de Brouilly. All the wines of southern
Burgundy are lighter than their northern cousins and suit less formal
fare. They are ideal as luncheon or picnic wines and particualrly
welcome with pâté, sausages, and cheese. They mature much more
quickly and should be substantially lower in cost.

Burgundy officially ends with the junction of the Saône and Rhône
rivers at the great gastronomic city of Lyon. But pursuing the Rhône
further south quickly brings one into another famous wine region
which bears that river's name. Like Burgundy, the Rhône Valley is
really a region comprised of three quite distinct districts: Côte Rôtie,
Hermitage, and Châteauneuf-du-Pape. Collectively, they represent the
most ancient wine region of France.

The Romans used the Rhône as their principal highway into the
Gallic interior and quite naturally brought their devotion to wine
making along with their conquering army, political system, legal code,
and imposing architecture. The climate in the Rhône Valley is as warm
as that of much of Italy and only heat-resistant grapes—almost all of
which are red—do well here. The wines are traditionally made from a
combination of grapes and are known for their rich flavor, full body,
and high alcohol content. Those of the Côte Rôtie and Hermitage are
especially long-lived and are regarded as the best of the Rhône. The
wines of Châteauneuf are more immediately appealing and produced in
much greater quantity. All of the Rhône wines work well with beef and
lamb dishes, but seem to have a particular affinity for game.

Crossing now to France's Atlantic coast, one comes into the country's largest, and what many believe is its finest, wine region. This is
Bordeaux, and here too viticulture began with the Romans, though
probably not until the fourth century A.D. An organized wine industry
did not emerge until about 800 years later when the English took
possession of this area and held it until the mid-fifteenth century. Two
hundred more years were required before the French began to lay the

foundation for the massive and highly sophisticated wine production center that Bordeaux has become today. Here quality wine making is practiced on a scale found nowhere else in Europe by a highly organized and regulated industry supported by major research facilities and one of France's largest wine-shipping centers.

The quality of Bordeaux wines is rooted in a unique combination of well-drained soils and the fact that the nearby ocean and the great Gironde river system moderate what would otherwise be an excessively hot southwestern climate. The region is comprised of 22 districts, of which only five are of real consequence for the international wine trade: Médoc, Graves, Sauternes, Saint-Emilion, and Pomerol.

Médoc is France's, and the world's, most famous source of red wines made from the noble cabernet sauvignon grape. It includes such renowned wine-producing townships as Saint-Estephe, Pauillac, Saint-Julien, and Margaux; and within them such awe-inspiring vineyards—referred to here as *châteaux*—as Mouton Rothschild, Lafite-Rothschild, Latour, and Margaux. There are, of course, a host of less well-known wines from the Médoc, many of which are of better quality in any given year than these great potentates of the wine world. They are ranked in five qualitative levels—*premier cru, deuxième cru,* etc.—based on a classification devised in 1855 which, understandably, has lost some of its reliability over the last century and a quarter.

All the Médoc wines share a drier nature than the reds of Burgundy, are usually held to be more complex in character, and are certainly longer lived. The classic rule is to begin drinking a fine Médoc only after it has passed its seventh birthday, and some have been known to live a century or more. Médoc wines complement the full spectrum of French cuisine. Some see them as the perfect foil for lamb, but it would be difficult to contend that they are any less ideal for beef, fowl, or veal. They may in fact be at their acme with some of France's most exotic cheeses.

The next important district along the left bank of the Gironde is Graves. As the name suggests, the soil is very gravelly and yields mainly dry white wines from a combination of the semillon and sauvignon blanc grapes. Some great red wines are also made here from the cabernet sauvignon grape, most notably Château Haut-Brion. Hard by Graves is Sauternes, whose name has become synonymous with sweet white dessert wines. Sauternes are also made from the semillon and sauvignon blanc; the technique here is to leave the fruit on the vine well into the fall to accumulate extra sugar. The most famous Sauternes, and surely the most sought-after dessert wine in the world, is Château d'Yquem.

Crossing over to the right bank of the river, one is once more in red wine country in the districts of Saint-Emilion and Pomerol. Saint-Emilion antedates the Médoc by at least 1,300 years and may have been the site of the vineyard cultivated by the Roman consul and poet Ausonius. In any event, a famous vineyard of this district, Château Ausone, now honors his name; it is qualitatively ranked with several other *premier grand cru* properties, including Château Cheval Blanc, Belair, Canon, Figeac, Pavie, and Trottevieille. In addition, there are about 70 other vineyards accorded *grand cru* status. One need not wait to savor these wines so long as those of the Médoc because they are made from the cabernet franc and merlot grapes, which produce wines that mature more readily and live somewhat shorter lives.

Saint-Emilion's companion district is Pomerol, which employs the same grapes to make its red wines. The stars in its firmament are Château Pétrus (preeminently), Clos l'Eglise, Conseillante, Gazin, Nénin, Trotanoy, and Vieux-Château-Certan. Its wines, like those of Saint-Emilion, work handsomely with a wide range of meat dishes, most notably lamb, veal, and pâté. Because they have a bit more sugar than Médocs and mature more quickly, they are sometimes referred to as the Burgundies of Bordeaux—a distinction useful only in suggesting the great flexibility these "right bank" wines have with all sorts of foods.

The last wine region in our clockwise tour of France is the Loire Valley. Here again there are a series of districts, this time arranged along the banks of what is the nation's longest river. The Loire rises in the deep south, runs 300 miles north, and then turns west to run another 300 miles before emptying into the Atlantic at the port city of Nantes. Most of the districts are situated along the river's westward course and we will begin with the twin districts of Pouilly and Sancerre. Here the sauvignon blanc grape we encountered in Bordeaux is grown to produce a quite different, even drier and more full-bodied, wine that is in great vogue at this time. It is a fine alternative to a good white Burgundy and somewhat lower priced. It is hard to beat as a companion to fish and fowl.

Next in order come the paired districts of Anjou and Touraine. Now we are in the famed châteaux country, the playground of the French nobility and what is still known as the "garden of France" because of its lushly scenic and richly productive land and waterways. The mild, white chenin blanc grape prevails here and makes soft white wines on the sweet side. The best known come from Saumur and Vouvray and are meant to be consumed in their youth to capitalize on their qualities of freshness and charm. Ideal summer luncheon or picnic wines, they go best with chicken, fish, veal, and light desserts.

Finally, we come to Muscadet at the mouth of the Loire. It, too, is a white wine district and produces what is sometimes referred to as the "poor man's Chablis." It is more affordable than that great classic because its vineyards are much larger and the muscadet grape bears more heavily. It is also Chablis-like because it goes so well with oysters, mussels, and other shellfish. It does not, however, offer the full bouquet or complex taste of the Burgundian classic. Many people find that Muscadet's best use is as an aperitif.

Our tour of the major French vineyards ends in the Loire Valley, but before moving on to another European wine country we owe some attention to the key words used in labeling French wines. Besides the place name under which the wine is sold and perhaps the name of the producer or shipper, the most important words to look for are *appellation contrôlée*. The French were the first to devise a legal system for regulating wine production—something the United States does not yet have on a comprehensive, national basis. The French system is intended to frustrate wine counterfeiters, protect legitimate producers, and insure consumer confidence. Basically, it is a three-tiered system which assigns wines to succeeding levels of quality and prescribes the production standards which must be met for those levels.

At the bottom are the *appellation simple* wines. As the name suggests, these are simple table wines which seldom get into international trade; the French government requires little more of their makers than that they maintain sanitary conditions in their wineries and not mix the wine named on the label with wine from other sources. The next level is *vin délimité de qualité supérieure*, or VDQS wines as they are colloquially known. Some of these are showing up in American wine shops and can represent good value. The standards for their manufacture are more strict than those for simple wines but not up to those prescribed for the uppermost tier of *appellation contrôlée*.

These "AC" wines are those on which France's viticultural reputation depends. A wine maker, in order to carry this designation on his label, must meet an exacting set of regulations governing the location of his vineyard; the kinds of grapes he may use; what planting, pruning, and spraying practices he may employ; when and how much of his crop he can harvest; and how he may vinify, mature, bottle, and describe his wine. He complies because, without the AC on the label, he knows that he can't get a top price for his wine or compete in international trade.

This system has been a tremendous boon to the buyers of French wines since 1935 and in recent years other European countries have adopted similar regulations. There are, of course, the occasional "wine scandals," but their discovery only proves the overall effectiveness of the system. It is important to recognize, however, just what the AC designation does and does not guarantee. It certifies that what is on the label is what is in the bottle and that the minimum required standards derived from tradition and codified by the government were employed in its manufacture. It does not say that the wine will be good or that it will please your palate. Still, it is the nearest thing to "truth in packaging" that the wine world has yet devised and it merits the respect that it has won.

Germany

One cannot discuss European wines without saying something about Germany. The area planted in vines is small in comparison with France's, and Germany makes really only one type of wine rather than hundreds. But what makes German viticulture special is the fact that it makes that one type so superlatively. Indeed, most experts agree that, bottle for bottle, no country makes better wine than Germany. Again, its superiority is an example of the excellence that can be achieved through specialization.

Germany, however, had no real choice but to specialize. Its best grape-growing areas are all along the middle Rhine and its tributaries, and the vines that have been planted there are the only ones that will prosper in what is the world's northernmost high-quality wine-producing region. At this latitude—roughly that of Montreal—only the smallest white wine grapes will ripen properly and only then when they are situated on southward-facing slopes in the shelter of steep-sided river valleys. Several grapes are used, but the riesling is by far the most important.

The region has four major districts: Mosel, Rheingau, Rheinhessen, and Rheinpfalz, with the first two producing the most distinguished vintages. The best German wines bear the names of the vineyards in which they are raised, preceded by the names of the towns in which the vineyards are situated. Thus the wine of the Himmelreich vineyard in the town of Graach is expressed on the label as Graacher-Himmelreich. A wine made from the products of several less distinguished vineyards can be sold under the town name alone as Graacher Riesling. The least distinguished wines are sold either under the names of the producing

districts or under traditional trade names like Moselblümchen or Liebfraumilch.

In 1970, Germany adopted a wine production control law modeled
on the French system. It, too, has three qualitative quality levels which
in ascending order are called *Tafelwein, Qualitätswein*, and *Qualitätswein mit Prädikat*. The higher two grades are the only ones likely to
reach America. As in France, the government's permission to use these
designations depends upon the producer's meeting certain standards in
his cultivation of approved grape varieties, the ripeness of the grapes
when harvested, the techniques employed in vitification, and the
alcohol content and other properties of the finished wine. The achieve-
ment of a minimum natural sugar content is all-important in so northern a climate and those vineyards that achieve it are also permitted to
label their wines with special words indicating increasing amounts of
sweetness. In ascending order, these words are Kabinett, Spätlese,
Auslese, Beerenauslese, and Trockenbeerenauslese.

German wines go very well with light meals and desserts, but their
sugar content can make them a bit cloying with some foods. Recogniz-
ing this, the Germans use beer with many of their meals and save their
wines for an aperitif or for drinking at any time of day for the sheer
pleasure of it. A sheer pleasure it can be, too, when you share a
distinguished Mosel or Rheingau with friends—perhaps most ideally on
a terrace or porch on a perfect spring or summer day. You'll find it one
of the most delightful experiences in the whole world of wine.

Italy

Finally, a few paragraphs must be devoted to this great country whose
citizens have done more than any other to propagate the wine in both
the Old World and the New. Too few people are aware that Italy is still
the greatest wine-producing nation on earth in terms of quantity and

surely among the top three or four in terms of quality. Our ignorance is excused by the fact that until recently Italy was exporting less than 10 percent of its enormous production and what reached our shores was usually labeled "Chianti"—and often was not even genuine Chianti at that. In this decade, however, Italy has decided to share its vinous wealth more widely and is actively exporting top-grade wines from its fabulously broad selection of red, white, rosé, sparkling, and fortified wines. Moreover, Italians are letting them go at very attractive prices which suggest that they will play an increasingly important role in American restaurants, home consumption, and entertaining.

Space does not permit an adequate description of the vast landscape of Italian viticulture. Suffice it to say that the better vineyards are in the north and that the three most important regions are in a triangular relationship delineated by the city of Florence in the north-central section of the country, Turin in the northwest, and Venice in the northeast. The region around Florence is called Tuscany and this is where the real Chianti is made—a fact which the Italians underline by labeling it Chianti Classico. In the northwest, the region is called Piedmont and is known for making Italy's most distinguished, long-lived red wines like Barolo and Barbera plus those delectable sweet, sparkling whites called Asti Spumanti. In the northeast, the key region is called Veneto and here the vintners concentrate on lighter, less formal reds like Valpolicella and Bardolino as well as what is probably Italy's best-known dry white wine: Soave.

Italy preceded Germany by seven years in instituting its version of the French AC laws. Its three quality grades are called *denominazione di origine semplice, denominazione di origine controllata,* and, at the top, *denominazione di origine controllata e guarantita.* Instituting this system has been a slower process in Italy than in Germany; this is understandable in view of the size and complexity of the Italian wine industry. Plenty of these newly regulated wines are now reaching America, however, and you will be well advised to look for these certifications of authenticity on the labels.

The Wine Market

Like any other market, today's wine trade is a creature of supply and demand. At its most basic level, it changes in response to purely agricultural factors. For example, several abundant harvests in one region may more than satisfy the demand for that kind of wine and its producers or shippers will lower its price in order to help move the excess. Conversely, when environmental circumstances reduce the quantity or quality of several vintages of a popular wine, the price of the remaining supply of good wine of that type is sure to go up. There are other, less obvious factors at work in the wine market, however, and some are even more unpredictable than the weather which can favor or flatten a vineyard.

Several recent developments are illustrative of the nonagricultural factors which affect what you may have to pay for wine. A good example of a major cultural shift occurred in the late '60s and early '70s when Americans suddenly decided they liked wine. This new demand set off the most frenzied expansion of vineyards and winery facilities in the history of viticulture as U.S. producers scrambled to increase their output. A huge capital investment was required and the consumer is now footing the bill in the higher cost of American wines. A similar response occurred abroad, especially in the case of Europe's most prestigious wines. The supply of these wines is fixed—in France, for example, by the AC regulations—and when American wholesalers, hotels, and restaurants unleashed huge new orders against a stock which legally cannot grow, prices had to rise. A happier development for the American consumer is Italy's recent decision to increase its wine exports substantially so as to improve its foreign exchange earnings. This is an example of a political-economic factor at work in the market which seems remote to the individual consumer but is likely to have an important effect on the prices he pays—and not only for Italian wines.

The point is that the cost of wine is constantly changing and there are no immutable rules for playing this market. Still, there are a number of tips that can be offered to help you make prudent buying decisions in the years just ahead as well as some general guidelines that can be offered to aid in keeping your home cellar stocked at the lowest possible prices.

First, with respect to domestic wines, good values are likely to continue in the generic wines being produced by California's central valley wine makers. Admittedly, these may not be the wines you will wish to offer for your most elegant dinner parties, but for many of the menus described in this book they will do very nicely and, dollar for dollar, they represent some of the best buys on today's wine market. Remember that the best savings exist in the larger-than-standard bottle sizes and that the risk of spoilage—any wine deteriorates with exposure to the air—of any unfinished portion is reduced in these California "jug wines" because most are lightly pasteurized. You can further slow down the rate of oxidation by keeping the opened wine in the refrigerator. European wines sold in such large bottles are not treated to resist spoilage and should be used on those occasions when all the wine is likely to be consumed.

The price outlook with respect to California's North Coast counties wines is not so favorable. Here the cost of investment in new land and equipment has been very high and yet the production of these quality-oriented vintners is necessarily low. That means that a high price per bottle is almost inevitable and the products of the superpremium vineyards are often in the $5 to $10 range. On the East Coast of the United States—where wines of comparable quality from Europe are available for less money—these California rarities are likely to have a hard time staying competitive. Still, for reasons of novelty and nationalism, even Easterners may want to make a point of serving these wines to guests.

With imported wines, the price picture is mixed. Some of the best values from France are the wines of Alsace and, being less well known, they offer the advantage in entertaining of being a point of interest for your guests. The wines of northern Burgundy are in such short supply relative to world demand that they almost always have to be reserved for special occasions. Southern Burgundy wines, on the other hand, are by no means out of reach—particularly those from the Côte Chalonnaise and Côte Maconnais. The Rhône has always offered good value, and even though the wines from its three best-known districts are no longer the bargain they once were, a good Côte Rôtie, Hermitage, or Châteauneuf offers tremendous satisfaction for the money. Moreover, there are some good regional wines—labeled as Côtes-du-Rhône—which are even less expensive.

Bordeaux prices depend very much on what you select from this, the largest single source of fine French wines. The world's fondness for Bordeaux is every bit as intense as that for Burgundy, but fortunately there is more than twice as much produced in an average year. This means that, with the exception of the most sought-after *châteaux*, the prices of Bordeaux have remained fairly reasonable—at least with respect to their principal qualitative competitor. Médocs fetch the highest prices, but the cost spread between the least- and best-known wines can be remarkable. The wise buyer recognizes this fact and seeks to find a wine to his or her taste at the lower end of this spectrum. The few Graves reds tend to track closely with the Médocs, but the whites are much more moderately priced. Sauternes used to be a great bargain when many people misunderstood their use and shunned them for being too sweet. Now, as people have extended their wine use to the dessert course, the best-known Sauternes are becoming quite costly.

Happier hunting for the bargain-conscious Bordeaux buyer can be found in Saint-Emilion and Pomerol. Prices there run about 10 percent less than for comparably good Médocs, and, unless you're buying wines for long-term cellaring, they represent a good alternative. Adventurous buyers will also find some very acceptable wines at comparatively low prices if they extend their search beyond these five best-known districts of Bordeaux. There are 17 others to choose from, and American wine shops are featuring more and more selections from districts like

Bourg, Blaye, Néac, Lalande-de-Pomerol, Entre-Deux-Mers, and Saint-Croix-du-Mont. Ferreting out the best among them is one of the happy challenges of intelligent wine buying.

The white wines of the Loire represent some of the very best values among French wines. Those of the Pouilly and Sancerre districts are the most expensive but still can be found for under $5. Vouvray and Touraine remain very easy on the pocketbook; and Muscadet, though inching up in price, is still one of the best buys in wine. Too many Americans know too little about the Loire and this gives the informed wine buyer a substantial competitive edge.

Elsewhere in Europe, the picture is also mixed. German wines are usually more expensive. Still, the finest Mosels and Rheingaus are less expensive than Burgundy and Bordeaux wines of comparable excellence and those of the Rheinhessen and Rheinpfalz are very reasonable indeed. Italy offers—almost across the board—the best wines for the money in the entire import market. This is not to say that they are universally good, but carefully chosen vintages with DOC on the label are likely to be among the happier surprises of your wine buying.

Whether you are seeking wines from America or abroad, there are some general guidelines to be followed if getting the best buy is important to you. First, identify the wine shop in your area with the most comprehensive selection and develop a good relationship with a competent member of the sales force. A good relationship, in this instance, means being candid about your preferences, the degree of your wine knowledge, and what you are willing to pay. Taking a wine merchant into your confidence in this way is almost always rewarding because he is then in a position to watch for good values in the areas of interest you have already established and perhaps lead you into wine types you had not yet considered. The relationship can be mutually profitable because he gets a steady customer if he makes it possible for you to get the best wines at the best prices.

Another good tip is to buy in quantity. Almost all stores offer a discount of 10 percent or better on bottles bought in case lots (12 bottles) and some extend the discounting to half cases or even smaller denominations. Next, watch for sales. The merchandising of wine varies considerably from one locality to another, but in those places where a free market prevails the competition between merchants leads to sales at which a substantial number of wines are sold at well below the everyday price. Finally, buy wines when they are young. Prices almost always rise on a wine as it matures—even if it is not one of those which improves with age. Inflation is partly to blame, but it is also a function of supply and demand. As the supply of any one vintage for which there is still a strong demand diminishes, the cost is sure to go up. So buying wines young is increasingly the practice among American wine buffs and some even go so far as to order wine "futures" before the cases have actually arrived for sale at their merchant's shop.

Keeping a Home Wine Cellar

Having a personal stock of wine at home is not as big an undertaking as you might suppose. A growing number of Americans do so and very few have the traditional underground storage facilities that you might have in mind from having seen pictures of the stately homes or famous wineries of Europe. All that is required is a space apart in your home where the light is low, the temperature is moderate, and there is nothing to make the bottles vibrate. The size of the "cellar" will be determined by your use of wine, the space available, and the money you can spend on stocking it.

But why go to the trouble in the first place? There are at least two good reasons in addition to the fact that, if you're going to follow the previously mentioned tips on buying wine economically, you're going to need a place to store your purchases. Just like the reserve food shelf discussed elsewhere in this book, a cache of wines at home means that you will be ready on short notice to make a simple meal special by the serving of wine. Secondly, you will discover that properly stored wines that have had a chance to rest and mature in your home will taste better than those that have just been brought from the store.

Understanding the latter point and deciding how and where to establish your own cellar require a little more information about the nature of wine. Unlike distilled spirits, wine is biologically and chemically alive and therefore responsive to the environment in which it is kept. It is not as sensitive as milk and other beverages which need refrigeration to stay fresh. In fact, it was wine's capacity to resist spoilage—due to the combination of alcohol and tannin in its makeup— which made it man's only safe beverage in the millenniums before refrigeration. But each wine has a life cycle depending on the grapes from which it was made and the method of vinification. This means that it is always in a process of change, with some light white wines coming to their maturity in only a couple of years and certain heavy reds lasting a century or more. It is this maturation process that can be disturbed by adverse storage conditions, and when this occurs the result is not as often a spoiled wine as one that cannot live up to its potential or your expectations.

Fortunately, wine is a great deal more tolerant of rough treatment— particularly when it is young—than some sources would have you believe. Still, it is a fact of life that between the time a bottle leaves a winery and the time it ends up on your table it gets a lot of rough treatment. The heat and knocking about in transport can be fierce and, sad to say, there are few wine merchants' shops which are equipped to provide proper storage after the wine arrives there. The obvious solution is to get wines home some weeks or months before you intend to use them, and to provide for the wines the rest that will allow them to shake off the effects of travel and reestablish the natural rhythm of their maturation process.

As indicated above, a good storage facility protects from excesses in light, temperature, and movement. Some protection from light is afforded by the dark green or brown glass in which most wines are bottled, but the conscientious merchant and consumer must also do their part by keeping the wine out of bright light—particularly sunshine. As for temperature, wine should ideally be kept at about 55 degrees F., and many wine lovers with large holdings install air conditioning equipment to assure this temperature. A more practical approach for most of us, however, is just to find a spot in our homes where the wine will be neither too cold nor too hot, i.e. between 50 degrees F. and 70 degrees F., and where any sudden change within this temperature range is unlikely. Finally, one should try to protect home-stored wines from motion sickness. This simply means picking a place away from slamming doors, rumbling electric motors, and heavy foot traffic. Likely spots to protect your wines from all these hazards are the bottoms of closets, the unused spaces under stairs, and the bookcases in rooms allotted chiefly to adults. Danger zones for wine storage include kitchens, laundries, family rooms, and any place near a heat source.

Now that you know how to situate your wine cellar, the only remaining questions have to do with stacking and stocking. In recent years, many types of wine racks have come on the market from the very simple to the unnecessarily elaborate. Budget and space constraints will probably dictate your choice, and there may be aesthetic considerations as well, depending upon the placement of the wine storage area within the home. Just remember that the only thing the bottle needs is to rest securely in a horizontal position. This is so because the cork must stay in contact with the wine. Without this contact the cork will dry and then shrink, losing its capacity to keep the bottle airtight, and wine exposed to air spoils in a matter of hours. Many people have made very effective and attractive storage facilities for their wines without resorting to store-bought racks. Plywood shelving, ceramic drain tiles, and even the wooden cases in which some wines are still sold make good construction materials.

As for stocking your own cellar, it would be ideal if you could assemble representatives from all of the wine districts mentioned in the foregoing discussion of American and European viticulture. Most people, however, will want to proceed more modestly, and that is certainly the prudent course if you are just beginning to explore the wine world. In deciding on your initial purchases of either domestic or imported wines, it will be helpful to recall the three qualitative categories used to describe California wines, i.e. "standard," "premium," and "superpremium." The point is that any home wine cellar should have a few bottles in the first category for family consumption, informal entertaining, and picnic use. The core of the collection, however, should be in the second category because what most of us need for most entertaining situations is wine that is of good quality but not too expensive. Finally, every cellar should have a few special bottles to accompany those great meals that are undertaken for the most important holidays, family celebrations, and the presence of honored guests.

What follows is one prescription for moderately-sized but well-balanced cellar. Obviously, personal preferences and available funds could result in many variations on this theme.

I. STANDARD WINE FOR "EVERYDAY" USE

Two cases of four 1.5 liter (ca. 50 oz.) jugs containing California generic wines. One case of white, preferably "Chablis", and the other of red, probably "Burgundy".

II. PREMIUM WINES FOR MOST ENTERTAINING

Three cases of twelve .75 liter (ca. 25 oz.) bottles, equally divided between foreign and domestic wines. Specifically, three bottles each of the following types:

American Varietals	*European Districts*
Whites	*Whites*
Chenin Blanc	Muscadet
Chardonnay	Macon Blanc
Johannisberg Riesling	Mosel
Reds	*Reds*
Zinfandel	Beaujolais Villages
Cabernet Sauvignon	St. Emilion
Barbera	Chianti Classico

III. SUPER-PREMIUM WINES FOR SPECIAL OCCASIONS

One case of twelve .75 liter (ca. 25 oz.) bottles, equally divided between foreign and domestic wines. Specifically, one bottle each of the following types:

American Varietals	*European Districts*
Whites	*Whites*
Fumé Blanc	Pouilly-Fumé
Chardonnay	Chablis Grand Cru
Johannisberg Riesling	Rheingau
Reds	*Reds*
Zinfandel	Barolo
Cabernet Sauvignon	Médoc
Pinot Noir	Côte de Beaune

Serving Wine at Home

For a number of wrong-headed reasons, a mythology has grown up about serving wines to the effect that it is a highly complicated process best left to tuxedoed waiters in restaurants. Nothing could be further from the truth and it is helpful, in regaining an appropriate sense of the simplicity of this process, to remember that most of the wine in the world is consumed in cultures where this beverage is as basic to the diet as bread and salt and is served in the same informal way. The following steps should take much of the mystery out of this process.

Let's start with the bottle. Ideally, getting it from the cellar—or, if you must, the store—should be part of your preparations on the day before the meal is to be served. This will give you the opportunity to make an unhurried choice and to serve the wine in its best condition. Of course, these preliminary steps—which differ for white and red wines—can be taken closer to the event if time requires.

In the case of the reds, getting the bottle a day early permits the wine slowly to take on the temperature of the room in which it is to be consumed. Personal preferences have their place, but almost nobody thinks of serving a red wine cold. This is because so much of the pleasure in reds is derived from the scent or "bouquet" of the wine and this quality is sharply reduced if the wine has been refrigerated. Of course, if you know the dining room is likely to be excessively warm, e.g. over 75 degrees F., you may place the bottle in the refrigerator for about ten minutes before serving—but no more.

A second advantage of getting red wines a day early is to allow any solid material in the wine to settle when it is moved from its horizontal resting place to an upright position. This solid material is absolutely harmless but can interfere with the visual and, to a lesser degree, the tasting pleasure your guests will take with a wine. The solids are merely the residue of the grape skins and pulp with which red wines are always made and from which they derive their color and their capacity for long life. White wines are made only from the juice of the grape and so, although they have no sediment, their life spans are generally shorter.

Today, most red wines, particularly those made in America, are so heavily filtered that a day standing on a sideboard or kitchen shelf will concentrate whatever sediment there may be in the bottom of the bottle and you can count on pouring out a clear wine so long as you do not agitate it. On occasion, however, you may encounter one of those well-aged, heavy-bodied European reds—Burgundy, Rhône, and Port wines are the worst offenders—and you may wish to take the extra step of decanting. This is just a fancy word for pouring the wine slowly from the bottle into another clean container and leaving the sediment behind. It must be one of those tasks reserved for the period directly before the guests arrive because older wines of this sort will not stand long exposure to oxygen. All that is required is a steady hand and a candle beneath the neck of the bottle so that you can see when all of the clear wine has been transferred to the new container and the "arrow" of sediment is nearing the lip of the bottle. That is the moment to stop short, put the stopper into the decanter, and enjoy the sight of an absolutely clear vintage red wine.

Preparing a bottle of white wine is simpler still. As indicated above, sediment is not a problem in whites and all that is necessary is to get the wine to a proper drinking temperature. Again, personal preferences have their place, but few people will argue with the proposition that white wines are best when chilled. The question is, however, how long they should be chilled, and too often the answer is too long. Basically, a white should be served cool but not cold, and 40 minutes in the average refrigerator, or 20 in a freezer, will do the job. As a last resort, whites can be immersed in ice as is so often done in restaurants. This shock treatment, however, seems to have an adverse effect on the bouquet and flavor of the wine.

With the wine fully ready in terms of clarity and temperature, all that remains is to open the bottle. Again, the procedure is different—at least with respect to timing—for red and white wines. Reds are usually opened about an hour or so before your guests arrive to let the wine begin to develop its bouquet by a limited exposure to the air. Younger reds seem to benefit most from this exposure, while fully mature wines can pass their peak if allowed to stand open too long. White wines do not require any of this "breathing" and can be opened immediately before serving. Pulling the cork is obviously the same procedure for both types and there are all sorts of devices to help you do the job. The choice of tool is up to you but the old-fashioned corkscrew is hard to beat. Whichever device you use, be sure first to cut away the lead foil surrounding the top of the bottle and to wipe the lip clean before and after pulling the cork.

A word is in order about glassware before moving on to the final step of pouring the wine. Glasses of all sorts have been made for all types of wine but one set will do for any occasion if it is properly designed. Simplicity, again, is the keynote. A good wine glass is clear, stemmed, and ample in size. Tinted or elaborately cut glass only obscures the diner's view of the color of the wine, and color is important. Observing it is one of the secondary pleasures in wine, and it offers important clues as to the wine's age and condition. Stemware is preferable to tumblers, not because it is more elegant, but because the stem serves as a handle and lets the diner keep his hand off the bowl of the glass and thus avoid raising the temperature of the wine. Finally, a good glass should be ample in size—six ounces at the very least—so that when it is half filled there will be a generous serving in the bottom half of the glass and room in the top for the bouquet to develop. It is also helpful if the glass tapers in near the top to concentrate the scent further and preserve it for the taster's pleasure.

Pouring the wine is no trick at all. The host pours a bit of wine in his glass first so that any odd bit of cork will not be received by the guests. He can also use this moment to taste the wine to be sure it is sound but this can well be accomplished before the wine is brought to the table. Wine baskets and other such paraphernalia accomplish nothing that can't be done as well or better by the human hand. If the bottle is cold and damp from chilling you may employ a napkin to improve your grip, but the label should remain visible so that the guests can see what they are being served. After pouring, the bottle should be left in full view for the same reason.

Wine pouring is a democratic procedure in which the host or hostess simply moves to each guest in order around the table without regard to status or sex. Again, no glass should be poured more than half full, however awkward this may seem at first to your sense of generosity. If the server gives a short twist of his wrist at the end of each pouring, he is likely to avoid any spills on the tablecloth. Any errors can be assuaged, however, by a quick application of salt to the spot. After the first serving, the host can decide, depending upon the formality of the occasion, whether to pour the subsequent servings or to follow a more venerable tradition, and leave the bottle on the table for the guests to help themselves.

A Guide to Pronunciation

The following aids to pronouncing the French, German, and Italian words in this chapter are intended for Americans who have not studied European languages. These approximations may not satisfy a linguist, but they will enable you to communicate with wine merchants and waiters, and to hold your own in dinnertable conversation.

Aloxe-Corton ah-lohx cor-tawn
Alsace al-sass
Anjou on-shoe
appellation contrôlée (AC) ah-pell-ah-see-own cawn-trohl-lay

appellation simple ah-pell-ah-see-own sahm-pl
Auslese ouse-lay-zuh
Barbera bar-bare-ah
Beaujolais bo-show-lay
Beaulieu bo-lyew
Beaune bone

Beerenauslese   baron-ouse-
   lay-zuh
Blanchots   blawn-show
Blaye   bligh
Bordeaux   bore-dough
Bougros   boo-grow
Bourgogne   boor-gone-yuh
Brouilly   brew-yee
brut   brute
Cabernet Sauvignon
   cah-bare-nay so-veen-yawn
Chablis   shab-lee
Chambertin   shawm-bair-tan
Chambolle-Musigny
   shawm-bowl moosey-nee
Chappellet   shap-puh-lay
Chardonnay   shar-dough-nay
Chassagne-Montrachet
   shah-san-yuh mont-rash-shay
Château Clos Fourtet
   shot-toe clo foor-tay
Château Haut-Brion
   shot-toe oh-bree-awn
Château Pétrus   shot-toe
   pay-trews
Château Saint Jean   shot-toe
   san shawn
Château Trotanoy   shot-toe
   tro-tan-wah
Château d'Yquem   shot-toe
   dee-keem
Châteauneuf-du-Pape
   shot-toe-nuff dew pop

Chénas   shay-nass
Chenin Blanc   shay-nan
   blawn
Cheval Blanc   shev-al
   blawn
Chianti   key-awn-tee
Chiroubles   sheer-roo-bl
Les Clos   lay clo
Clos de Vougeot   clo duh
   voo-show
Conseillante   cawn-say-yawnt
Côte de Beaune   coat duh
   bone
Côte Chalonnaise   coat
   shall-lone-nayz
Côte Maconnais   coat
   mac-cawn-nay
Côte des Nuits   coat day
   nwee
Côte du Rhône   coat dew
   rone
Côte Rôtie   coat roh-tee
denominazione di origine
   semplice   day-naum-eh-not-
   zee-own dee or-ee-gene
   sem-pleech-ay
Deuxième Cru   doo-zee-em
   crew
Entre-Deux-Mers   on-truh
   duh mare
Figeac   fee-shock
Fleurie   flur-ree
Fumé Blanc   foo-may blawn

Gazin   gaz-an

Gevrey-Chambertin   shehv-ray shawm-bair-tan

Gewurztraminer ge-vertz-trah-miner

Gironde   she-rawnd

Graacher Himmelreich gr-ahsh-er Heem-ml-rishe

Grand Cru   grahn crew

Graves   grah-v

Grenouilles   gren-wee-yuh

Juliénas   shule-yay-nass

Lafite   la-feet

Lalande-de-Pomerol   la-lawnd duh paum-eh-rawl

Liebfraumilch   leeb-frow-milsh

Loire   lwahr

Macon Blanc   mac-awn blawn

Margaux   mar-go

Mayacamas   my-ah-cahm-ahs

Médoc   may-dawk

méthode champenoise may-toad shawm-puh-nwahz

Meursault   mare-so

Montrachet   mont-rash-shay

Morgon   mor-gawn

Mosel   mo-zell

Moselblümchen mo-zel-blyoom-shen

Moulin-à-vent   moo-lan ah vawn

Moutonne   moo-tawn

Muscadet   muss-cah-day

Le Musigny   luh moosey-nee

Néac   nay-yack

Nénin   nay-nan

Nuits-Saint-Georges   nwee san shorsh

Pauillac   paw-yak

Pavie   pah-vee

Pinot Blanc   p'no blawn

Pinot Noir   p'no nwar

Pomerol   paum-eh-rawl

Pouilly-Fuissé   poo-yee fwee-say

Premier Cru   preh-myay crew

La Preuses   lah pruh-z

Qualitätswein   quali-tates-vine

Qualitätswein mit prädikat quali-tates-vine mit pray-dee-caught

Rheingau   rine-gow

Rheinhessen   rine-hess-en

Rheinpfalz   rine-pfahltz

Richebourg   reesh-burg

Riesling   rees-ling

La Romanée-Conti   la roman-nay cawn-tee

Sainte-Croix-du-Mont   sant crwa dew mawn

Saint-Emilion   sant aye-me-lee-on

Saint-Estephe   sant ace-teff

Saint-Julien san
  shoe-lyan
Sancerre sawn-sair
Saône sone
Saumur so-myur
Sauterne saw-tairn
Sauvignon so-veen-yawn
Savigny-les-Beaune
  sah-veen-yee lay bone
Semillon seh-me-yawn
Soave swa-vay
Spätlese shpayt-lay-zuh
La Tâche la tahsh
Touraine too-rain
trockenbeerenauslese
  trawk-en-baron-ouse-lay-zuh
Trotanoy tro-tan-wah
Trottevielle trawt-vee-ay

Valmur val-myur
Valpolicella vahl-po-
  lee-chel-la
Vaudésir vo-day-zeer
Veneto vain-nay-toe
Vieux-Château Certan
  vyuh shot-toe sair-tan
vin délimité de qualité
  supérieure (VDQS) van
  day-lee-mee-tay duh
  cahl-lee-tay sou-pay-ree-er
vin ordinaire van
  or-din-nair
Vosne-Romanée vone
  ro-mah-nay
Vouvray voo-vray
Wehlener Sonnenuhr
  vay-len-er zawn-neh-nur

INDEX
